World Hunger Series 2006

Hunger and Learning

**A co-publication
of the World Food Programme, Rome
and Stanford University Press
Stanford, California
2006**

Map A - Hunger and learning across the world

Prevalence of underweight

Countries with underweight prevalence above 30%

School life expectancy

High: more than 12 years

Moderately high: 9 to 12 years

Moderately low: 6 to 9 years

Low: 4 to 6 years

Very low: less than 4 years

NA

The boundaries and the designations used on this map do not imply any official endorsement or acceptance by the United Nations.
Map produced by WFP VAM.

Data source: UNESCO, WHO

Acknowledgements

This report was prepared by a team at the United Nations World Food Programme. Stanlake Samkange, Director, Policy, Strategy and Programme Support Division, oversaw and guided the effort. Paul Howe, Policy Adviser, was the lead author and team leader. Gyorgy Dallos, Senior Economist, and Carlo Quirici, Consultant, were responsible for data. Michael Hutak, Communications Specialist, coordinated production. Elena Borsatti, Marco Cavalcante, Valeria Silvestri and Miranda Sissons all made valuable contributions as team members. Ester Fiorito, Cinzia Mandri, Arduino Mangoni, Flor de Maria Ramirez and Laura Segatori provided administrative support.

Numerous experts provided comments and advice on the report's contents. The lead reviewers for the report were Fernando Mönckeberg and Amina Ibrahim. The expert reviewers group included: Harold Alderman, Indra de Soysa, Joy del Rosso, Peter Easton, Lawrence Haddad, Beryl Levinger and Krishna Rao. Background papers were prepared by Carmen Aldinger, Marc Cohen, Paul Howe, Ute Meir, Bjorn Nordtveit and Brian Gray, Roger Shrimpton and Jane Lucas, and Nalan Yuksel-Hughes. Luka Biong Deng, Fernando Mönckeberg and Sibylle Riedmiller wrote case studies.

Several World Food Programme staff provided helpful comments and guidance, including: Patrick Webb, Petros Aklilu, Martin Bloem, Nicholas Crawford, Francisco Espejo, Adama Faye and Robin Jackson. Regular feedback and support was given by Lynn Brown, Ugo Gentilini, Brian Gray, Ute Meir, George Simon and Christine Van Nieuwenhuyse.

Anthea Webb and Cristina Ascone from WFP's Communications Division worked with the designers and printers. Bruce Ross-Larson from Communications Development Incorporated provided editorial services.

About the World Food Programme

Founded in 1963, the World Food Programme (WFP) is the world's largest humanitarian organization and the United Nations' frontline agency in the fight against global hunger. WFP uses food aid to meet emergency needs and support economic & social development. Operational in more than 80 countries, it relies exclusively on donations of commodities and money. In close collaboration with other members of the UN family, governments and NGOs, WFP works to put hunger at the centre of the international agenda, promoting policies, strategies and operations that directly benefit the hungry poor.

Foreword

There is no more important task than ensuring our children have the nutrition and education they need to make the very most of what the world has to offer. When children are well fed and educated, not only are their own lives immeasurably better, but those of future generations are improved in concrete ways.

Almost all of the Millennium Development Goals can be linked to two basic issues — hunger and education. Eradicating extreme poverty and hunger, guaranteeing all children a basic education, empowering women, reducing child and maternal mortality, combating HIV/AIDS and other diseases are all dependent on people having good nutrition and an opportunity to learn.

It is fitting then that the first edition of this new publication, the World Hunger Series, focuses on 'Hunger and Learning'.

Every child deserves to eat and go to school. The World Hunger Series aims to demonstrate to experts in development, education, health, nutrition, economics and to the general public that this can be achieved. It proves that the benefits will be felt by individuals, communities, nations and economies for generations to come.

How well a mother is nourished during pregnancy has a life-long impact on her baby's ability to learn. Hunger and the need to contribute to the family's income are among the principal reasons many poor children do not go to school. Even those that do attend classes have trouble concentrating when their bellies are empty. Poor, malnourished, uneducated children are, for the most part, destined to remain that way. Alarmingly, scientific evidence is emerging that the less education a child receives, the more likely he or she is to contract HIV.

One of the most surprising elements of this new publication is the opportunity that learning presents to curb hunger. Simple stimulation through play and exposure to colour helps prepare an infant's brain for future cognitive development, especially if it is linked with good nutrition. Schooling opens children's minds to new, better ways of doing things — like improved agricultural techniques or hygiene — and gives them the building blocks to implement them. The number of years a woman attended school, for example, can reduce the likelihood that her child will be malnourished by up to 40 percent. It is never too late to learn; microcredit, income-generation and agricultural extension programmes can improve poor and hungry people's abilities to feed themselves.

At a time when the number of hungry people throughout the world is on the rise again, it is imperative that we take action to stop it. The best way of doing that is to focus our efforts on children and mothers.

James T. Morris
Executive Director
UN World Food Programme

Contents

Figures

Contents

Maps

Boxes

Preface

During the 'hungry season', when the grain from the previous year has been consumed and the crops of the new harvest have not yet matured, farmers in southern Sudan sometimes tie pieces of cloth tightly around their waists. The rags are fastened so that the pressure of the knot is felt on the stomach. It helps control the pain of hunger, they say. Bound this way, they can often work in their fields for a couple of hours. If too weak to stand, they can at least sit in one place to weed the patch of land around them. Although rarely fatal, these bouts of hunger have debilitating effects on adults — on their health, their cognitive functioning, their psychological state and their livelihoods. For children, the damage can be life-long.

Similar hunger, more or less severe, of shorter or longer duration, exists in many parts of the world at the start of the twenty-first century. From rural India to urban Brazil, the Food and Agriculture Organization estimates that 852 million people were undernourished in 2000-2002. The stubbornness of these problems troubles policymakers from local governments to global agencies. Yet progress has been made in many places, demonstrating that hunger can be tackled. It is estimated that the proportion of hungry people in the world has come down from one-fifth to one-sixth over the past 20 years. But the knowledge of how these gains have been achieved has not been well enough disseminated or consistently translated into effective action. In Sudan it is only when the new harvest or some external assistance arrives that farmers can undo the pieces of cloth and discard them for another year.

This report series is about untying knots — about working through the real-life choices and practical constraints that make it difficult to address hunger effectively. It is aimed at policymakers in developing and developed countries. It attempts to fill an important gap in existing reports on hunger. While other reports monitor trends towards international goals or serve primarily as advocacy tools, the World Hunger Series (WHS) will focus on practical strategies to achieve an end to hunger. Each report in the new series will examine a key hunger-related issue — such as learning, health, markets, trade, crises and social exclusion. It will present state-of-the-art thinking on that year's theme, combined with an analysis of the practical challenges to implementing solutions. Based on this analysis, it will identify realistic steps to address hunger.

There is a danger that in focusing on the practical constraints and acknowledging the challenges, we will tacitly offer ready-made excuses to policymakers, who do not want to engage in the difficult task of dealing with hunger. If the challenges are so well-known, they might argue, it is not surprising that they have struggled and failed like others. Our intention is otherwise: to show that no excuses — 'we need to eradicate poverty before hunger' or 'we do not have the expertise' — can justify the neglect of hunger issues, because ways exist to address them.

Another danger, through our emphasis on the practical, is that we could create the impression that hunger is simply a technical issue amenable to mechanistic solutions. This characterization removes the political elements — the way hunger reflects the priorities of nations and the world community. Not discussing the sustained political effort required to deal with hunger would misrepresent and underestimate the difficulties presented by these issues. This report series will take seriously the challenges of generating political will and support for relevant programmes. And it will itself stand as a reminder of world hunger and be an urgent call to action.

Overview

"Understanding the relationship between hunger and learning requires a long-term perspective: what happens at one stage of life affects later stages, and what happens in one generation affects the next."

When most people think about hunger, they focus on its physical manifestations: the emaciation of famine-affected populations, the small stature of chronically malnourished people. But for those who survive hunger, perhaps its most damaging impact is its legacy for learning. Hunger in childhood can lead to irreversible mental stunting, lower intelligence quotients (IQs) and reduced capacities to learn. The effects are tragic for individuals and staggering for nations. It is estimated, for example, that the average IQs of the populations in over 60 countries are 10-15 points lower than they could be because of iodine deficiencies alone (UNICEF and Micronutrient Initiative 2004).

The impacts are especially great because hunger and learning have a two-way relationship. Hunger impairs learning at each stage of life; yet learning is an effective means of addressing hunger. A vicious cycle can be created: hungry children become damaged adults with limited opportunities and capacities, who end up having hungry children of their own. Such a cycle undermines human and economic development. But this cycle can also be reversed, with good nutrition and enhanced learning reinforcing each other through the generations and leading to long-term national development.

The problem of hunger is not going away

In recent decades, there has been some improvement in the global hunger situation. The proportion of undernourished people has been reduced from one-fifth to one-sixth over the past 20 years (UN Millennium Project 2005a), while the number of underweight preschool children in the developing world declined from 162.2 million to 135.5 million between 1990 and 2000 (UNSCN 2004). While this progress is important, it is not nearly enough to achieve the targets that the international community has set for itself as part of Millennium Development Goal 1: halving, between 1990 and 2015, the proportion of people who suffer from hunger.

Why is progress not on track? Part of the explanation is the increase in humanitarian crises, but by far the most important reason is the choices of political leaders. Hunger is a multidimensional problem that requires intersectoral interventions in relevant areas, such as health, markets, learning and emergency preparedness. But too often the necessary investments have not been made. While all these issues must be addressed in a comprehensive approach to hunger, this inaugural edition of the World Hunger Series focuses on one that offers the most promising opportunities to achieve substantial and lasting improvements: the two-way relationship between hunger and learning.

Hunger takes a lifelong toll on learning

Understanding the relationship between hunger and learning requires a long-term perspective: what happens at one stage of life affects later stages, and what happens in one generation affects the next. Consider, first, hunger's impact on learning.

- **Nutrition during pregnancy and the first two years of life strongly influences future mental capacity.**

Along with genetics, stimulation and socio-economic factors, the nutritional conditions during pregnancy and infancy have an important impact on the growth of the brain. After early childhood, it is still possible to improve children's cognitive development, but their fundamental capacity has in many ways already been determined.

- **Hunger keeps children out of school and limits their ability to concentrate once there.**

At school age (5 to 17 years old), hunger keeps children from making the most of opportunities to learn and develop their minds. Many do not attend school, since their parents need them to stay home to help on the farm or to earn money to purchase food. Even when children make it to classrooms, they cannot concentrate on lessons if they are hungry.

- Hungry adults are not able to take advantage of learning opportunities and therefore transmit hunger to the next generation.

Hunger in adulthood (18 years and older) does not have the long-term damaging impact on mental capacity that it does in earlier stages of life. But it can make it difficult to take advantage of opportunities to learn. Hungry adults have less time to focus on activities that do not have a direct payoff in improved nutrition. And they have more trouble concentrating during training. This means that they do not acquire the skills needed to address hunger for themselves and their children.

But learning offers a way to escape from hunger

At each stage of life, learning can contribute to the fight against hunger.

- Stimulation builds the basic capacity to learn in the future.

Stimulation involves relatively simple techniques such as play, conversation, and exposure to colours or shapes. Yet it is critical to making the connections between neurons in the infant's developing brain. It does not teach any particular skills relevant to addressing hunger, but it lays the foundation for future cognitive development, allowing a person to acquire the knowledge needed to escape hunger later in life.

- Schooling allows children to acquire the skills and openness necessary to address hunger at this stage of life and in the future.

Schooling imparts a greater openness to new ideas (such as new agricultural techniques or improved hygiene) and a greater capacity to understand and apply them. A recent study demonstrated that women's level of schooling accounts for more than 40 percent of reductions in childhood malnutrition (Smith and Haddad 2000).

- Adults can acquire the specific skills needed to improve their nutrition — and that of the next generation.

Microcredit programmes, agricultural extension, and income-generating activities can improve production or increase the resources available to buy food. Other learning opportunities can teach better nutritional practices, such as improved hygiene and exclusive breastfeeding for the first six months. These changes in livelihoods and behaviour contribute to improvements in the nutritional status of adults — and feed back into improved prospects for their children.

Relatively simple and tested interventions exist

Interventions can be identified to address each of these problems — to reverse the vicious cycle of hunger and reduced learning, and create a virtuous one.

- Early childhood

To ensure that children reach the proper birthweight and are adequately nourished in infancy, a range of interventions can be considered: food supplements; micronutrient fortification and supplementation; antenatal care (including health services and advice); exclusive breastfeeding for six months; and post-natal care (including immunizations and advice). The importance of stimulation also needs to be emphasized at postnatal clinics and in early childhood development programmes.

- School age

At this stage of life, interventions need to alter parents' calculations about the value of schooling. There are several ways to offset the opportunity costs of sending children to school, depending on the context: school feeding, take-home rations, cash transfers and reduced fees (combined with investments in educational infrastructure and capacity). School feeding can also help children concentrate once there. Children in school will become adults with greater openness and cognitive ability. And, even while in school, they can acquire skills and knowledge about hunger-related issues, such as HIV/AIDS, sanitation and hygiene.

• Adulthood
Learning at this stage creates opportunities to acquire and apply skills and knowledge that lead to increased agricultural production, higher incomes, better nutritional practices, and improved health and sanitation. This knowledge feeds back into improved conditions for the next generation. Adults can be motivated to take advantage of opportunities by offering economically-relevant training and, in some cases, by providing take-home rations.

Creating a virtuous cycle is critical for national development

This relationship between hunger and learning affects more than the potential of individuals or households; it also helps determine the prospects for nations.

• Human development
Improved nutrition and learning are associated with new possibilities — to take on more fulfilling and productive work, to be able to read books, to participate in local council meetings, to protect loved ones from infections, to choose more nutritious foods, to enjoy an evening free from worry. These returns improve prospects for the next generation, which grows up less hungry and more knowledgeable and has even greater potential to secure a better future for their own children. At an aggregate level, these improvements in nutrition and learning expand opportunities and choices for millions of people — national development, in the truest sense.

• Economic growth
The relationship between hunger and learning shapes a nation's economic growth in two ways. First, improved nutrition leads to a better-educated workforce that has a higher level of talents and

skills, or human capital. And high quality human capital is a critical factor in economic development (Barro 1998; Lucas 1988; Lucas 1990; Romer 1986; Romer 1993). The talents and skills create a productive workforce more capable of generating high-value outputs. By contrast, the economic burdens and human capital losses due to illiteracy and ill-health can drain a government of resources. Second, greater learning contributes to a better nourished, stronger workforce. As a result, more people are able to actively participate in the economy, and the effectiveness and efficiency of those who are already engaged increases dramatically (Fogel 2004).

A developed society often has more capacity to put resources back into addressing hunger and inadequate learning at the start of the lifecycle. Economic development leads to the potential for a greater tax base. At the same time, broad indicators of social development such as fertility rates and infant mortality also tend to improve in societies that have addressed hunger and learning issues. These changes help to reduce the burden of population growth and ill-health. The nation is better able to support the next generation, and the cycle is renewed and reinforced. Development, then, is a process, requiring a long-term vision informed by an understanding of how these relationships help to sustain it.

But it requires political will to take the necessary actions

It is easy to identify potential interventions and to point out the critical importance of action for national development. But a concerned policymaker will immediately respond with a barrage of legitimate queries: How can we create political support for these interventions? How can we pay for them? How do they relate to other initiatives? The answers are critical to successful interventions in the real world. Lessons from a number of countries offer some suggestions.

• **Creating political will.**

Several strategies exist. One is to identify champions —high-ranking officials who understand the importance of the issues and can move them up the political agenda. Another strategy is to engage the support and interest of the media, used in both Chile and Thailand to raise awareness about the severity of the nutritional problem — and to mobilize action. Perhaps the most effective way to ensure attention to hunger and learning issues over the long run is to have relevant programmes legally mandated and therefore protected.

• **Overcoming resource constraints.**

Resource concerns sometimes arise from a misunderstanding about costs and benefits. Nutrition interventions for early childhood, for instance, have long-term benefits that far exceed the initial costs. In some cases, programmes such as school feeding can be made more affordable through cost-saving measures. It is important to remember that a number of countries (including Chile, Indonesia and Thailand) have made these investments in nutrition and learning while they were still relatively poor; their economic growth was more a result than a cause of these investments, at least at the outset.

• **Promoting intersectoral work.**

Consideration must go, in the first place, to sequencing interventions. For instance, training hungry adults on income-generating activities or literacy will have limited value if no opportunities yet exist to apply that knowledge to improve livelihoods and reduce hunger. Once a sequenced strategy is developed, the challenge is to find ways to involve all the necessary ministries for intersectoral interventions. Champions for a programme need to ensure that different ministries (e.g. education, health and agriculture) recognize the value of the interventions for achieving their own goals.

In the end, the decision to act is political. Where these investments have been made, the improvements in human and economic terms have been enormous. But these actions required far-sighted leaders who recognized that the greatest returns would be seen 10 or 20 years in the future — and that these benefits would be more than commensurate with the patience and commitment of the effort.

Box 1 — What is hunger?

Most people intuitively understand the physical sensation of being hungry. But specialists who work on hunger issues have developed a range of technical terms and concepts to help them better describe and address the problem. Unfortunately, there is some disagreement on what these terms mean and how they relate to each other. This box provides a short glossary of how these terms and concepts are used in this report. It cannot claim to be the only 'correct' usage, but it does offer a relatively clear and consistent way of understanding the issues.

HUNGER. A condition in which people lack the required nutrients (protein, energy, and vitamins and minerals)[1] for fully productive, active and healthy lives. Hunger can be a short-term phenomenon, or a longer-term chronic problem. It can have a range of severities from mild to clinical. It can result from people not taking in sufficient nutrients or their bodies not being able to absorb the required nutrients.

MALNUTRITION. A clinical condition in which people experience either nutritional deficiencies (undernutrition) or an excess of certain nutrients (overnutrition).

UNDERNUTRITION. The clinical form of hunger that results from serious deficiencies in one or a number of nutrients (protein, energy, and vitamins and minerals). The deficiencies impair a person from maintaining adequate bodily processes, such as growth, pregnancy, lactation, physical work, cognitive function, and resisting and recovering from disease.

UNDERNOURISHMENT. The condition of people whose dietary energy consumption is continuously below a minimum requirement for fully productive, active and healthy lives. It is determined using a proxy indicator that estimates whether the food available in a country is sufficient to meet the energy (but not the protein, vitamin and mineral) requirements of the population. Unlike undernutrition, the indicator does not measure an actual outcome.

SHORT-TERM HUNGER. A transitory non-clinical form of hunger that can affect short-term physical and mental capacity. In this report, it often pertains to school children who have missed breakfast or have walked long distances to school on a relatively empty stomach.

FOOD SECURITY. A condition that exists when all people at all times are free from hunger — that is, they have sufficient nutrients (protein, energy, and vitamins and minerals) required for fully productive, active and healthy lives.

What is the difference between hunger and undernutrition?
Undernutrition is the clinical form of hunger. It can be measured using indicators such as:

- weight-for-age (underweight);

- height-for-age (stunting); and

- weight-for-height (wasting).

However, hunger also includes milder forms that do not register clinically, but nevertheless impair physical and mental activity, often on a short-term basis.

In some cases, undernutrition can be caused by disease, which can influence the adequacy of food intake and/or its absorption in the body (and therefore the level of hunger). Disease affects the adequacy of food intake by altering metabolism (thus increasing the requirements for the intake of nutrients) and reducing appetite (thus often lowering the amount of food ingested). At the same time, disease may cause problems of absorption through the loss of nutrients (e.g. vomiting, diarrhoea) or its interference with the body's mechanisms for absorbing them. Of course, disease often has many other serious and debilitating effects not directly related to its impact on hunger.

What is the difference between hunger and food insecurity?
The concept of food security provides insights into the causes of hunger. Food security has four parts:

- Availability (the supply of food in an area);

- Access (a household's ability to obtain that food);

- Utilisation (a person's ability to select, take-in and absorb the nutrients in the food); and

- Vulnerability (the physical, environmental, economic, social and health risks that may affect availability, access and use) (WFP 2002; Webb and Rogers 2003).

Food insecurity, or the absence of food security, is a state that implies either hunger (due to problems with availability, access and use) or vulnerability to hunger in the future.

How are undernutrition, hunger and food insecurity related?
Undernutrition, hunger and food insecurity are 'nested' concepts. Undernutrition is a subset of hunger, which in turn is a subset of food insecurity. As we have seen, hunger includes both clinical forms (undernutrition) and milder forms, while food insecurity occurs when a person is either hungry or vulnerable to hunger in the future (see diagram below).

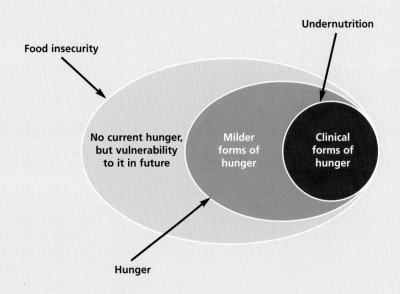

PART I: The Global Hunger Situation

"Too often, analyses of hunger focus exclusively on its physical manifestations, without examining its damaging legacy for learning."

Part I sets the context for the report by surveying global hunger in 2004. **Chapter 1** shows that addressing hunger is a key to human development. Hunger irreversibly limits human potential, causing millions of deaths, stunting physical development and reducing learning capacity. However, not enough progress is being made to meet the Millennium Development Goal for hunger. The chapter identifies two principal reasons: an increase in humanitarian crises — and, more importantly, the choices of political leaders.

1. Hunger and development

Hunger feels like pincers,
like the bite of crabs.
It burns, burns, and has no fire.

— Pablo Neruda

As an impoverished student in Santiago in the 1920s, the Chilean poet Pablo Neruda sometimes went without food. At the time, hunger was widespread in his country, especially in urban centres and rural mining districts to the north. Having experienced hunger directly, Neruda could convey the physical sensation in evocative imagery. But the line quoted above also suggests another important aspect of hunger: it does not draw attention to itself, it "has no fire".

Except in severe crises, the physical symptoms of hunger are hard to recognize. The life-long damage that it does to the mental development of children cannot be seen. It is only when the problem is explained, and solutions developed, that it can be adequately addressed. Decades later, recognizing the profound loss of human potential to hunger, Neruda's country identified it as a priority and, despite political turmoil, made consistent investments that have had enormous long-term benefits for its population.

Many developing countries today face the choices Chile did two generations ago. The story of the challenges and benefits of making these investments is the focus of this year's report. In particular, the report emphasizes what might be called the 'other side' of hunger — the relationship between hunger and mental development. Too often, analyses of hunger focus exclusively on its physical manifestations, without examining its damaging legacy for learning. This report discusses the profound, mutually reinforcing benefits that investments in hunger alleviation and learning have for individuals and nations. And it offers an agenda for concrete actions at the national and international levels.

The report has four principal parts:

- The Global Hunger Situation surveys the current state of hunger in the world.

- Hunger and Learning explores the two-way relationship between hunger and learning through the lifecycle.

- An Agenda for National Development examines the role of hunger reduction and learning in national development and provides concrete steps for moving forward.

- A Resource Compendium contains technical annexes and supporting data.

To set the stage, this first chapter assesses the current hunger situation. It begins by explaining hunger's critical role in development and assessing progress in meeting international targets related to hunger. It then examines two major reasons for the persistence of hunger: humanitarian crises and political choices.

1.1 Hunger's role in development

Development can be understood as the process of expanding the real choices that people enjoy (Sen 1999). In this view, 'development' is not an achieved state, a clear-cut level, which once surpassed qualifies one or one's nation as 'developed' (even though we speak of 'developed' and 'developing' countries as a linguistic convenience in this report). Instead, it is the accumulation and expansion of freedoms that constitute development. Addressing hunger is an integral part of achieving development for individuals and nations — both as a developmental end in itself and as a means to realize other key aspects of development, such as education, health and poverty alleviation.

Hunger greatly reduces the opportunities of individuals and nations — and thus limits development — by causing deaths, physical stunting and mental retardation. Each year nearly 11 million children die before they reach the age of five (*Lancet* Editor 2003). The main cause of death varies from region to region, but more than half of these young children (roughly 6 million) die of factors linked directly to undernutrition.

Box 1.1 — Hunger limits opportunities around the world

There are …

- 852 million undernourished people in the world (FAO 2004a), who cannot fully engage in their livelihoods.

- 135.5 million underweight preschool children (UNSCN 2004), who are suffering mental damage.

- 32 percent of children under 5 in the developing world, who are moderately or severely stunted (UNICEF 2004) and who will never grow to their genetic potential, may never achieve their full mental capacity, and will probably suffer more often from chronic illness in the rest of their lives.

- 75 million people, who needed food aid to save their lives and/or livelihoods in the context of humanitarian crises (WFP, annual two-year average).

For those who survive, hunger causes physical and mental damage that can last a lifetime. There are approximately 150 million children under 5 years old who are physically stunted — too short for their age (UNSCN 2004). Nutritional shocks in early childhood can permanently limit the size and stature of the future adult. A smaller stature has been proven to lead to lower income returns and opportunities, especially in manual labour (Scrimshaw 1997; Strauss and Thomas 1998; Sachs 2001). Stunted individuals also appear to be more prone to chronic diseases. The impact of inadequate nutrition, especially in the earliest years, on mental development is much less widely publicized. But evidence strongly indicates that undernutrition can irreversibly limit the mental capacity of an individual. (This is the subject of this year's report and will be discussed in detail in subsequent chapters.)

These physical and mental limitations can create a 'hunger trap' in which hunger is transmitted from one generation to the next. The trap has at least three reinforcing dimensions. First, adults who were damaged by hunger as children are less productive and less able to create adequate livelihoods. As a result, they do not have the resources or skills to care for themselves or their children. This means that their children will likely be hungry and grow up damaged as well.

Second, because of their narrow margin of survival, hungry adults are extremely risk averse, unable to take chances that might improve their situation. The hungry poor find it difficult to send their children to school, to treat health problems, to invest in new production techniques, or to take measures that will protect them from future crises, because these activities use scarce resources for investments that may not have an immediate return. Yet these are precisely the investments that they need to make to address hunger in the long term for themselves and their children.

Third, the hungry poor are so risk averse because they are vulnerable to shocks, such as crop failures or a death in the family. Unfortunately, their cautious strategy does not pay off, since each time the hungry are hit by a shock, they are forced to employ negative coping strategies — such as reducing food consumption, selling productive assets or removing children from school (Corbett 1988; Walker 1989; Rahmato 1991) — that further diminish their asset base and make them more vulnerable to the next shock. As a result, their livelihoods become even more inadequate to meet the needs of themselves and their children. Moreover, the shocks disproportionately affect young children and those developing in the womb, leading directly to physical

Figure 1.1 — Progress on undernourishment and underweight is not rapid enough in the majority of developing countries

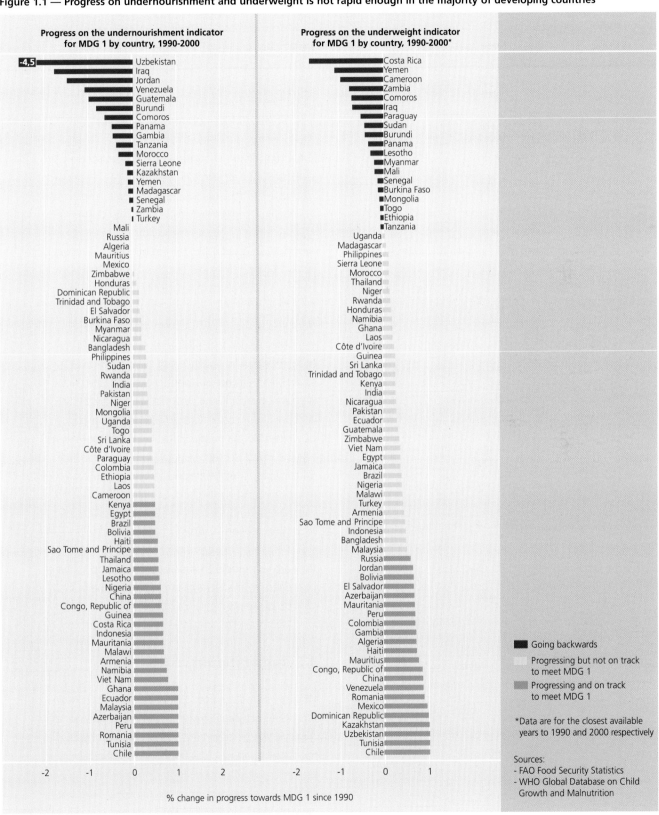

Progress on the undernourishment indicator for MDG 1 by country, 1990-2000

Progress on the underweight indicator for MDG 1 by country, 1990-2000*

% change in progress towards MDG 1 since 1990

Going backwards

Progressing but not on track to meet MDG 1

Progressing and on track to meet MDG 1

*Data are for the closest available years to 1990 and 2000 respectively

Sources:
- FAO Food Security Statistics
- WHO Global Database on Child Growth and Malnutrition

and mental stunting and reduced opportunities for them in the future. In all these ways, hunger is transmitted to the next generation. When aggregated, these impacts limit the progress of nations — economically, socially and politically.

1.2 Measuring progress on hunger

Development, while conceptualized as expanding choices, can be measured through the proxy of the Millennium Development Goals. At the Millennium Summit in September 2000, world leaders committed their nations to a new global partnership to reduce poverty, improve health, and promote peace, human rights, gender equality and environmental sustainability. They identified eight goals relating to these topics. Millennium Development Goal 1 (MDG 1) refers to "halving poverty and hunger" between 1990 and 2015.

The indicators for the hunger target of MDG 1 include:
1. The proportion of people undernourished (an indicator of estimated shortfalls in caloric intake); and
2. The prevalence of underweight preschool children (a composite measure reflecting both chronic and acute undernutrition).

Using these indicators to assess progress, there have been some improvements in the global hunger situation, but not enough to meet the goals. The proportion of undernourished people (or people without sufficient caloric intake) has been reduced from one-fifth to one-sixth over the past 20 years (UN Millennium Project 2005a). The number of preschool children who are underweight (or who have a lower weight than normal for their age) in the developing world declined from 162.2 million to 135.5 million between 1990 and 2000 (UNSCN 2004).

But these global trends disguise a much more troubling picture at the national level. In fact, if the progress made by China is excluded, the number of undernourished people in the world has actually increased by 18 million since 1990 (FAO 2004). Of 76 developing countries examined in this report, 63 percent (or 48 countries) are not on track to meet the undernourishment target, while 71 percent (or 54 countries) are not making enough progress to reach the underweight target. Some countries, including Burundi, Yemen and Zambia, are actually regressing on both indicators (see Figure 1.1).

Why are so many countries not on track? There are at least two explanations: the increase in humanitarian crises and the choices of political leaders.

1.3 Humanitarian crises

Whether natural or man-made, humanitarian crises represent a major cause of hunger and a serious threat to the development process. Although some natural disasters, such as floods and earthquakes, may be over in a matter of days or even minutes, communities may require years to recover from the damage that they cause to their livelihoods and food

---

Box 1.2 — Hunger and the other Millennium Development Goals

The focus in this report is on MDG 1, but hunger also influences:

- MDG 2 (universal primary education) by reducing school attendance;

- MDG 3 (gender equality in education) since girls are more likely to drop out of school due to hunger than boys;

- MDG 4 (child mortality) by causing millions of deaths;

- MDG 5 (maternal health) by leading to the deterioration of the health of pregnant mothers;

- MDG 6 (HIV/AIDS, malaria and other diseases) by reducing the body's capacity to fight infections.

security. During that time, new crises may emerge, further aggravating the situation. The problems are often magnified when conflict is involved. Conflict has been described recently as 'development in reverse' (Collier and others 2003), suggesting its far-ranging negative impacts, which often include hunger.

• Current situation

Humanitarian crises involving hunger continued at near record highs in 2004 (Map 1.1). WFP relief interventions alone — themselves just a fraction of public and private humanitarian aid — reached an average of 75 million people a year in 2003 and 2004. These interventions responded to some of the most visible manifestations of hunger — the effects of wars, natural disasters and sudden economic crises in the poorest countries (Figure 1.2).

Figure 1.2 — Conflict and natural disasters top the list

Hunger Emergencies: Major WFP Interventions in 2004

Expenditure rank	Country or region	Expenditure (million US$)	Type of Emergency
1	Sudan	354.3	Conflict
2	Tsunami-affected countries	274.4 [a]	Tsunami
3	Ethiopia	147.9	Drought
4	Democratic People's Republic of Korea	121.4	Economic failure/Drought
5	Afghanistan	119.1	Economic failure/Drought
6	Uganda	83.0	Conflict
7	Angola	73.5	Conflict
8	Zimbabwe	70.6	Economic failure/Drought
9	Kenya	56.6	Drought/Conflict
10	Eritrea	44.9	Drought/Conflict

[a] The tsunami occurred in late 2004 but expenditures were incurred largely in 2005.

Source: WFP

At least 70 countries had major emergencies involving hunger in 2004. Almost half (46 percent) resulted from socio-political instability (i.e. economic failure or conflict). These kinds of emergencies arose in Iraq and Darfur, Sudan, for example. Around 26 percent involved natural disasters, such as the tsunami in the Indian Ocean, the locust infestations in the Sahel and the earthquake in Iran. The remaining 28 percent were caused by a combination of socio-political instability and natural disasters, as in Afghanistan.

• Trends

These record numbers reflect longer-term trends. The past decade and a half has seen an overall increase in natural disasters leading to a rise in the number of humanitarian crises involving hunger.

Longer-term data analyzed by the International Federation of Red Cross and Red Crescent Societies (IFRC) show that the number of hydrometeorological disasters (e.g. storms and droughts) has multiplied sevenfold since 1960 and that of geophysical disasters (e.g. earthquakes and volcano eruptions) fivefold (see Figure 1.4). In the last decade, this trend has begun to assert itself more forcefully. From 1994 to 2003, the number of natural disasters has grown dramatically from just above 200 reported disasters a year to more than 400 in recent years (CRED-EM DAT 2005). Disasters in countries with low human development are increasing at the fastest rate (IFRC 2004). At the same time, conflicts remain a problem. While the number of major armed conflicts has declined since the end of the cold war, there were still close to 20 ongoing in 2004 (SIPRI 2005).[2] The conflicts in Afghanistan, Iraq and Darfur, Sudan, required some of the most significant relief operations of the last decade.

These developments in natural and man-made disasters have made it necessary to expend more resources on emergency response efforts, hampering attempts to address the root causes of hunger.

Map 1.1 — Hunger crises around the world in 2004

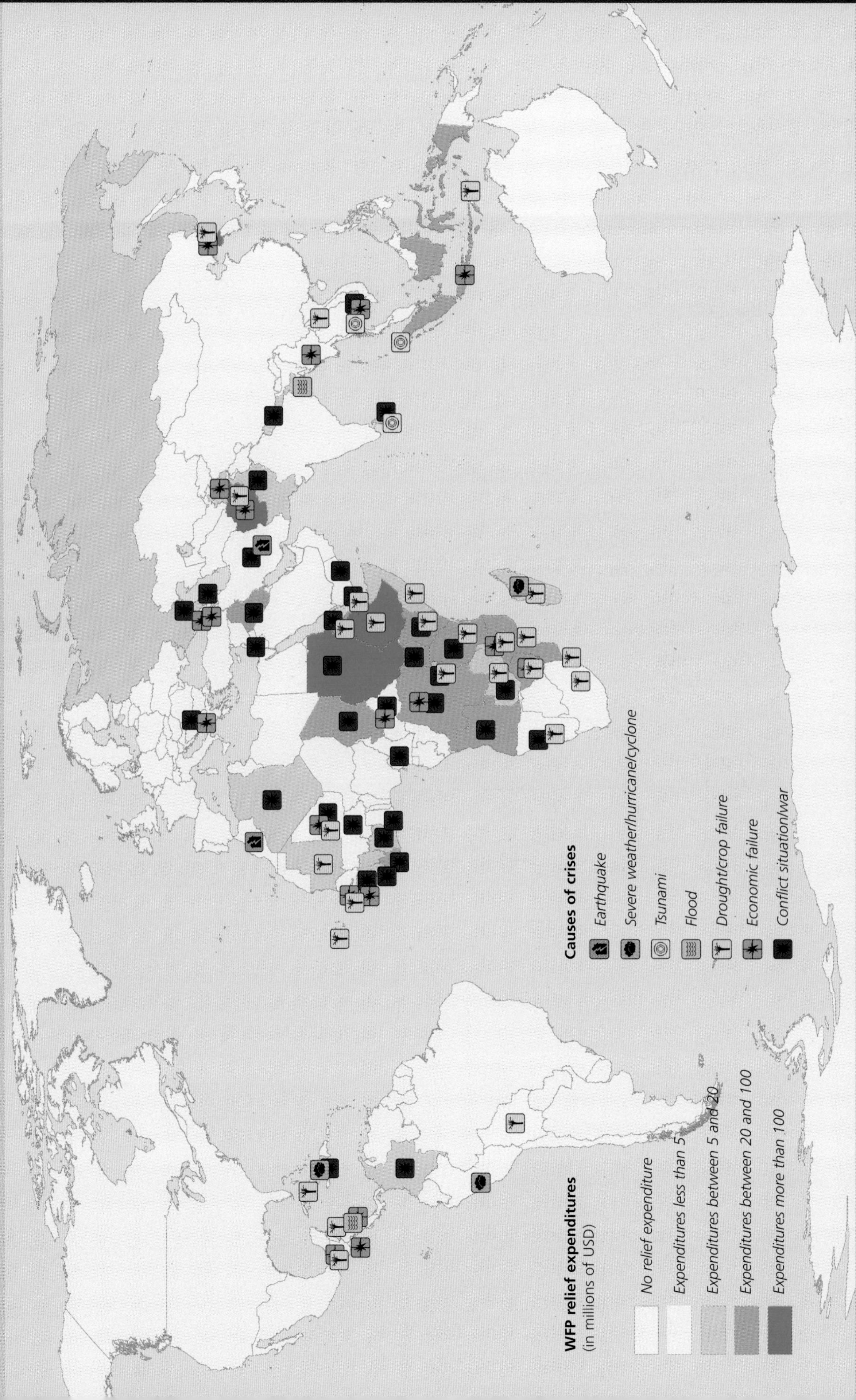

Causes of crises

- Earthquake
- Severe weather/hurricane/cyclone
- Tsunami
- Flood
- Drought/crop failure
- Economic failure
- Conflict situation/war

WFP relief expenditures
(in millions of USD)

- No relief expenditure
- Expenditures less than 5
- Expenditures between 5 and 20
- Expenditures between 20 and 100
- Expenditures more than 100

Data source: WFP

1.4 Political choices

But humanitarian crises account for only 10 percent of the hunger suffered worldwide (UN Millennium Project 2005a). The majority of people suffering from hunger are caught in ongoing 'silent emergencies' of chronic undernutrition and ill-health (see box 1.3). The choices of national and international policymakers are the most critical factor in the continued existence of this kind of hunger. In the past, many concerned governments focused exclusively on economic growth as a means to reduce hunger. It was believed that economic progress would 'trickle down' to the poorest, leading to improvements in undernutrition. But the evidence does not support this view. Macroeconomic growth does not

translate in linear fashion into improvements for the poorest of families. One study found that changes in economic growth, food availability and child nutrition are only weakly correlated over time (Haddad, Webb and Slack 1997).

Similarly, using household data from six developing countries, Appleton and Song (1999) showed that stunting was not confined to poor households; it was also present in 32 percent of non-poor households. Alderman and Christiaensen (2001) found that in Ethiopia a 10 percent increase in expenditure among the poor only reduces the gap between average stunting rates and international reference standards by 1.2 percent. Although GDP per capita in developing countries rose by more than 60 percent between 1980 and 2000, the number of

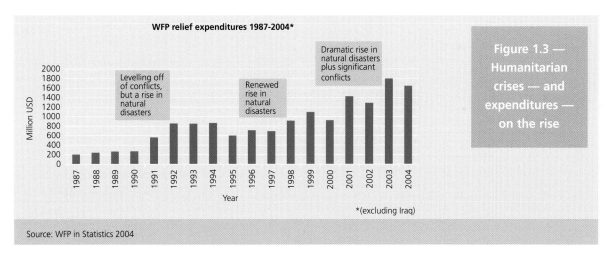

Figure 1.3 — Humanitarian crises — and expenditures — on the rise

Source: WFP in Statistics 2004

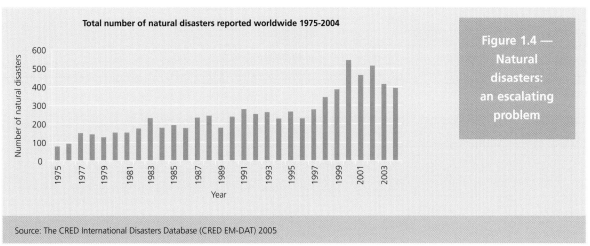

Figure 1.4 — Natural disasters: an escalating problem

Source: The CRED International Disasters Database (CRED EM-DAT) 2005

31

Box 1.3 — Silent emergency in India

Most preventable deaths of hungry people take place outside emergencies. This startling fact is at the centre of a paradox in India. Renowned for its Famine Codes that have prevented famine for more than 60 years, India nevertheless faces an ongoing 'silent emergency' of chronic hunger and suffering. A major famine has not occurred in India since the one in Bengal in 1943, but even more people die each year from malnutrition than were lost in that crisis (Drèze and Sen 1989). There are currently 221 million undernourished people in India (FAO 2004) — some 27.5 percent of the world's total. India has 35 percent of all underweight children, with only 17 percent of the world's people. The country has taken numerous steps to address these issues. It has an extensive food-based safety net system. The system is designed, in theory, to protect a person through the life-cycle, with assistance to young children and expectant and nursing mothers, followed by school feeding for children, and then seasonal public works projects and a Public Distribution System (PDS) for those in need as adults. In practice, the performance of the national system has been uneven. However, several state systems, such as the one in Tamilnadu, have shown remarkable impact through careful management, targeting and comprehensive programmes (Mahendra Dev and others 2004).

hungry people fell by only 10 percent. In other words, economic growth is not enough.

Needed, as well, are targeted policies that focus specifically on hunger-related issues. Hunger is a multi-dimensional problem that requires political commitment for inter-sectoral interventions in relevant areas ranging from health and markets to learning and emergency preparedness (see Figure 1.5). Hunger has a two-way relationship with many of these factors that create it — that is, hunger is both their cause and effect. Hunger contributes to problems in areas such as learning, health, the environment and agriculture; yet each of these factors affects the availability, access and utilisation of food. This report series aims to provide

policymakers with the information they need to make the right choices in addressing hunger in their specific contexts.

The UN Millennium Project Hunger Task Force and others have identified recommendations for achieving the Hunger Target of Millennium Development Goal 1 (cf. UN Millennium Project 2005a). This report series will complement these efforts by examining the individual issues in-depth and providing concrete steps for actions. While a number of factors must be addressed to tackle hunger effectively, this inaugural report focuses on one of the most promising areas to achieve substantial and lasting improvements: the two-way relationship between hunger and learning.

Figure 1.5 — The relationship between hunger and its causes

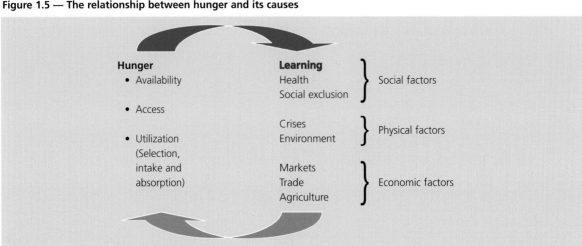

Intermezzo 1: Humanitarian crises in South Asia and Sudan

Two of the major crises involving hunger in 2004 occurred continents apart. The Indian Ocean tsunami and the emergency in Darfur, Sudan, illustrate not only the geographical spread of hunger crises, but also their differing causes at the start of the millennium.

The Indian Ocean tsunami

At 0800 local time on 26 December 2004, a powerful earthquake measuring 9.1 on the Richter scale shook the coast of Aceh Province in Indonesia, setting off a series of large tsunamis across the Indian Ocean. Areas as far away as India and Somalia were severely affected by wave surges, some as high as 6 metres. The wave surges struck some of the poorest and most heavily populated coastal communities in Indonesia, Sri Lanka, the Maldives and elsewhere (quoted, in part, from WFP 2005a).

For many along the coast, it was as if an angry ocean had taken a deep breath: all the water was sucked away from the shore, leaving fishing boats and vessels temporarily on dry land. People described an eerie feeling as birds squawked and circled, and monkeys scampered instinctively towards higher ground. When the ocean exhaled, it was with a surge of water that overran houses, fields, tourist hotels, businesses, roads, sanitation facilities and other infrastructure along the coast. More than 250,000 people died in the wave surges, or drowned in the powerful undertow that dragged others into the ocean.

In the aftermath the main concerns for hunger focused on more than 2.2 million people who were in need of food aid. A UNICEF study indicated that, as a result of this shock, 13 percent of children under five suffered from acute malnutrition in Banda Aceh, Indonesia (Schlein 2005). Those whose access to food had been cut off and who were deemed most at risk included displaced people in evacuation centres and shelters, people whose homes had been damaged or destroyed, and children who had lost their parents and families in the disaster (WFP 2005a).

Assistance would also have to be provided to displaced people as they returned home and to fisherpersons, farmers and other poor people, as they re-established their livelihoods. Assessment missions determined that the tsunamis did not significantly damage inland agricultural fields and national food availability — and that much of the required food aid could be bought through local purchase.

Since the tsunami, it has become clear that several issues need further investigation in order to make responses to similar natural disasters more effective in the future.

• Appropriate aid

Though few questioned the provision of food aid in the weeks immediately following the tsunami, the debate quickly shifted to the merits of alternative strategies. Would the influx of cash contributions and cash-for-work programmes — in areas where functioning markets remained — be enough to maintain the nutritional status of the population? What were the possibilities for local purchase of needed food aid commodities? How could governments and donors introduce agricultural and fishery recovery programmes that actually improved rather than simply restored long-term productivity? The answers to these types of questions are being explored in the tsunami-affected countries and others around the world.

• Early warning and contingency planning

Widespread calls were made for a tsunami early warning system, based on the ones that exist for the Pacific Ocean. But some also pointed out the importance of improving contingency planning (Choularton 2005). Currently, and predictably, contingency planning tends to focus on more likely events. However, in the future, planning must also take into account low-probability but potentially catastrophic contingencies — such as the tsunami.

The crisis in Darfur, Sudan

Unlike the tsunami, the crisis in Darfur, Sudan, was man-made, with political origins. In 2002, citing a history of political and economic marginalization, two rebel groups (the Sudan Liberation Movement/Army and the Justice and Equality Movement) in the Darfur region of Sudan began fighting for greater regional autonomy and investment. The government retaliated with air attacks and apparent support for proxy militia, known as the Janjaweed, who have looted and razed villages.

In 2003, the principal access that aid workers had to the victims of the violence was through the refugee camps along the border of Chad. Apart from the horrific tales of the refugees, relatively little was known about what was occurring across the sands in Darfur. Since then, aid agencies, journalists and researchers have gained better access, and the dimensions of the crisis have become clearer.

In terms of hunger, an estimated 3.2 million people are in need of assistance (WFP and UNICEF 2005). The main group of concern is internally displaced persons, forced to flee their villages, disrupting their livelihood opportunities and their access to food. They are generally living in camps, being hosted by residents or sheltering in schools and other public buildings of government-controlled towns. A second group of concern is the resident population. They have not moved from their respective villages, but their access to food (through markets, agriculture, labour and hunting) has been constrained due to the war and insecurity. Some of the residents are also hosting internally displaced people, placing an additional burden on their scarce resources (quoted, in part, from WFP 2005b).

Though larger than many other complex emergencies, the challenges of addressing hunger in Darfur are similar to those in many conflict-affected areas around the world:

• **Maintaining minimal nutritional standards during a crisis to avoid long-term development losses**

An in-depth joint assessment in 2004 determined that the global acute malnutrition rate was 21.8 percent, while the severe acute malnutrition rate was 3.9 percent among residents and internally displaced people. Both were well above the internationally accepted range, indicating an alarming nutritional situation. Micronutrient deficiencies for women and children were also unacceptably high, with 26 percent of women suffering from iodine deficiency and an estimated 16 percent with clinical vitamin A deficiency. Anaemia was also found in 26.8 percent of the

women and 55 percent of the children (WFP 2004b, WFP 2005b). As this report shows, malnutrition, especially in young children, can lead to long-term mental as well as physical damage.

Fortunately, a major multi-sectoral response effort appears to have made some progress in improving the situation (WFP and UNICEF 2005). A joint assessment in 2005 showed that global acute malnutrition had declined to 11.9 percent and severe acute malnutrition had fallen to 1.4 percent. Over 70 percent of the households had adequate iodized salt. And school feeding programmes for over 350,000 children are set to begin.

• **Access, protection and sovereignty**

Given the precariousness of the situation, a central concern is how to obtain — and maintain — humanitarian access and deliver assistance in a situation where both sides, but principally the government and its militias, have been accused of crimes against humanity and even genocide. On the one hand, there is an imperative to protect the affected populations from attack and to hold the responsible parties to account. On the other hand, raising these concerns sometimes compromises access to those in need of humanitarian assistance.

The issues raised in both the tsunami and Darfur are illustrative of the challenges facing affected populations and aid workers in the fight against hunger in the early 2000s.

PART II: Hunger And Learning

"Undernutrition during pregnancy and infancy causes the most harm to the long-term learning capacity of individuals ..."

While **Part I** demonstrated how, despite some progress, hunger remains widespread and continues to undermine development, **Part II** examines an often overlooked but critical aspect of hunger: its two-way relationship with learning. **Chapter 2** explains how hunger seriously (and often irreversibly) impairs learning, from early childhood to adulthood. **Chapter 3** shows how learning can be used to overcome hunger. **Chapter 4** provides practical interventions that can be implemented to create a positive cycle between hunger alleviation and learning. These discussions set the stage for **Part III**, which explores steps to address the links between hunger and learning at the national level.

2. Hunger's impact on learning

Henry David Thoreau, the eminent American thinker, once famously wrote that "There are a thousand hacking at the branches of evil for one striking at its roots!" It is not enough to deal with the immediate manifestations of hunger, he would likely argue; it is also necessary to address its root causes. Societies frequently use their scarce resources to cope with the damaging consequences that early undernutrition has for learning — to rehabilitate malnourished children, help them recover from associated delays in intellectual development and address learning problems in later life.

Figure 2.1 — Hunger's impact on learning

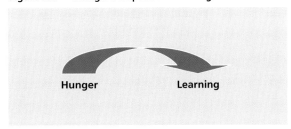

Taking corrective action is essential. Children who survive early nutritional deprivation perform more poorly at school, have lower cognitive capacity and greater poverty in adulthood, and create poorer nutritional conditions for the next generation — thus perpetuating the cycle of hunger. The challenge, however, is to reorient the focus of current efforts from mainly curative, reactive strategies to more preventive, proactive ones — that is, to get at the root causes of the problem. The evidence clearly shows that, in addressing hunger's impact on learning, it is best to intervene early, targeting mothers and infants as the first priority, but that intervening at other stages of life is also critical. This chapter explains these linkages in more detail (see Figure 2.1).

In examining each stage of the lifecycle, it is necessary to distinguish between hunger's impact on a person's future *capacity* to learn (brain structure) and the impact on a person's ability to make use of specific *opportunities* to learn (school, training).

Hunger tends to have its greatest influence on capacity in early childhood and, to a lesser degree, during school age. The impact on opportunities to learn is more pronounced among school-aged children and adults.

2.1 Early childhood

Nutritional conditions in early childhood (in addition to genetics and stimulation) can affect both a person's future capacity to learn and immediate opportunities to develop cognitive ability.

Capacity to learn

Undernutrition during pregnancy and infancy causes the most harm to the long-term learning capacity of individuals. It is the time when the brain is forming and rapidly developing. Without sufficient nutrients, its structure and size can be irreversibly damaged. Signs of trouble include: low birthweight, growth faltering and micronutrient deficiencies.

• Low birthweight

Low birthweight means that a child's weight at the time of birth is less than it should be. (Technically, it occurs when the newborn weighs less than 2.5 kilograms.) While low birthweight in industrial countries is usually the result of premature births, in developing countries it is more likely the result of the foetus not growing properly in the womb. This inadequate growth can result from several factors, but nutritional deficiencies in the mother are a primary one.

Because the brain is at a formative stage during pregnancy, early malnutrition sometimes causes damage that can last into later life. Until recently, low birthweight was primarily seen as a concern because it is a risk factor for poor growth after birth, which (as the next section shows) can lead to reduced mental ability[3]. However, there is now

2. Hunger's impact on learning

Box 2.1 — Hunger's impact on learning in more detail

This chapter looks at hunger's impact on learning. To fully understand the relationship, it is important to examine the impacts broken out by stage of life. The basic stages of life considered here are early childhood (zero to five years old); school age (six to 17 years old); and adulthood (18 years and older). As discussed in the main text and shown on the diagram below, hunger at each stage can lead either to a reduced capacity to learn in the future or to fewer opportunities to learn at that time.

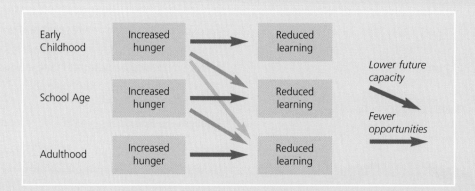

A complete representation needs to consider hunger's impact on the various components of learning. Learning occurs when there is availability, access, and utilization of learning opportunities. That is, for learning to take place, opportunities to learn must be available (e.g. schools with teachers must exist in an area). People must be able to access them (e.g. students must be able to afford the fees). And people must be able to utilize the opportunities (e.g. once at school, students must have the attention span and learning capacity to benefit from the lessons). Hunger affects these aspects of learning at each stage of life.

Early childhood: Hunger in this stage of life, indicated by low birthweight, growth faltering and micronutrient deficiencies, can cause damage to a person's basic learning capacity (i.e. their ability to utilize future learning opportunities). Hunger can also limit an infant's opportunities to explore the world around them (i.e. to gain access to stimulation) and to concentrate on those interactions (i.e. to utilize those opportunities).

School age: At this stage of life, vitamin and mineral deficiencies may limit future capacity to learn (i.e. affect a learner's basic characteristics and therefore their ability to utilize future learning opportunities). Hunger also reduces opportunities to learn while in school by leading to low enrolment, attendance and retention (i.e. limited access) as well as to poor attention spans (i.e. inability to fully utilize the opportunity).

Adulthood: Hunger in adulthood does not affect basic mental capacity, but it does limit opportunities to learn by raising the opportunity cost of engaging in learning activities (i.e. affecting access) and by decreasing attention spans (i.e. affecting the ability to utilize opportunities).

Figure 2.2 — Birthweight can affect cognitive ability into adulthood

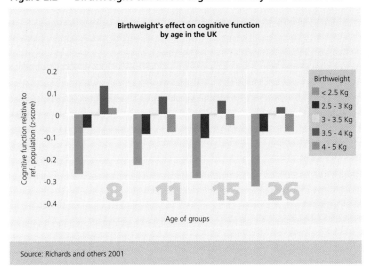

Source: Richards and others 2001

increasing evidence that low birthweight itself is a sign of longer-term mental damage.

One of the most striking illustrations is the apparent relationship between low birthweight and future academic performance. Researchers examined a data set that traced the intellectual development of some 5,000 people born in the same week in March 1946 in England, Scotland and Wales. Controlling for a number of socio-economic factors, the study attempted to assess the impact of birthweight on future intellectual ability (Richards and others 2001), by examining the test results of the group at ages 8, 11, 15, 26 and 43. Surprisingly, the authors found that the damaging effects of low birthweight persist through adolescence and into adulthood, influencing school performance and even university entrance (Figure 2.2)[4] — although many of these differences disappear by midlife.

• **Growth faltering**

Once a child is born, the dangers are not over. Growth faltering is the term used to describe the failure of a young child to grow to its potential after birth. It is a physical indication that a child is not receiving the necessary nutrients; it also means that the child is probably suffering some mental damage. Low birthweight explains much of the growth

faltering in early childhood (Shrimpton 2001), but proper nutrition after birth matters as well. Inadequate nutrition alters the structure and limits the growth of the young brain, especially the parts linked to cognitive functioning and the development of motor skills.

Growth faltering was once thought to begin at about three months. More recently, however, an analysis of 39 countries determined that stunting (a form of growth faltering) begins immediately after birth (see Intermezzo 2). Stunting leaves a damaging legacy — making people not only shorter, but also mentally impaired. Preschool children with stunted growth in Kenya and Mexico were behind their peers in cognitive and behavioural measures. They played, verbalized and interacted less frequently— and cried or did nothing more often (Allen and others 1992).

The greater the severity of stunting, and the earlier its onset in the child's life, the greater is the effect on future cognitive development (Mendez and Adair 1999). Philippino children, for example, were given a test in which they were shown cards with five objects drawn on them. They had to choose the object that did not fit in logically with the rest. For instance, one card showed four types of shoes and a hat. Children who had experienced severe stunting when they were less than two years old performed significantly worse than their colleagues on these tests when they all reached the ages of eight and 11 — though the gap diminished somewhat over time.

In developing countries, around one-third of children under five, as many as 180 million, exhibit growth faltering. Among children under five in the least developed nations, and especially in South Asia, almost half are stunted (UNICEF 2004). The high rates show that conditions affecting the cognitive development (and growth and health) of children in developing countries remain poor, limiting the ability of millions of people to function at their full potential as adults (de Onis and others 2000).

• Micronutrient deficiencies

In addition to contributing to low birthweight and growth faltering, vitamin and mineral deficiencies during pregnancy and infancy can have specific effects on the cognitive structures involved in learning (Grantham-McGregor and others 2000; Pollitt and others 1989; Sheshadri and Golpaldas 1989). Iodine deficiency can be particularly serious, since the micronutrient is required for the proper development of the foetus's brain and nervous system during pregnancy (WFP 2004e).

Expectant mothers in developing countries are often deficient (like the rest of the population) because there is not enough iodine in the soil and water where they live and therefore in their food. If the deficiency occurs early in pregnancy, it can sometimes cause cretinism, a form of severe mental retardation. But even moderate deficiencies in the mother can have lasting consequences for the mental development of children (Delange 2000; cf. Grantham-McGregor and others 2000; Pollitt and others 1989; Sheshadri and Golpaldas 1989).

A study from China graphically illustrates this point. Researchers compared the IQs of primary school students in villages that were similar in social and economic terms, but that had different prevalences of iodine deficiency. The children in the iodine deficient villages would likely have been affected during pregnancy. When the researchers plotted the students' IQs, they found that the curves were similar, but the one for the iodine deficient villages was shifted back — by more than 10 points (Figure 2.3).

A lack of iron in infancy is another one of the most common and damaging deficiencies. Inadequate iron, because of its effect on brain enzymes, slows neural impulses and is thus associated with delayed psychomotor and cognitive development and behavioural problems (Algarín and others 2003). Young children are slower to learn to crawl and are more likely to be tremulous. They process information more slowly and are less likely to show appropriate reactions to their experiences. Even with early treatment, the adverse effects of iron deficiency in infancy appear irreversible (Lozoff and others 2000). Other micronutrient deficiencies (including vitamins A and B12) in infancy and early childhood also negatively affect cognitive development.[5]

Opportunities to learn

Although hunger's impact in early childhood is greatest on a person's future capacity to learn, it also limits the immediate learning opportunities of the young child.

Hunger (and associated illnesses) can prevent children from exploring and participating in learning opportunities in the world around them — from picking up a toy, investigating a basket of clothing, or playing with their friends. Even when presented with such opportunities (for example, when an adult reads a book to them), hunger can distract a child's attention, preventing them from making the most of those occasions to learn.

Figure 2.3 — Iodine deficiency lowers student intelligence

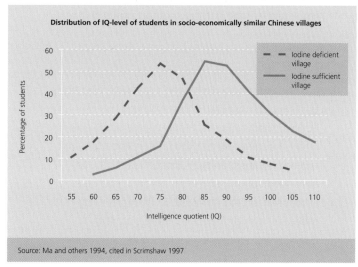

Source: Ma and others 1994, cited in Scrimshaw 1997

2.2 School age

School age is also a sensitive period in children's development. Their fundamental capacity to learn is still being shaped, and hunger can prevent them from making the most of their opportunities to learn at school.

Capacity to learn

While it is not clear whether nutritional deficits cause any damage to long-term mental capacity at this age, good nutrition for school-age children can affect their long-term ability by providing a chance to compensate for some previous damage through 'catch-up growth' (Jukes and others 2002). That is, children can recover some of their potential both in terms of physical size and mental development. Although it seems clear that catch-up growth can occur, it is less certain how much takes place. Researchers have arrived at different conclusions. While there is strong evidence that substantial recovery is possible (cf. Simondon and others 1998), it unfortunately does not appear that full catch-up growth occurs (Drake and others 2002) — even in terms of mental development.

Opportunities to learn

Hunger also reduces children's ability to take advantage of learning opportunities, by reducing school attendance (i.e. their access to these opportunities) and limiting attention spans (i.e. their ability to make the most of them).

• Reduced school enrolment and attendance

In 2000, an estimated 100 million school-age children around the world were not enrolled in school (UIS 2003). In many countries, especially in Africa, more than 30 or even 50 percent of primary school-age children are not enrolled (see Map 2.1), in large part because of hunger.

Hungry families face a number of barriers to sending their children to school. For one thing, they often have to pay tuition or other fees for their children to attend. These fees can amount to 5-10 percent of the family's household income, or even 20-30 percent for poorer families (UNICEF 2002a). In Uganda, Bangladesh, Zambia and Nepal, education was found to be one of the top three major household expenditures (Herz and Sperling 2004).

In addition to these direct fees for schooling, there are such indirect costs as contributions to parent-teacher associations, as well as the expense of transport, clothing and safety escorts (especially for girls). Perhaps most importantly, sending children to school incurs opportunity costs for hungry families, since the children could be performing household chores or earning wages (UNICEF 2002c). These costs all add up and may become a deterrent to enrolment for students from hungry households.

If they can overcome these barriers, children suffering from undernutrition are still more likely to enrol later in school than their peers (Del Rosso and Marek 1996). One of the reasons is simple but telling: malnourished children do not seem old enough for their parents to send them to school (Jukes and others 2002). Indeed, people unfamiliar with stunting are often shocked to learn that a child who looks seven years old is actually 12.[6] Partly as a result of this and other factors, a study in Ghana found that a 10 percent increase in stunting was associated with a 3.5 percent increase in age at first enrolment at school (Glewwe and Jacoby 1995).

Moreover, once hungry children enrol, they are more likely to drop out. Hungry children tend to perform more poorly, due to the previous damage to their basic cognitive capacity and to current hunger which affects attention spans (see next section). Feeling pressure to help at home and not succeeding at school, children can become de-motivated and attend less often. A recent study in the United States showed that children at nutritional risk had significantly poorer school attendance, punctuality and grades at school —

and more behavioural problems (Kleinman and others 2002). Children suffering from undernutrition therefore not only enter schools later, but complete fewer years of schooling (Pollitt 1990; Jukes and others 2002; Glewwe and Jacoby 1994).

There are, of course, other factors besides undernutrition that can limit school enrolment and attendance. Schools do not function well without adequate infrastructure (buildings, facilities), materials (textbooks), and human resources (teachers, principals) (UNESCO 2004). Moreover, the class size, teaching methods and other constraints may affect the quality of the education and therefore the value that parents and children attach to it. These factors must also be considered in any analysis of enrolment and attendance.

• Reduced attention spans

Even when children make it to school, short-term hunger can affect their attention spans, making it hard to learn. Short-term hunger often arises because a child has missed breakfast or walked a long distance to school on a relatively empty stomach. Studies in Peru and the United States showed that when nine to 11 year old children had not eaten overnight or in the morning, they were slower in memory recall and made more errors on tests (Pollitt and others 1998). The effect was particularly strong for children nutritionally at risk. It has also been observed that children who skip breakfast are less able to solve simple visual tasks, focusing more on peripheral information not relevant to the problem at hand (Pollitt 1990; Simeon and Grantham-McGregor 1989, Del Rosso and Marek 1996).

By contrast, children who do not suffer from hunger are better able to learn and score higher on tests of factual knowledge (WHO 1998; Pollitt and others 1993). A study in Jamaica showed that children had more creative ideas when they received breakfast for two weeks than when they did not (Fernald and others 1997). A separate study in Jamaica also demonstrated that undernourished children's performance on a test of verbal fluency increased significantly when they received breakfast (Chandler and others 1995).

2.3 Adulthood

The relationship between hunger and learning in adulthood has been less studied than the link at earlier stages of life. By adulthood, an individual's cognitive capacity to learn is already largely established. Undernutrition will not significantly impair future potential, but it does have a large immediate impact on the ability to participate in opportunities to learn and apply learning.

Opportunities to learn

Hunger limits opportunities both through its effects on mental functioning and on attendance at adult training activities.

• Impaired mental functioning

Adults can acquire new skills through lifelong learning classes, such as literacy training, micro-credit programmes or agricultural extension. But the effects of hunger can make it difficult to concentrate and therefore to make the most of the learning opportunities. A classic and much-cited study on the correlation between a lowered caloric intake and productivity took place in Minnesota in 1950, when a group of young male volunteers was put on a semi-starvation diet of 1,550 calories over 24 weeks, and then 'stabilized' on a 1,800 calorie diet. The individuals adapted to this diet (which did not lack micronutrients) through lower work output and more apathetic behaviour.

The study showed that the intelligence level and learning curve stayed the same for undernourished

Map 2.1 — Around the world, not enough children are enrolled in school

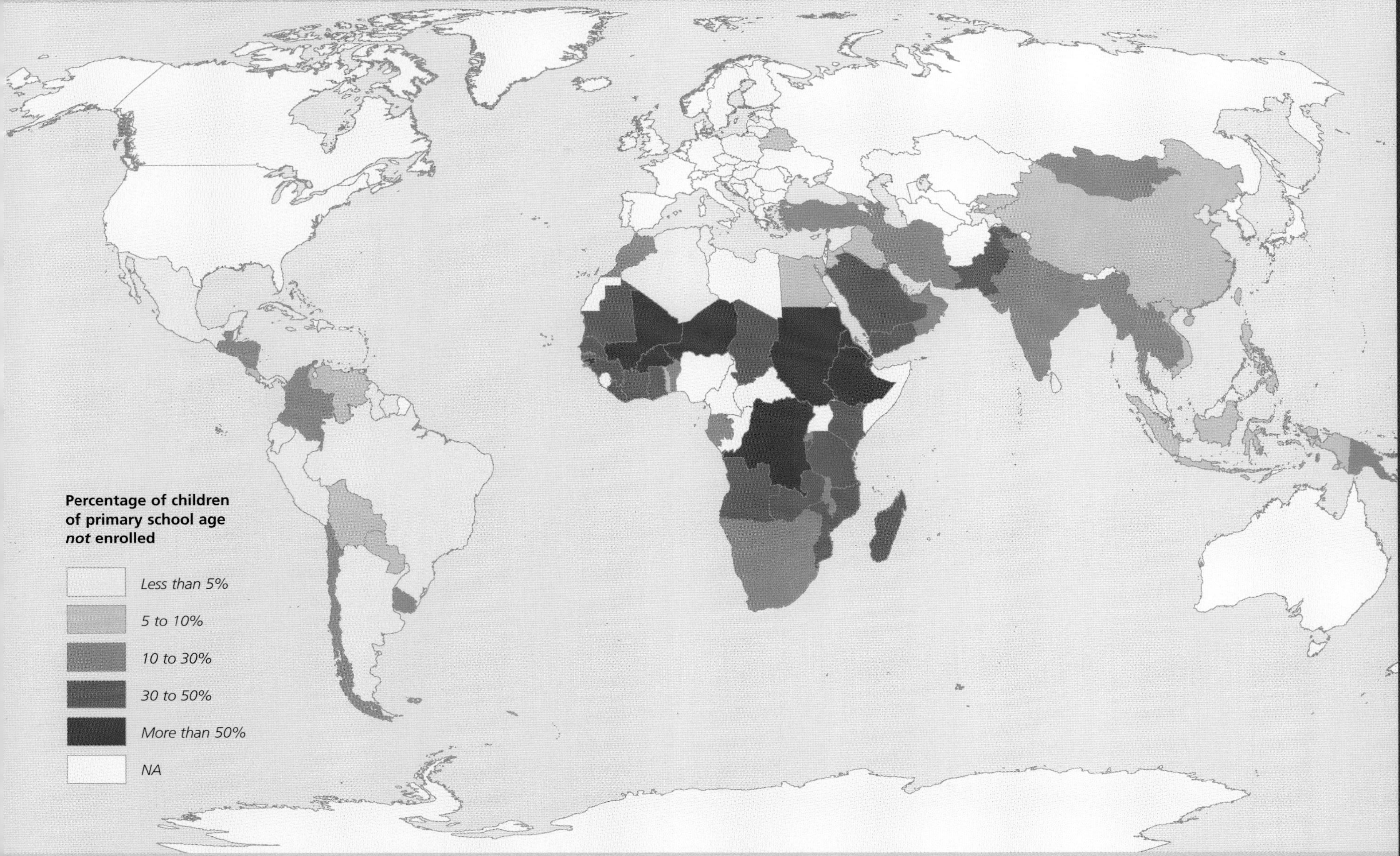

**Percentage of children
of primary school age
*not enrolled***

Less than 5%

5 to 10%

10 to 30%

30 to 50%

More than 50%

NA

The boundaries and the designations used on this map do not imply any official endorsement or acceptance by the United Nations. Map produced by WFP VAM.

Data source: UNESCO

adults, but that their ability to engage with learning opportunities and to apply learning diminished:

> "In summary, the measured intellective performance did not change importantly in either starvation or rehabilitation. The complaints about intellective inefficiency rose in starvation and declined during the rehabilitation period. Spontaneous mental effort and achievement declined during starvation, remained at a low level during the early phase of rehabilitation (R1 to R12), and only gradually returned to 'normal.'"
> (Keys and others 1950: 862-63).

These findings have been supported by several other studies.

Micronutrient deficiencies can also make it difficult to learn. Research has found evidence that not only people who are anaemic, but also those who suffer from moderate iron and zinc deficiencies could show signs of tiredness and lethargy. "In adults, mineral deficiencies can lead to a variety of alterations in behaviour including irritability, reduced attention span, fatigue, memory impairments, and depression. These consequences can be rapidly reversed by providing sufficient quantities of the mineral in the diet" (Kanarek and Marks-Kaufman 1991: 75).

• **Reduced attendance**

Adults may also be less able to participate in training because of the costs. Participants' costs for training are usually divided into two categories: fees and opportunity costs. Some providers charge a fee for attending courses. In developing countries the fee for attending adult training courses is usually very low and is generally used to ensure the learners' continued attendance (frequently, both cash and in-kind payments are accepted). It is assumed that someone willing to invest a small amount to participate in the course will continue to attend to try to maximize his or her return on the investment.

Opportunity costs, however, are often much higher than the direct costs. They correspond to the value of what the learners must sacrifice by attending classes. Participants may give up some of their time that could be used for work-related purposes, such as farming or shop keeping, and therefore attendance in adult learning courses can have a negative immediate impact on earnings. Recognizing this problem, classes are now often arranged at the end of the work day. Still, the learner will have to sacrifice time that could be devoted to leisure, rest, or the family.

Intermezzo 2: The 'window of opportunity' for nutrition[7]

It is well-established that growth faltering in early childhood is associated with a range of problems in later life, including reduced mental ability. However, the results from a worldwide survey suggest that the critical 'window of opportunity' for interventions opens earlier and shuts more quickly than previously suspected.

Over the past few decades, nutritionists have become more and more convinced of the importance of intervening early to address childhood malnutrition. One of the principal tenets has been that growth faltering begins at three months of age. A set of interventions, including growth monitoring programmes, has been developed to identify problems at this period. However, there had never been a systematic worldwide study of the phenomenon as a basis for this approach.

In 2001, Roger Shrimpton at the United Nations Children's Fund in New York and colleagues based in Brazil and Switzerland decided to make a comparison using 39 national datasets, spanning three continents. What they found surprised them.

Weight faltering begins during pregnancy

A comparison of the mean birthweights of different continents showed that on average people in Asia start life with a disadvantage. Their birthweights were less than Africa's and substantially less than Latin America's (see Figure 2a.). They likely suffer all the associated negative effects. Moreover, the patterns of weight faltering ran parallel across the first 60 months of life, suggesting that the initial starting point was a major factor in determining the degree of faltering that would be experienced. These findings argue for putting more focus on inter-uterine growth, or the development of the foetus in the womb. Interventions need to pay particular attention to the nutritional status and behaviours of pregnant mothers.

Figure 2a — The critical periods for nutrition come early

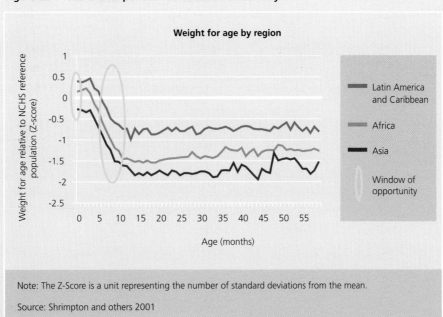

Note: The Z-Score is a unit representing the number of standard deviations from the mean.

Source: Shrimpton and others 2001

Length faltering begins immediately after birth

In terms of length, the newborns from the three regions clustered around the mean of the reference population. This finding suggested that, unlike weight, length was somehow 'pre-programmed' and not strongly affected by conditions in the womb. However, it offered another surprise: the drop-off was almost immediate, and did not stabilize for 18 months. In this period, children in Asia drop to more than 2 standard deviations below the reference population. For Africa, the faltering is almost as severe.

This finding indicates that waiting until the three month target to address growth faltering misses the most critical period in terms of length. In fact, it points to the need for interventions that focus on the period from birth to 18 months.

Taken together, the conclusions of the study suggest that the window of opportunity for intervening with maximum impact opens during pregnancy and begins closing around two years of age.

Source: Shrimpton and others 2001;
World Bank 2005c

Figure 2b — Length faltering begins very early

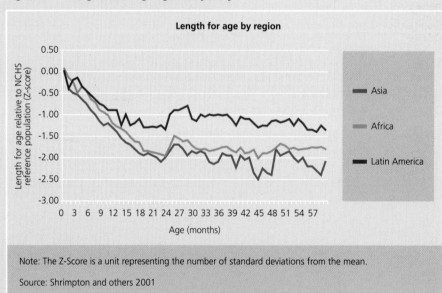

Length for age by region

Note: The Z-Score is a unit representing the number of standard deviations from the mean.

Source: Shrimpton and others 2001

3. Learning's impact on hunger

In Mali a certain tribal community lives along the Senegal River. The river, which flows from western Mali to the Atlantic Ocean, is filled with fish and provides an ample source of water for irrigating their fields. And yet the people face a paradox: despite these resources, a number of the villagers are malnourished. A team that investigated the situation discovered that what the villagers needed most was not food, but education on how to make the best use of their resources and to ensure good nutrition for the adults and children.[8]

Figure 3.1 — Learning's impact on hunger

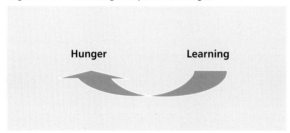

The previous chapter demonstrated how hunger impairs learning throughout the lifecycle. Yet one of the best solutions to hunger is to improve the knowledge and skills of those affected. To promote a virtuous cycle, and break the intergenerational transmission of hunger, it is thus important not only to address hunger but also to ensure that learning is supported. This chapter explores how learning in early childhood, school age and adulthood can help people escape this cycle (see Figure 3.1).

At each stage of life the learning may either build a person's basic *cognitive capacity* to handle a range of issues, including hunger, in the future or impart *specific skills and knowledge* that allow them to address hunger more directly. In early childhood, learning develops the capacity to acquire and apply messages later in life. For school-age children, learning primarily increases their cognitive capacity and problem-solving ability, but it also imparts some specific knowledge and skills that can be applied to help address hunger. In adulthood, general cognitive capacity can still be developed (for example, through literacy training). However, many adults prefer skills-based training that not only increases their mental development, but can also be more directly applied to address their own hunger and their children's.

3.1 Early childhood

In early childhood, learning helps to develop the cognitive structures that will be important in later life to acquire the skills and knowledge to address hunger.

Cognitive capacity

It has become clearer to researchers that much of the brain's development occurs before a child is born and in the first few years of life (World Bank 2005b). One author describes a newborn as having trillions of neurons "all waiting to be woven into the intricate tapestry of the mind. Some of the neurons have already been hard-wired … but trillions upon trillions [that] remain are … of almost infinite potential" (Begley 1996: 55). Early childhood is a critical stage of life for learning vocabulary (ages 0-3), math and logic (1-4), emotional control (0-2), and music (3-10) (Begley 1996; World Bank 2005b). Stimulation (an activity generating and strengthening cognitive function) is essential to develop these neurons and create the appropriate circuits within the brain. Otherwise, the neurons, and learning potential, can begin to wither.

Stimulation encompasses a range of fairly simple techniques for a caregiver to help improve child learning: play, conversation, exposure to colours or shapes and other activities. Some researchers have identified elements of an interactive style that caregivers can use to ensure that a child is stimulated: "providing rich language environments …; responding to children's requests and signals promptly and sensitively; maintaining and expanding on children's interests …; avoiding negative or restrictive behaviours; providing opportunities for choice … when children are more capable of beginning to direct their own learning; and monitoring children's behaviour" (Landry 2005).

Box 3.1 — Learning's impact on hunger in more detail

This chapter looks at learning's impact on hunger at each stage of life: early childhood, school age, and adulthood. As shown on the diagram below, learning at each stage can either provide the specific skills and knowledge necessary to address hunger or develop the future capacity to address it.

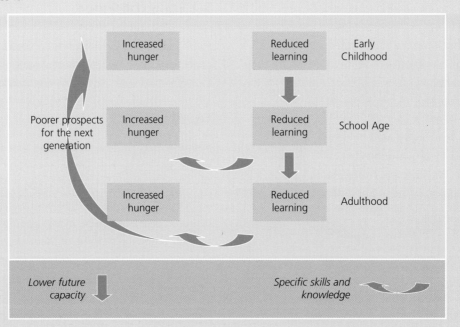

A complete presentation of the relationship also needs to show learning's impact on the various requirements to prevent hunger: availability, access, and utilization of nutrients. That is, to prevent hunger, food must be available (e.g. it can be produced or found in the market). Hungry people must also be able to access this food (e.g. they have the money to buy it). And hungry people must be able to utilize it properly (e.g. they select the right foods, consume a sufficient quantity and their bodies absorb the nutrients).

Early childhood: The learning in this period does not lead directly to reduced hunger, but instead forms the basic cognitive foundation for future learning to address hunger (i.e. to improve availability, access, and utilization of nutrients). Insufficient stimulation in this period will compromise this foundation.

School age: In this period, learning continues to strengthen the cognitive foundation that will be used in later life for improving the availability, access and utilization of nutrients. It also offers specific skills and knowledge on health, sanitation, and nutrition (all of which relate to better utilization). Without this learning, a child's current and future ability to address hunger will be impeded.

Adulthood: Learning at this stage creates opportunities to acquire and apply skills and knowledge that lead to increased production (i.e. greater availability), higher incomes (i.e. improved access to nutrients), better nutritional practices (i.e. better utilization), and improved health and sanitation (i.e. better utilization). This knowledge allows parents to improve conditions for themselves and the next generation. However, if learning does not occur, the lack of knowledge will lead to increased hunger for adults and their children.

In many cases, at the earliest stages of infancy, the main caregivers are parents or relatives. There is a growing understanding of the more basic effects of a positive relationship between a primary caregiver, usually the mother, and her child on the child's nutritional status and cognitive development. Compared with mothers who develop close emotional ties to their infants, mothers who fail to bond with their newborns are less responsive caregivers, with consequences for stimulation and cognitive development. But stimulation is also provided by teachers (and other students) in preschools, crèches and other early childhood development programmes.

Research has dramatically demonstrated that psychosocial stimulation can improve mental (and physical) development (Pelto and others 1999). A nutrition study in Jamaica compared the results of psychosocial stimulation and food supplements on the delayed cognitive development of stunted children. As it turns out, stimulation produced a greater effect than supplementation on the mental recovery of the stunted children (Figure 3.2). Children who received both interventions nearly caught up to the cognitive developmental level of non-stunted children (Grantham-McGregor and

others 1991). However, the control group (which did not receive any interventions) remained far behind.

Reviewing the results of the evaluations of a number of programmes in the developing world — including those in Bolivia, India, Turkey and Jamaica — the World Bank (2005b) suggests that early childhood development programmes (which include stimulation) have benefits that last into the next stages of life: higher intelligence scores, higher and timelier school enrolment, reduced drop-out and repetition rates, improved school achievements and greater adult productivity. These impacts, as we will see in the next sections, improve the chances of addressing hunger.

3.2 School age

In this stage of life, learning can help to address hunger and food insecurity through several pathways. Some — such as increased awareness of health and HIV/AIDS — can be applied immediately to have an impact on hunger. But most — such as improved livelihoods and smaller families — are gains achieved later in life as a result of having increased cognitive ability, openness to new ideas and problem-solving skills from staying in school. So, many of the benefits that make school age such a critical time of life emerge in later adolescence and adulthood.

Cognitive capacity

Schooling strengthens a person's cognitive capacity to deal with hunger in later life through several pathways related to future livelihoods, timing and size of families, nutrition, empowerment and views towards learning. The precise reasons for schooling's impact are not always clear, but there is a strong base of evidence for these relationships.

Figure 3.2 — Stimulation helps in Jamaica

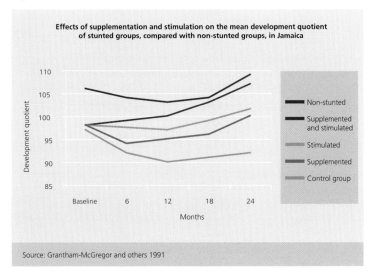

Source: Grantham-McGregor and others 1991

3. Learning's impact on hunger

• **Pathway to improved livelihoods**

The first pathway is through learning's impact on future livelihoods. Strengthening livelihoods ensures that households are able to produce more food or to have more income to buy it in the market. A recent report from the Food and Agricultural Organization of the United Nations (FAO) describes the lifetime costs of childhood hunger: "Every year of missed schooling during childhood cuts deeply into lifetime earnings" (FAO 2004: 11). This is especially true for girls (Herz and Sperling 2004). One study found that if women had the same education as men, staple food production could rise by 22 percent (Quisumbing 1996). In sub-Saharan Africa women produce three-fourths of all food, yet they have less education than men. So, there are high potential productivity gains from providing access to education to girls in African countries (Saito and others 1994).

Why is schooling so effective in strengthening livelihoods? At least part of the answer is that schooling influences attitudes and skills related to income generation and food production, such as the propensity to adopt technical innovations or new production methods. A study of Indian farmers during the green revolution (Foster and Rosenzweig 1996) found that education increased productivity for workers in the agricultural sector when technologies, such as new seed varieties, were introduced. Learning equipped some with the capacity to understand the new technology and the openness to try it (see also Box 3.2). These farmers improved their production significantly, while those without education fell behind.[9]

• **Pathway to smaller families**

Learning can also reduce hunger in later life through its influence on the timing and size of families. Educated mothers tend to get married later and have fewer children. A World Bank study of 100 countries found that when women gained four years of education, their fertility dropped by about one birth (Klasen 1999). Reduced fertility rates mean that mothers can concentrate more attention on each child and that the available food is shared among fewer household members. The delay in becoming

---

Box 3.2 — How primary education helps farmers solve problems

"Farmers in Kenya were shown a diseased plant and asked about the cause of the disease and the measures that might control or prevent it. An unschooled Kenyan farmer mentioned three possible causes of damage to maize — weeds, birds, and hailstones — none of which was responsible for producing the symptoms in the specimen shown. The farmer gave these as generic causes of crop damage and did not attribute particular kinds of damage to specific causes.

"By comparison, a Kenyan farmer with seven years of primary education made a complex causal model that correctly identified the cause of damage and a possible solution:

This is what Amodonde, the stalk borer [bug], does. It attacks the stem and makes it whither at the buds, sometimes without you knowing it. You buy chemicals from the store and apply when the maize is small, two or three feet. You spray the buds after the first weeding, from the top, when it is about to rain so the chemicals don't dry up. You can also put sulphur ammonia. It is also good for top dressing.

"This farmer's understanding of how technology could improve productivity was enhanced by a primary curriculum that taught science in conjunction with farming practice and that emphasized scientific theory over memorization."

Source: Eisemon 1989, quoted in Lockheed and Verspoor 1991: 6

pregnant also provides time for their own physical development (including the enlargement of the pelvis bone), which is essential for the nutrition and safety of both mother and child.

• Pathway to better nutrition and health

A third pathway is the impact of learning on the future mother's knowledge of nutrition and health. "Research evidence makes it clear that the single most important factor in determining a child's health and nutritional status is its mother's level of education" (WHO 1998: 9). Schooling equips mothers to take measures to improve their situation: to wash hands before preparing meals, to select the right types of food, to prevent parasitic infections in children, and so on. Women's schooling is associated with almost 43 percent of the reduction in child malnutrition in developing countries from 1970 to 1995 (Smith and Haddad 2000). This relationship is also borne out in comparisons of the stunting rates for children under five and female enrolment in secondary school (Figure 3.3), which suggests that stunting decreases with education.

• Pathway to empowerment

A fourth pathway is through learning's effect on women's empowerment. Studies in South Asia, sub-Saharan Africa, Latin America and the Caribbean, show clearly that a higher social status of women (often associated with more schooling) has a significant, positive effect on children's nutritional conditions. It appears that women with higher status take better care of themselves and have better overall nutrition (Smith and others 2003). This may improve the nutritional situation for their children in several ways. For one thing, a better nourished mother is able to offer better nutrition for the foetus and richer breastmilk for her infant. For another, empowered women also may have greater influence within a household and therefore be able to ensure that resources are focused on children.

Figure 3.3 — Female learning is correlated with better child nutrition

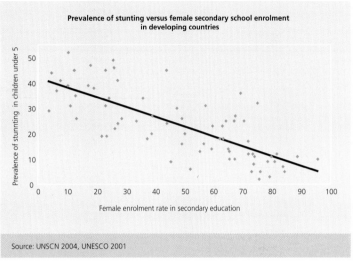

Source: UNSCN 2004, UNESCO 2001

Moreover, their incomes may be greater, allowing them to provide higher quality care.

• Pathway to positive views towards learning

Educated parents are more likely to send their own children to school and thus create a virtuous cycle of education. This relationship holds particularly for women and the educational opportunities of girls. A mother's level of schooling has a greater impact on the education of her daughters than her sons — and her impact is slightly greater than the father's (UN Millennium Project 2005b). The mother's learning seems to be important for three reasons. First, she earns more income and can therefore invest in schooling. Second, being educated, she serves as a positive role model for her daughter. And, finally, she is better able to help her children with their homework and other learning activities (UN Millennium Project 2005b).

Specifics skills and knowledge

While these pathways lead to future parents who will have a greater ability to provide good nutrition for their families, learning for school-age children can also have an immediate effect on hunger. They can be taught specific skills that will allow them to better handle hunger-related issues such as HIV/AIDS, nutrition, and pregnancy.

HIV/AIDS, for example, can undermine a family's ability to feed itself (Gillespie and Kadiyala 2005). When a parent or another productive member of the household becomes sick, the entire family suffers from lower food production and income. Yet the person who is ill requires additional care and food — which has costs in both time and money. These demands can be hard for a household to manage, putting them at much greater risk of hunger. If children can be informed of the means of transmission, they may be able to take steps to protect themselves and others from infection.

As other examples, children can learn the importance of eating fruits and vegetables; they can be taught to wash their hands after using the latrine and before eating; they can also understand the importance of protecting food from flies. These practices can help them improve their nutritional status immediately. Adolescent girls can also be taught the importance of delaying pregnancy. Waiting to have their first child will greatly enhance the child's and their own health and nutrition status.

3.3 Adulthood

Adulthood is the stage in the lifecycle where earlier investments in learning show their returns — through the pathways described earlier. Opportunities for learning in adulthood can strengthen these pathways, contributing to good nutrition for adults and helping to break the transmission of hunger from one generation to the next. In these cases, the learning is not so much creating future capacity to deal with hunger issues (though it does do this); it is providing skills and knowledge that adults can apply directly to improve their situation — and that of their children.

Specific skills and knowledge

Adult learning activities can strengthen livelihoods in two principal ways. First, through agricultural extension and other programmes, it can improve crop production, increasing the availability of food for the household. Second, through microcredit and other schemes, it can increase household income, improving their access to food in the market. By increasing the food security of households in these ways, it ensures that they can draw on more resources to meet the nutritional needs of both parents and children.

However, in most contexts these adult learning activities need to be accompanied by other development programmes to be effective. It is particularly important to transfer responsibility for organizing local economic activities to local people. The opportunity to assume economic powers and to command resources — which may be quite modest at the outset, as so many examples of microfinance demonstrate — stimulates the demand for education and makes adult learning relevant.

Relevant adult learning can also help ensure that hungry people are able to use food most effectively. Training can help them select the right types of foods to grow or purchase, so that they are better meeting their own needs for energy (macronutrients) as well as vitamins and minerals (micronutrients). It can also assist mothers in identifying the most appropriate foods for their children. In addition, training can help them consume the right amounts of food, recognizing, for instance, that women need to take in more nutrients when they are pregnant than they normally do.

It can also provide knowledge on how to improve hygiene and sanitation and prevent diseases, which are often contributing factors to undernutrition. And learning, whether in literacy classes or other activities, has other benefits as well. Literacy tends to make parents more appreciative of the value of learning. That respect for learning often translates into more support for their children's schooling (UN Millennium Project 2005b).

Intermezzo 3: The Jamaican study

For decades, the treatment of malnutrition had focused on providing essential nutrients and curing disease. But a landmark study of children in Jamaica highlighted a largely overlooked component of recovery — the role of psychosocial stimulation.

In later life, Frank Lloyd Wright, the famous American architect, attributed some of his international success to playing with his mother as a child. Even as an infant, he said, she held Froebel blocks above his crib as he watched in fascination. He traced his future spatial ability to those kinds of early interactions. While on the face of it the claim may seem far-fetched, researchers have increasingly recognised the importance of stimulation in the long-term mental development of children.

This insight was central to one of the most important studies on stimulation and malnutrition. In 1975, fifty-four young children ended up in a university hospital in Kingston, Jamaica. Thirty-five of them were severely malnourished. Researchers wanted to test whether stimulation would help the children recover from the mental damage caused by malnutrition.

The children were divided into three groups: a control group of 19 children who were not malnourished; a non-intervention group of 17 children who were malnourished; and an intervention group of 18 children who were also malnourished. Unlike the non-intervention group, the children in the intervention group received stimulation at the hospital as well as home visits over a three-year period once they were released. During the visits, the careworkers played with the children using homemade toys and showed mothers new techniques that they could try.

To assess the longer-term impact of the intervention, the researchers followed up on the children six years and 14 years after leaving the hospital. They found that, during the three years of the intervention, the IQs of the children increased significantly, even catching up with and overtaking the levels of the control group that had never experienced malnutrition. After six years (three years after the end of the intervention), however, their IQs had declined substantially. At 14 years, their IQs were even slightly lower, but the decline had been arrested, and the level had stabilized and begun to show some increase.

Figure 3a Stimulation led to higher IQs — even in the long run

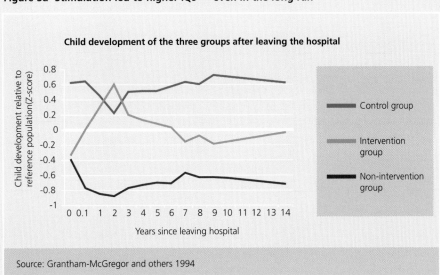

Source: Grantham-McGregor and others 1994

57

The most significant fact about these findings is that the intervention group consistently outperformed the non-intervention group — at a statistically significant level. The non-intervention group's IQs declined rapidly in the years immediately following hospitalization. While the levels subsequently recovered somewhat, a large difference continued to exist between them and the intervention and control groups — even 14 years after leaving the hospital. Similar differences were found in specific areas such as reading, spelling and arithmetic.

Based on these findings, the researchers concluded that "psychosocial stimulation should be an integral part of the treatment of severely malnourished children." The importance — and challenge — of providing this kind of stimulation in areas of severe malnutrition and famine has often been overlooked in the past.

Source: Grantham-McGregor and others 1994

Figure 3b — Stimulation increases achievement across a range of areas

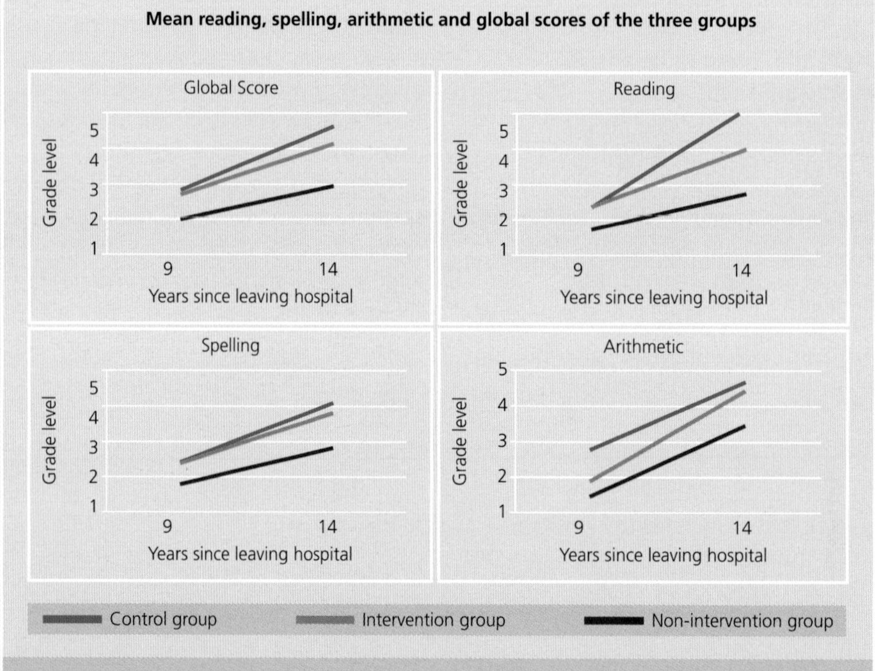

Mean reading, spelling, arithmetic and global scores of the three groups

Global Score

Reading

Spelling

Arithmetic

Grade level

Years since leaving hospital

Control group   Intervention group   Non-intervention group

Source: Grantham-McGregor and others 1994

4. Practical interventions

In a village in the Indian state of Rajistan, a supplementary feeding programme for young children is housed in a former temple. On the walls, illustrations of different foods and common childhood ailments compete for attention with the images of deities. In some ways the juxtaposition of human troubles and divine powers is an appropriate comment on the seriousness of the situation: several children attending the feeding centre show visible signs of chronic undernutrition, and at least one is mentally retarded.

Policymakers may be faced with an array of worrying anecdotes and statistics about the state of their adults and children. The previous chapters demonstrated that it is critical to address both poor nutrition and inadequate learning at each stage in the lifecycle. But what precisely should be done? This chapter describes effective interventions for ensuring nutrition and learning for early childhood, school age and adulthood.

4.1 Early childhood interventions

For early childhood, interventions need to be selected to address each of the main problems that lead to reduced mental capacity: low birthweight, growth faltering, micronutrient deficiencies and inadequate stimulation. Some of the key interventions that have proven effective are summarized in Figure 4.1. In many cases, multiple problems will require multiple interventions, and packages of interventions appropriate to the context will need to be developed.

Low birthweight

The nutrition and health status of mothers has the most direct influence on the growth of the foetus in the womb, its birthweight, and any related harm caused to the developing brain. It is therefore important to ensure good nutrition for the mother

Figure 4.1 — Summary of interventions for early childhood

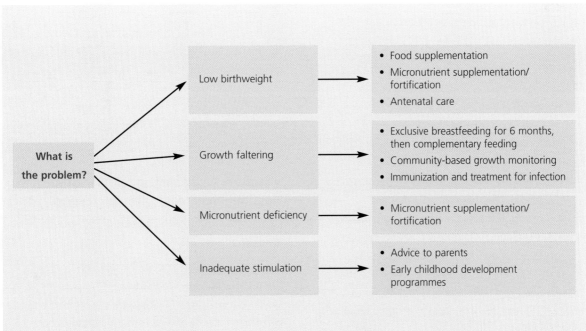

4. Practical interventions

throughout pregnancy. Several interventions should be considered depending on the context: food supplementation, micronutrient supplementation or fortification, and antenatal care.

• Food supplementation

In places where pregnant women suffer from undernutrition, supplementing their diets with balanced protein-energy foods helps the foetus grow in the womb and reduces the risk of low-weight births (de Onis and others 1998). One of the most encouraging recent studies comes from The Gambia, where 1,460 chronically undernourished women were given a locally prepared food supplement: a biscuit consisting of groundnuts, rice, flour, sugar, and groundnut oil. Although they received the supplement only in mid-pregnancy, the results were impressive. Low birthweight decreased by 39 percent — and by 42 percent in the hungry season (Ceesay and others 1997). Meta-analyses of other trials support the finding that food supplements can reduce low birthweight (Allen and Gillepsie 2001).[10]

• Micronutrient supplementation and fortification

Micronutrient supplementation and fortification can also help to maintain the pregnant mother's nutritional status and help prevent low birthweight. Until recently, there had been little clear-cut evidence on whether vitamins and minerals could improve birthweight (Allen and Gillepsie 2001). However, recent studies appear to demonstrate the benefits of interventions involving multiple micronutrients. A study of Bhutanese refugees in Nepal, for example, showed how the introduction of a fortified blended food into the rations helped to reduce the number of low birthweight babies from 18 percent to 8 percent (Shrimpton and others 2003; see Box 4.1). Another recent study in Nepal found that a multivitamin given during pregnancy had a greater effect on improving infant birthweight than single supplements (Osrin and

others 2005).[11] Individual supplements such as iron and zinc have a more mixed record.[12]

• Antenatal care

During pregnancy, antenatal care (i.e. care given before the birth of a child) can help ensure adequate nutrition for both the pregnant woman and her foetus by offering monitoring, advice and treatment. Informed health providers at local clinics, using weighing scales and other simple equipment, can assist the pregnant woman in monitoring the development of the foetus. They can also provide advice about resting, avoiding smoking while pregnant, and eating more, and determine whether additional supplementation is required[13]. Antenatal clinics can also help mothers prevent and treat infections. Malaria, for instance, can have a particularly damaging effect on birthweight, and women who are pregnant for the first time have decreased immunity to the disease.[14]

Growth faltering

After birth, a young child faces many nutritional risks. Growth faltering is a sign that children are suffering physical and possibly mental damage, but there are interventions that work. They include: exclusive breastfeeding for the first six months, subsequent introduction of complementary foods, regular assessment of progress through community-based growth monitoring programmes, and the provision of health services.

• Exclusive breastfeeding for the first six months, then complementary feeding

Exclusive breastfeeding contributes to cognitive development in three ways. First, the fatty acids in breastmilk contribute to the development of the infant's brains. Some studies have shown that the breastfeeding can have a positive effect on intelligence quotients (Anderson and others 1999). Second, by lowering the infant's susceptibility and exposure to infection, it reduces the likelihood that disease will contribute to undernutrition. In this respect, establishing lactation within the first few hours of birth is particularly important. Colostrum, the initial breastmilk, has a higher protein and lower fat content, and immune cells make up a large portion of the protein. Initiating breastfeeding early therefore lowers the risk of diarrhoea, respiratory infections and other common diseases of early childhood (Holman and Grimes 2001). Breastfeeding also reduces the opportunities for infection from contaminated utensils. Third, it helps create a bond between the mother and child, and provides stimulation (see section below).

Yet only about a third of the world's infants are exclusively breastfed up to age six months (UNICEF 2004; see also Map 4.1).[15] Breastfeeding campaigns (where messages are disseminated by a variety of means, including clinics, radio and television) have been effective in Chile, Mali and many other places.

At about six months of age, breastmilk alone is no longer sufficient to provide essential nutrients to support the active, growing child. From this time to about two years of age, children also need nutrient-rich complementary foods. There is evidence from observational studies that improving complementary feeding practices could reduce malnutrition by up to 20 percent at one year of age (Caulfield and others 1999a). Where the composition or amount of complementary foods is inadequate, supplements need to be considered. The effects on children's intelligence can be dramatic.

A long-term study was done with children in the impoverished Mexican village of Tezonteopan (Chavez and others 1995). Half of them received supplements up to age two in the form of vitamin- and mineral-enriched milk, while the other half did not. All the children were breastfed, received stimulation and were treated for any health problems. In later life, the mental age of the children who received nutritional supplements was significantly higher than their contemporaries in the village (Figure 4.2).[16]

• Community-based growth monitoring

Community-based growth monitoring allows mothers and other caregivers to identify any faltering in the development of children and to get advice on appropriate ways to respond. Some basic elements include conducting weight monitoring monthly for the first 18-24 months, using growth charts to measure progress, taking inadequate growth as the indicator for action and providing guidance for mothers and caregivers. The programmes are most effective when they give recommendations for the individual's growth and help generate broader community actions to support child growth and secure livelihoods (Allen and Gillepsie 2001). Careful design and a willingness to make adjustments are essential, since many growth monitoring programmes have faced practical difficulties in the past (cf. Ruel 2005).

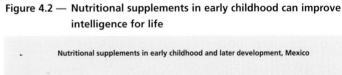

Figure 4.2 — Nutritional supplements in early childhood can improve intelligence for life

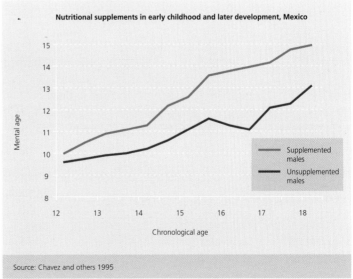

Source: Chavez and others 1995

Box 4.1 — Micronutrient fortification reduces low birthweight among Bhutanese refugees in Nepal

An analysis of medical records of Bhutanese refugees in Nepal uncovered a surprising result that refutes the idea that it takes several generations to reduce low-birthweight rates. The analysis showed that low-birthweight rates among the refugees had dropped from 18 percent in 1995 to 8 percent in 1998. By contrast, in hospitals in the same area of Nepal, low birthweights were greater than 30 percent. The refugees had arrived only between 1992 and 1993 from Bhutan, where low-birthweight rates were also around 30 percent. So, the changes must have occurred during their five years as refugees.

The medical records of mothers were investigated to solve the mystery. The improvements in birthweights of children born in the camps were at least partly the result of changes in the foods included in the general ration of the camps (since few other things changed in this period[17]). An outbreak in 1993 of beri beri, scurvy and angular stomatitis (diseases associated with nutritional deficiencies) led to the substitution of parboiled rice for polished rice and the addition of UNILITO, a micronutrient fortified blended food, to strengthen the general diet of the refugees in 1994. After changes in the general ration, birthweight steadily increased from 2.8 kg to 3.0 kg during the period from 1994 to 1998. In 1998, however, UNILITO was removed from the general ration and birthweights stabilized.

Figure 4a — Birthweight can be improved

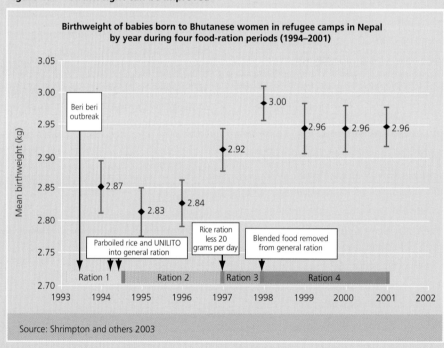

Birthweight of babies born to Bhutanese women in refugee camps in Nepal by year during four food-ration periods (1994–2001)

Source: Shrimpton and others 2003

The results seem to suggest that micronutrient supplementation does improve birthweights rapidly and that dramatic improvements can be achieved in refugee settings.

Source: Shrimpton and others 2003

Map 4.1 — A 'world' of improvement still possible in breastfeeding

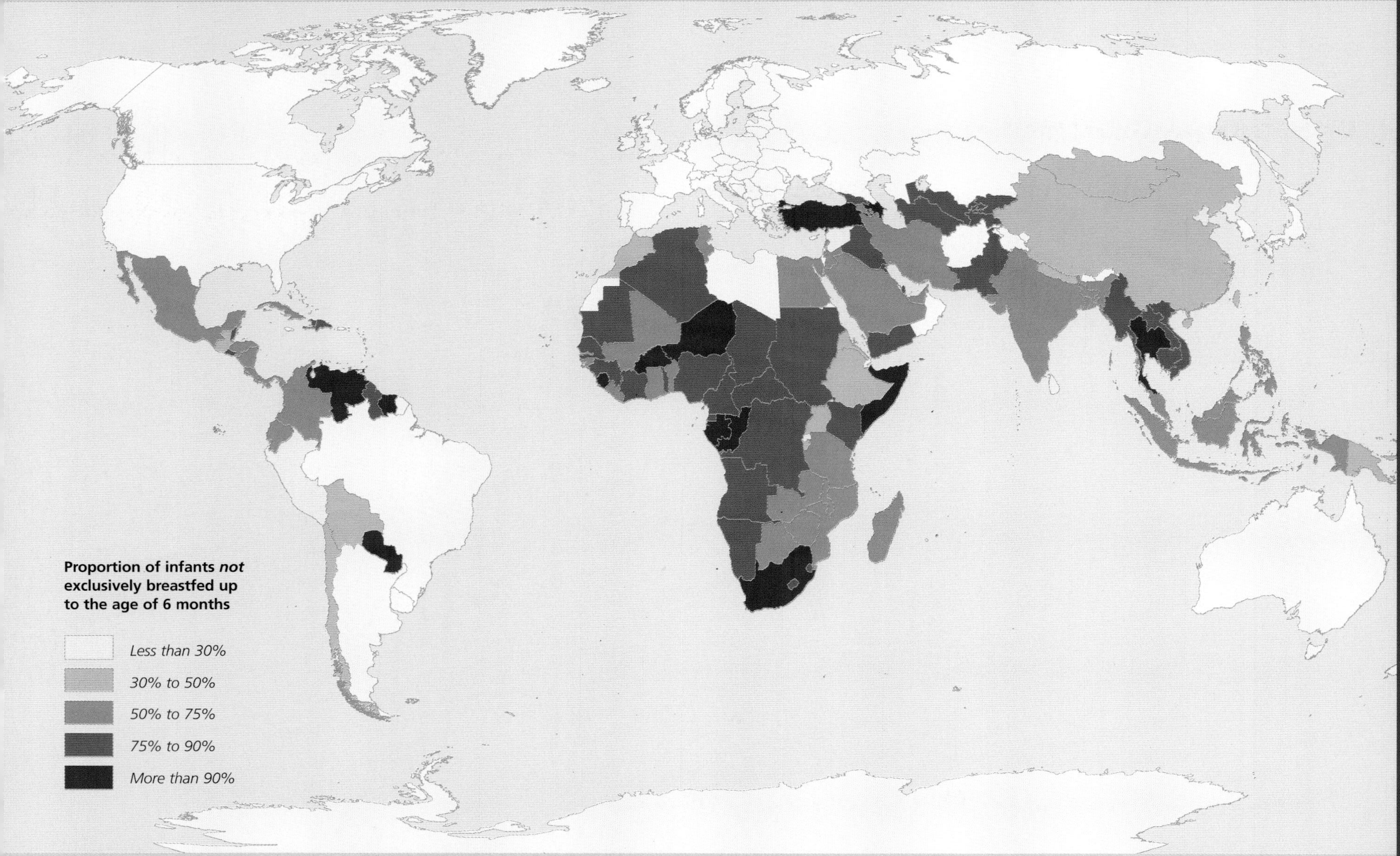

Proportion of infants *not* exclusively breastfed up to the age of 6 months

Less than 30%

30% to 50%

50% to 75%

75% to 90%

More than 90%

The boundaries and the designations used on this map do not imply any official endorsement or acceptance by the United Nations. Map produced by WFP VAM.

Data source: UNSCN

4. Practical interventions

- **Immunization and treatment for diseases that contribute to growth faltering**

Diseases, such as diarrhoea, malaria and pneumonia, can contribute to undernutrition by affecting the adequacy of food intake (through reducing appetite and increasing metabolic requirements) and the ability to absorb the food (through expelling nutrients or inhibiting absorption in other ways). It is therefore important to fully immunize children and to ensure that they receive treatment for common diseases (UN Millennium Project 2005a).

Micronutrient deficiencies

While many vitamins and minerals (including zinc and vitamin A) affect early childhood development, iodine and iron deficiencies are among the main causes of reduced mental capacity.

- **Iodine fortification or supplementation**

The most effective means to reduce iodine deficiencies in a population is to fortify the salt with iodine — that is, to 'iodize' it. Almost all developed countries and an increasing number of developing ones, including India, have ensured 'universal' salt iodization, which in practice means that over 80 percent of households have access to iodized salt (Allen and Gillepsie 2001). In isolated regions an alternative is to inject people with iodized oil, which has positive benefits lasting up to four years. Injections before pregnancy have been shown to prevent endemic cretinism in some areas (Allen and Gillepsie 2001). A study of the impact of iodized oil on the cognitive skills of children in the northern part of the former Zaire showed that it leads to significant improvements (see Figure 4.3).

- **Iron fortification or supplementation**

Both supplementation and fortification can be used to address iron deficiencies. Anaemic pregnant women can benefit from the provision of iron supplements (UN Millennium Project 2005a). They have been proven to raise the mother's iron status

in numerous tests, but there is less evidence about their impact on the foetus. Iron supplements can also be provided for preschool children, where iron deficiency is a problem. Iron fortification has been successfully conducted with powdered milk in Chile, complementary foods in Ghana, salt in India, and wheat and maize in Venezuela (Allen and Gillepsie 2001). In Chile, the fortification reduced childhood anaemia from 27 percent to almost zero. Where appropriate, at-risk mothers and children can also be encouraged to eat more animal products (Allen and Gillepsie 2001).

Inadequate stimulation

Psychosocial interventions during early years are essential to ensuring that the neurons in a developing brain are adequately stimulated and will provide the basic cognitive capacity for the next stages of life. Interventions can focus on providing advice to parents and offering specific programmes for children.

- **Advice to parents**

Stimulation, as we have seen, can have a dramatic impact on the cognitive development of young children, especially ones that have suffered undernutrition (see Figure 3.2 and Intermezzo 3). And it can take very simple forms: playing with children, speaking to them, taking an interest in their explorations of the world around them. Breastfeeding can also help establish a strong bond between the mother and child and offer early opportunities for stimulation. Yet, unless parents are aware of the importance of stimulation, they may neglect it in their efforts to provide enough food for the family. Mothers' groups, community health volunteers, and health providers at local clinics can all offer advice about stimulation and should have it integrated into their support efforts.

- **Early childhood development programmes**

Early childhood development (ECD) programmes, usually for children over three years old, can help to ensure continuing cognitive development. Evaluations have found them effective in producing lasting benefits for intelligence and future productivity (World Bank 2005b). Some programmes, such as the Integrated Child Development Programme in Bolivia, provide a complement of psychosocial, health and nutrition interventions. Others focus specifically on providing adequate stimulation opportunities to the children (World Bank 2005b). The Mother Child Education Programme in Turkey and the Early Childhood Education Project in India actually teach mothers how to interact with and better stimulate their children (World Bank 2005b). For younger children, crèches are also a possibility, linked where possible to local health clinics that can provide de-worming and other services.

Multidimensional problems

In many cases, there is not a single problem, but several working together to increase hunger and reduce learning in early childhood. These situations require a package of interventions.

• Integrated nutrition and care

Integrated programmes bring together various interventions. When an expectant mother receives supplementary feeding, it is also a good time to provide her with advice about how to care for herself and her child during pregnancy and infancy. A child can receive nutritional support, while also having

stimulation. The programmes can take a number of forms depending on the situation. Mother Child Health and Nutrition programmes, the Integrated Management of Childhood Illness, and Early Childhood Development programmes all are efforts to provide an appropriate package of interventions for the particular context.

4.2 School-age interventions

For school-age children, the interventions need to address problems related to poor enrolment and attendance, limited attention spans, micronutrient deficiencies, and a lack of specific skills and knowledge to address hunger. Some of the most effective interventions, based on field experience, are presented in Figure 4.4. Each intervention is effective at meeting certain objectives, and an appropriate combination may need to be found for particular contexts.

Poor school enrolment and attendance

Several interventions have proven especially effective at increasing school enrolment and attendance in areas where hunger is prevalent: school feeding, conditional transfers (take-home rations and cash transfers) and fee reductions. However, the absence of critical inputs, such as teachers or schools, will also negatively affect enrolment and attendance.

Figure 4.3 — Iodized oil increases the mental ability of children

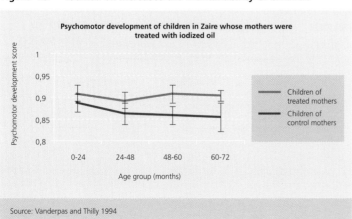

Source: Vanderpas and Thilly 1994

• School feeding

School feeding involves providing a meal or snack to students during the school day. The meal acts as an incentive to attend, leading to increased school enrolment, particularly for girls, in places where hunger and undernutrition are problems (see Figure 4.5). In Bangladesh, a school-feeding programme involving 6,000 schools raised enrolment by 14.2 percent (Ahmed 2004). The Global Food for Education Programme reported that enrolment increased on average by 10.4 percent — and by 11.7 percent for girls — in the 4,000 schools surveyed. Other studies have found positive results in the Peruvian Andes (Pollitt and others 1996), Malawi (UNICEF 2002b) and India (Laxmaiah and others 1999).

However, the programmes are much more effective in achieving these kinds of results when certain conditions are met. First, the meals need to be provided with enough regularity to serve as a genuine incentive for students to enrol and stay in school. Second, the meals must have sufficient financial value to offset the opportunity costs for families of sending children to school.[18] For this reason, and third, school feeding is often more effective where there is serious, but not extreme, hunger and poverty (Levinger 1986; WFP and others 1999). When people are suffering from abject conditions, the meals cannot offer a sufficient compensation to families, so they keep the children at home to work. Fourth, school feeding has its greatest impact on enrolment and attendance in areas where many children are out of school. If most of the children already attend school, a feeding programme will have only a marginal impact (Levinger 1986; WFP and others 1999). Finally,

parents and communities need to be aware of the benefits and limitations of the programme and be actively involved in its functioning (WFP and others 1999).[19]

• Take-home rations and cash transfers

Take-home rations and cash transfers can also help get children into school — though as with school feeding, they have been most effective when targeted to malnourished children and poor households. Take-home rations are quantities of food given to school children at set intervals to take back to their families. They are sometimes called a conditional transfer, since the food is given on the 'condition' that the parent sends the child to school regularly. In Cameroon, take-home rations increased the enrolment of girls by an average of 27 percent (FAS Online 2005). In Pakistan, the family of each female student who attended school for a minimum of 20 days received a 5-litre tin of vegetable oil per month, a precious commodity for local households. This helped to change parental attitudes about female education and made it more acceptable for families to educate their daughters (WFP 2001). Similar results have been obtained in Morocco and Niger (WFP 2001).

Figure 4.4 — Summary of interventions for school-age children

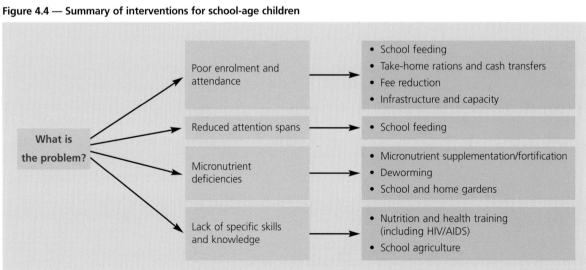

Cash transfers may also increase school enrolment. Scholarships and stipends can help cover indirect and opportunity costs. In Bangladesh a stipend that covers tuition, books, uniforms and transportation saw girls' enrolment rise to twice the national average (World Bank 2003). In Mexico the Opportunidades programme (formerly called PROGRESA) provides cash awards to poor families to compensate for the opportunity costs associated with sending children to school. It has especially increased the enrolment of girls and now serves as a model for other cash transfer programmes across Latin America (Schultz 2004; Morley and Coady 2003).

When well-targeted and adapted to local conditions in these ways, take-home rations and cash transfers (as well as school feeding) can lead to rapid increases in enrolment and attendance. But this increase can have potential downsides too. One fear is that overcrowding will reduce the quality of education, defeating the educational aims of the programme and, ultimately, leading parents to remove their children from school. Few studies have investigated this issue systematically, but a recent one in Bangladesh (see Box 4.2) suggests that overcrowding, in and of itself, does not lead to reduced educational achievement. However, the impact of new students with lower ability in the classes may (if unchecked) reduce the quality of education. Another concern, discussed in more detail below, is that the resources for the educational system may be overwhelmed by the increases in enrolment and attendance.

• Fee reduction

Reducing or eliminating school fees is another way to enable children to attend school. A report with evidence and policies from *What Works in Girls' Education* states: "The fastest and most direct way for governments to boost school enrolments is to reduce the direct, indirect, and opportunity costs to

parents" (Herz and Sperling 2004: 9). In Uganda enrolment increased 70 percent after fees were cut as part of major school reforms (Bruns and others 2003; Deininger 2003). In Tanzania, attendance doubled after eliminating fees (Bruns and others 2003).[20]

While these increases represent an important achievement, they can place a strain on the educational system. The burden is twofold: on the one hand, there are more children in school requiring resources, and on the other hand, a principal means of obtaining resources — school fees — has been lost. In general, the benefits of reducing fees (and providing school feeding, take-home rations and cash transfers) outweigh the costs, but it is necessary to plan for the consequences for the system (UN Millennium Project 2005b).

• Infrastructure and capacity improvement

The benefits of increased school attendance from school feeding, take-home rations, cash transfers, and reduced fees, can not be realized if the basic inputs for learning are not available.

Figure 4.5 — School feeding brings both boys *and* girls to school

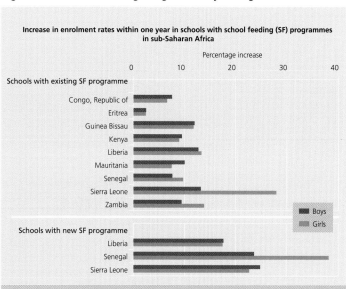

Source: WFP School Feeding Survey Results 2004

Box 4.2 — Do crowded classrooms crowd out learning? Evidence from Bangladesh

In 1993, the Government of Bangladesh began a Food for Education (FFE) programme designed to increase attendance at schools. The programme was simple: it offered a free monthly food ration to poor households in rural areas, on the condition that children enrolled in school and attended 85 percent of the time. The parents could choose whether to consume the ration or to sell it to buy other essential items.

In one sense, the programme was highly successful. Attendance rates increased, especially for girls, with beneficiary children making up 13 percent of primary school students when the programme ended in 2002. But the success created another problem: overcrowding in the classrooms. Schools with the FFE programme had 22 percent more students in their classes than non-FFE schools. The fear was that the overcrowding would reduce the quality of education.

In fact, multivariate analysis conducted by the International Food Policy Research Institute (IFPRI), demonstrated that those concerns were unfounded. There was no significant effect on education due to class size. However, another problem emerged: the children participating in the programme had, on average, lower ability — in part because they had suffered nutritional deprivation earlier in life and in part because their parents were less involved in their studies. This lower ability had an effect on the educational experience of non-FFE students, since the teacher often had to go over material more slowly. The study found that the effect became significant when the proportion of FFE students reached 44 percent.

This effect was partially offset by the fact that schools were required to meet minimum performance criteria in order to qualify for the programme. Overall, the conclusion of the study was that overcrowding has limited impact, and the effect of the poorer abilities of FFE students on educational quality can be largely offset by ensuring performance standards in FFE schools.

Source: Ahmed 2003

These requirements include: physical infrastructure and facilities, teaching and learning materials, human resources (principals, teachers), and school governance (UNESCO 2004). Without them, the quality and value of education diminishes. Government strategies for increasing attendance must be combined with sufficient resources to maintain the capacity of the educational system.

Reduced attention spans

Even if a child makes it to school, they can often be affected by short-term hunger, which results from missing a meal or walking long distances to school on a relatively empty stomach. This type of hunger is a primary cause of short attention spans and an inability to concentrate in the classroom — and often results in poor academic performance. School feeding interventions can help in this area, too.

• School feeding

There is now increasing evidence that school feeding programmes effectively address short-term hunger and thereby improve the attention span and cognitive function of students. In Bangladesh a school feeding programme that reached about one million students increased test scores by 15.7 percent (Ahmed 2004). In one Jamaican study, children who received a school meal showed improved arithmetic scores (and school attendance) after one semester, compared with the control classes (Simeon 1998). However, other studies have shown less conclusive results (WFP and others 1999). Some of the reasons may be associated with methodological problems; others may arise from flaws in the design of the particular programmes.

These findings highlight the importance of designing the programmes as effectively as possible. One key is to provide the meals early in the day — that is, prior to or during learning time.

A review of empirical studies showed that breakfast has a short-term effect in improving selected learning skills (especially memory), nutritional status and school attendance (Cueto 2001). Other studies have found similar results (cf. Grantham-McGregor and others 1998 in Jamaica; Noriega and others 2000 in Mexico).[21] It is also essential to tailor the size and the composition of the snacks or meals to the local nutritional requirements.

Micronutrient deficiencies

Micronutrient deficiencies, which make it difficult to achieve 'catch-up growth' and reduce the academic performance of students, can be addressed through supplements and fortification, deworming, and school and home gardens.

• Micronutrient supplements and fortification

Some of the most effective ways of addressing deficiencies in iodine and iron include fortification and supplementation. Iodised salt can be delivered through school feeding programmes or take-home rations. Iron supplements can also be provided to children at school clinics or as part of the school meals. In India iron supplements almost eliminated the differences in school performance between

deficient and non-deficient children (Sheshadri and Golpaldas 1989, cited in Del Rosso and Marek 1996). Foods such as wheat can also be fortified with iron.

• Deworming

Intestinal worms, sometimes referred to by their scientific names, such as schistosomes and helminth, can contribute to severe micronutrient deficiencies, including anaemia. Affecting about 400 million children around the world, worms can be ingested from contaminated river water or picked up from the soil. They make it difficult for children to absorb the nutrients in their food. Deworming treatments (usually involving tablets) can be an effective way of addressing this problem. An evaluation of a pilot project in Niger showed that the average prevalence rate of schistosomiasis declined in the most affected areas from 67 percent to 4 percent (WFP 2005e). Similar success has been achieved with helminth in Sierra Leone and elsewhere (WHO 2005a).

• School and home gardens

Diversifying diets is the most fundamental way to address the problem of micronutrient deficiencies (UNICEF and Micronutrient Initiative 2004). Vegetables from gardens provide a greater variety of vitamins and minerals than is normally found in the

---

Box 4.3 - What school feeding can *not* do ...

School feeding has the potential to address factors affecting learning such as low school enrolment and attendance, short-term hunger and micronutrient deficiencies. But it is not always appropriate for meeting other objectives:

- The evidence is mixed as to whether it leads to long-term improvements in students' *nutritional status*.

- It does not improve vital components of the *quality of education*, such as the curriculum, learning materials, school infrastructure and teacher training.

- It may not always reach all of the *very poorest of the poor children*, since the meals may not provide sufficient immediate compensation to these households to offset the direct and opportunity costs of sending their children to school.

Source: Allen and Gillespie 2001; WFP and others 1999; Levinger 1986

staple diets of hungry children. Home gardens are particularly effective, since the children will have access to more diverse foods on a more regular basis. School gardens can also provide needed micronutrients, though the amounts are more limited and less consistently available. Measures must also be taken to ensure that the children (rather than school officials) benefit from the produce from the gardens.

Inadequate skills and knowledge to address hunger

Children can obtain skills and knowledge that can be applied immediately to help address hunger, through HIV/AIDS training, pre-pregnancy advice for adolescent girls as well as other nutrition and health training.

• Nutrition and health training

Developing the knowledge, attitudes and skills to improve health, hygiene and nutrition can start with simple things, like teaching children to wash their hands or to store food safely. A successful health promoting schools project in Madagascar taught children about the importance of using iodized salt (see Box 4.4). These interventions equip children

with the skills to improve their utilization of food, by helping them select the most appropriate types (iodized rather than regular salt) and avoid becoming ill (through poor hygiene or food storage practices), which allows them to absorb the nutrients into their bodies.

School-based programmes also provide an opportunity for preventing and reducing the spread of HIV, which has so many damaging effects for food security (WHO 1999). Primary school can be a 'window of opportunity' to reach young people before they become sexually active and when they are least likely to be infected (WFP 2004a). Adolescent girls can also learn at school about the benefits of delaying their first pregnancies and their nutritional requirements if they do become pregnant (Shrimpton 2001).

• School agriculture

School gardens, in addition to diversifying diets to a certain extent, provide an opportunity for children, especially in rural areas, to learn about agricultural production techniques and to identify ways to treat crop diseases (cf. Desmond and others 2004). In some cases, the gardening is integrated into the curriculum through lessons on agriculture; in others, it is an optional activity. Either way, these programmes need to be carefully managed or they run the risk of simply using the students' labour to produce crops for school teachers and officials.

Multidimensional problems

In many cases several problems will co-exist and it will make more sense to create packages of interventions that mutually reinforce each other to address the problems.

• Integrated Programmes

By bringing children together, schools are often an effective platform for a range of interventions. Two integrated programmes

---

Box 4.4 — FRESH ideas: Using schools to address iodine deficiencies in Madagascar

Iodine deficiency can lower IQs by 15 points, but iodine supplements are often prohibitively expensive. In developed countries the problem is solved by iodizing salt. A FRESH (Focusing Resources on Effective School Health) programme in the Fort Dauphin prefecture in Madagascar brought the issue of addressing iodine deficiency into the classroom in a developing country. Teachers provided a lesson on the damage that the deficiency can cause and then asked students to bring a sample of their table salt from home. Using a test-kit developed by UNICEF, the teachers and students found that none of the salt was iodized. The students informed their parents, and sales of normal salt faltered in the market. Merchants scrambled to stock their stands with iodized salt. By 2002, up to 232 schools had tested local salt supplies.

Source: World Bank 2002

demonstrate the types of measures that can be undertaken. The FRESH framework identifies four components that should be made available together, in all schools, to the extent possible (UNESCO and others 2000): health-related school policies; provision of safe water and sanitation; skills-based health education; and school-based health and nutrition services. The 'Essential Package' initiative combines a range of interventions including: school feeding, deworming, health and nutrition education, micronutrient supplementation, and HIV/AIDS awareness.

4.3 Adulthood interventions

The problems that must be addressed in adulthood relate to lack of specific skills and knowledge, and poor concentration and attendance. All of the proven interventions for dealing with them (Figure 4.6) must be seen in the context of broader development activities. Learning must be part of an intersectoral approach (agriculture, health, natural resource management and local governance) that complements training with increased opportunities to apply it. Adult learning programmes undertaken in isolation will likely fail.

Lack of specific skills and knowledge

Sometimes the major constraint for households dealing with hunger is their livelihood. They simply do not produce enough food — or earn enough income to purchase it — to make sure that all members of their families are adequately fed. In these cases, adult learning should focus on skills training and literacy. Sometimes, however, the limiting factor for a hungry household is not its livelihood, but its knowledge related to nutrition. They may not eat the right foods, use the proper sanitation techniques, or know how to prevent certain diseases. In these case, nutrition training and literacy can be particularly helpful.

Box 4.5 — Nutrition training changes behaviours in Mali

In Mali, the Government and concerned NGOs realized that rural villagers were becoming malnourished, not because of a sudden disaster but because they did not know the basic facts about nutrition. The National Communications Project was designed to convey to villagers a set of simple nutritional messages, such as the benefits of breastfeeding, cures for vitamin A deficiency and men's responsibilities for women's and children's nutrition. Women were reached primarily through counselling sessions, while men took part in role plays, village mobilization meetings and radio shows — including one dramatic series entitled *Saheli Sama (Elephant of the Desert)*, which became a nationwide favourite.

An evaluation of the impact of the programme after five years found:

- Acute malnutrition for children under 3 declined from 38 percent to 28 percent in programme villages but remained unchanged in others;

- Chronic malnutrition, or stunting, fell from 46 percent to 31 percent percent in the programme villages but did not change in others; and

- The number of children receiving the initial breast milk (or colostrum) increased from 25 percent to 58 percent in the programme villages but only rose from 30 percent to 42 percent in others.

Overall, the assessment found the nutritional learning programme to be highly successful, with cost-effectiveness comparable to other early childhood nutritional interventions.

Source: Parlato and Seidel 1998

4. Practical interventions

• Skills training

Skills training, in the form of microcredit, agricultural extension, or income-generating activities, can strengthen livelihoods and address hunger, since they increase production of food (e.g. agricultural extension) or the resources to buy it in the markets (e.g. microcredit and income-generating activities). A review of skills and literacy training for better livelihoods found that "programs that start from livelihood skills seem to stand a stronger chance for success. They can, after all, demonstrate an immediate reason for learning" (Oxenham and others 2002: 2).[22]

• Literacy training

Adult literacy programmes are often a necessary complement to skills (and nutrition) training. But some studies of literacy classes on their own contend that there is little evidence of a correlation between literacy classes and higher earnings (Valerio 2003).[23] Without the motivation of a practical goal, the level of learning in adult literacy classes is often very low and the relapse into illiteracy high (Abadzi 2003). Ensuring 'demand' for literacy training is therefore essential.

However, there is evidence that literacy training on its own does confer other benefits, including an increase in parents' support for schooling, increased social and political engagement, and healthier families (Ahmed 1975; Lauglo 2001). All these findings suggest that adult literacy can assist in breaking the intergenerational transmission of hunger.

• Nutrition training

Nutrition training aimed at mothers and fathers can improve the nutritional status of their children. Recent studies suggest that the nutritional training of mothers on its own improves outcomes for the next generation of children — in a way previously thought possible only with more formal education (Webb and Block 2004). The training can take several forms. In some cases, it is integrated into other health programmes, such as ante- and postnatal care for mothers and their children. But it can also be combined with outreach in other development activities, not specifically related to nutrition. A nutritional learning programme in Mali achieved good results without combining the training with any direct nutritional interventions (see Box 4.5).

Poor concentration and attendance

Opportunity costs are often much higher than the direct costs of training and correspond to the value of what the learners must give up by attending classes. They include lost income (from time not spent working in the fields or tending the shop) and lost opportunities for leisure.

Figure 4.6 — Summary of interventions for adulthood

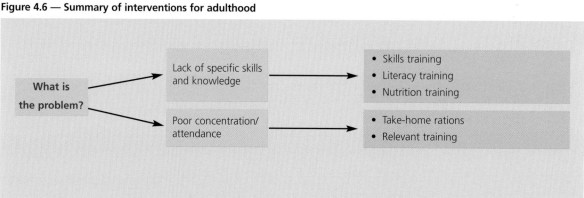

From 2000 to 2004 the World Food Programme and other partners provided food aid (in the form of take-home rations) to participants at adult literacy centres in 25 of Burkina Faso's poorest and most food-insecure provinces. The aims were to increase attendance (by reducing the opportunity cost) and to improve performance (by addressing short-term hunger), especially for women. An evaluation of the activity, comparing the results in food-supported centres with rates in non-supported centres at the national level, found:

- In 2000-2001, the food support led to a 7 point increase in the number of people who completed both phases of the literacy course (84 percent compared with 77 percent). The difference was 10 points for women.

- The drop-out rates were 4 to 5 percentage points lower in most phases of the course in food-supported locations than in other national centres.

The results suggest that food aid can increase attendance and performance in adult literacy classes in certain circumstances.

Source: Silvereano-Velis 2003

• Relevant training

Training programmes for the hungry poor therefore need to offer clear and immediate reasons for enrolment and perseverance in attending the course — with the expected returns in reduced hunger and improved livelihoods outweighing the costs of attending.

• Take-home rations

It has also been demonstrated that take-home rations can, to some extent, counter the effects of opportunity costs and raise attendance. The opportunity costs for the hungry poor are often related to gathering food for daily subsistence, and a take-home ration offsets some of these costs. Many training programmes have reported higher attendance and better results after they began to distribute food to the participants (see Box 4.6).

Hunger can also make it difficult to concentrate once a person enrols in a training course. The participant may feel lethargic or be inattentive, finding it hard to truly absorb what is being taught. Take-home rations ensure that the participants have enough food so that they can focus on the material discussed and benefit more from the learning.

Multidimensional problems

When possible, the various types of training — skills, literacy and nutrition — can be combined into what are sometimes called 'empowerment programmes'. These programmes recognize that problems are multidimensional, and that the individual elements of a multidimensional strategy reinforce each other. Literacy provides the skills and confidence to undertake income-generating activities. The empowerment arising from success in these areas leads to greater openness to new ideas and, for women, to greater bargaining power to make changes in behaviours in the household that will improve nutrition. Take-home rations can also be used, where necessary, to improve attendance and concentration.

4. Practical interventions

Intermezzo 4: Increasing adult literacy and reducing hunger in Uganda

Uganda's successful Functional Adult Literacy programme has equipped people with knowledge, attitudes and practices that help them fight hunger. But despite good ideas and strong results, the challenges of decentralization could slow progress towards the Government's goal of universal literacy — and hunger reduction.

Like many developing countries, Uganda faces a number of difficult problems: from poor nutritional conditions to high levels of unemployment and poverty. Life expectancy at birth is only 45.7 years. To address these kinds of difficulties, the Government introduced programmes to modernize agriculture (a sector in which 75 percent of the population works) and to stimulate rural development through microcredit schemes. These programmes had great potential for addressing hunger (in addition to other problems). However, in the beginning, they mostly benefited literate people, since others lacked the training and skills to take advantage of them. Several studies demonstrating the strong link between the literacy rate, economic development and social wellbeing, convinced the Government that increasing literacy was a way to improve the situation of Uganda's illiterate poor and hungry.

The programme

Literacy programmes have a long history in Uganda, dating back to courses provided by religious missionaries in the late 19th century. However, it took a successful pilot project of UNESCO, UNICEF, the German Adult Education Association (DVV) and the Government in the early 1990s to identify an appropriate approach for the Functional Adult Literacy (FAL) programme. Begun in 1996, FAL attempts to integrate literacy education with relevant training (e.g. on income generation and nutrition), which can be applied to address hunger.

FAL has achieved some important successes. According to UNESCO, the literacy rate in Uganda in 2004 was 68.9 percent — an increase of more than 10 percent from 1990. Much of this improvement is due to the FAL. A 1999 evaluation, conducted by the World Bank, found that the participants' performance is much better than that of non-literates in the same community in terms of knowledge, attitudes and practices — many of which directly improve food security and reduce undernutrition.

In terms of functional knowledge, two-year literates, or people who had been literate for two years, had a greater understanding than illiterates of topics such as which foods give energy to the body (35 percent as opposed to 27 percent); what the major benefits of breastfeeding are (87 percent to 70 percent); and what apart from fertilizer you can use to improve crop production (57 percent to 52 percent). The attitudes of two-year literates were also different than illiterates on hunger-related topics. More literates, for instance, felt that fruits are not only for children (91 percent to 82 percent) and that breastfeeding is better than bottle feeding (90 percent to 77 percent). The literates also seemed to value education more — both for boys and girls.

The knowledge and attitudes translated into practices that better address hunger: 73 percent of the two-year literates used fertilizer, while only 41 percent of illiterates did. As a result of the training, 71 percent of the sampled people declared that the classes helped them to boost their production and earn more money. A large number of non-farm income-generating activities have been started in the communities, which provide the graduates with the resources to better address hunger.

Even beyond the direct benefits for food security, the functional adult literacy training seems to contribute to broader social and political development. Even two years after graduating, literate women of child-bearing age were more likely than illiterates to practice family planning (39 percent to 15 percent), and two-year literates were far more likely than illiterates to be members of social groups (69 percent to 25 percent). In addition to improved social development indicators such as fertility rates and social capital, the literacy training also appears to contribute to greater political engagement. Literates took part more often than illiterates in elections (91 percent to 79 percent at the local level), and were also more likely to attend council meetings (58 percent to 32 percent) and speak up once there (62 percent to 31 percent).

This greater social and political involvement ensures that the literates will have a greater say in how resources at the community level are used to address problems such as hunger.

Challenges

In spite of these successes, the programme faces a number of challenges that need to be overcome. One relates to the instructors. They are unpaid, and very few of them have sufficient training to teach. While the use of volunteers keeps the costs down, it may limit the effectiveness of the programme.

A second concern is that most of the participants are people that have already been to school. Almost three-quarters of the graduates have some education. The danger is that the programme has missed the original target group of totally illiterate people.

The third, and largest, problem relates to the financing of the programme. The Government's decentralization policies during the 1990s led regions and districts to take increasing financial responsibility for programmes such as FAL. However, some districts are not spending enough money to make up the difference and are sometimes cutting the programme funds. As a consequence, the programme works well in the better-off districts, while it appears to be less effective in the poorer ones — increasing inequality and limiting the ability of the programme to reach those most in need.

Ways must be found to motivate local governments to prioritize adult literacy — if the real achievements of the programme in many areas, including hunger reduction, are to be sustained.

Sources: Okech and others 2001;
Oxenham and others 2001

Figure 4b — Knowledge, attitudes and practices improve with functional literacy

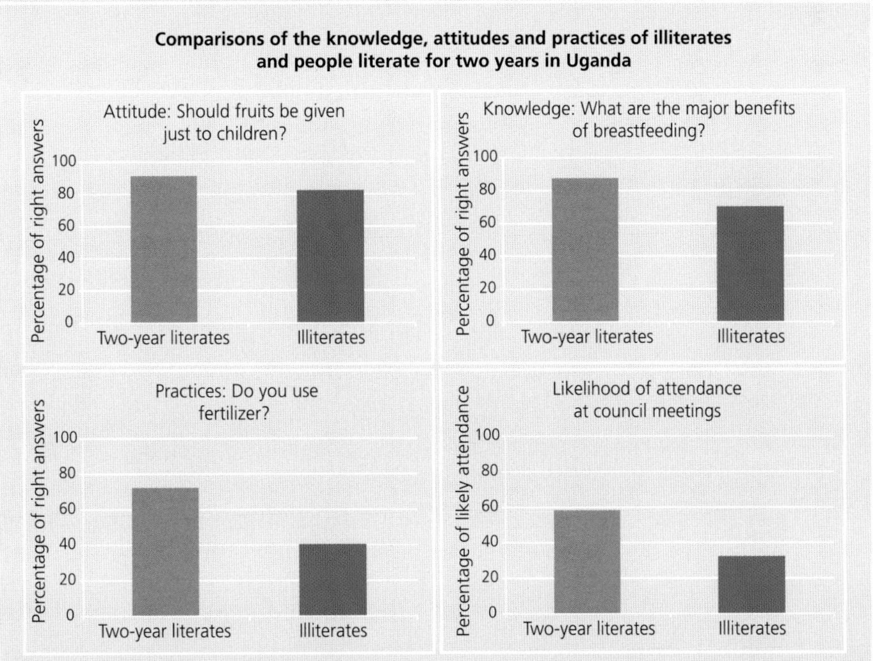

Comparisons of the knowledge, attitudes and practices of illiterates and people literate for two years in Uganda

Source: A. Okech and others 2001

PART III: An Agenda For National Development

"...addressing both hunger and inadequate learning can lead to improvements in human capital and greater economic growth"

Part I demonstrated the profound impacts of hunger on development. **Part II** focused on hunger's two-way relationship with learning, describing the theory as well as identifying concrete interventions for addressing problems. **Part III** turns to the link between hunger, learning and national development. **Chapter 5** shows how the relationship between hunger and learning affects the processes of long-term national development. **Chapter 6** examines the political choices that must be made to create a virtuous, rather than vicious, cycle that will reinforce these processes. **Chapter 7** concludes by outlining steps that can be taken at national and international levels.

5. Hunger, learning and national development

In 2000, over forty years after the end of a divisive conflict, North and South Korea began taking tentative steps towards closer relations, as part of South Korean leader Kim Dae-Jung's so-called 'Sunshine Policy'. Some of the initial gestures of goodwill included the exchange of family members who had been separated during the long period of closed borders and fragile ceasefires. When the families were reunited, they may have been struck by an astonishing fact: those who had grown up in North Korea were considerably shorter than their counterparts in the South. A detailed study, comparing North Korean refugees and South Koreans, demonstrated that differences in height were up to 6 centimetres in the youngest generations (Pak 2004).[24] These physical differences, among genetically similar populations, suggest that mental damage may also have occurred.

Figure 5.1 — Hunger and learning's two-way relationship

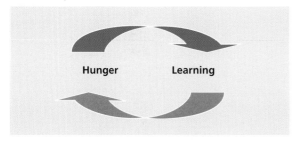

When the country was divided, the North and South took very different developmental paths. South Korea, like many of the eventual 'East Asian Tigers', made investments in learning and nutrition. Combined with a reasonably stable government and export-led growth, the country developed rapidly in economic terms. By contrast, North Koreans suffered under a political system in which investments in education and agricultural production were often mismanaged or compromised by other events. At the time of the exchanges, the country had just begun to recover from a great famine that is believed to have claimed from 250,000 to 3 million lives (Natsios 2001).

What explains the difference in the fortunes of North and South Korea? What explains the success, over the long run, of other countries such as Chile and Thailand? While inevitably there are a large number of factors at work in each of these cases, the successful countries appear to have shared a common understanding of the relationship between hunger, learning and national development — and used it to inform their larger development strategies.

The previous part of the report laid out the two-way relationship between hunger and learning (Figure 5.1). This chapter turns to the link with longer-term national development. It shows how a virtuous, self-reinforcing cycle can be created across the generations, contributing to human and economic development — or how a negative cycle can lead to national decline.

5.1 Investing to expand people's opportunities and promote national development

We have seen how the two-way relationship between hunger and learning affects the prospects of individuals (see Box 5.1). When aggregated over the wider population, and looked at in a more temporal perspective, it becomes apparent that the outcomes at each stage of life affect subsequent stages and ultimately the next generation. Over time, these interactions shape the developmental trajectory of a nation.

Figure 5.2 is called a 'vision' diagram, because it requires seeing beyond the immediate circumstances to pay-offs that will be realized in the future. It shows that what is done today will have a profound impact on the nation's potential a generation from now. Early childhood is the most critical period for laying the foundation for future development. Nutrition and stimulation affect learning capacity (and the ability to address hunger) at school age and even into adulthood.

Box 5.1 — The two-way relationship between hunger and learning in detail

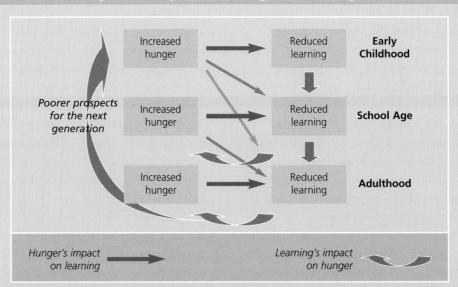

Combining the two diagrams in Boxes 2.1 and 3.1 allows us to see the interrelationships between hunger and learning throughout the lifecycle. In examining the two-way relationship, it can be helpful to look at how hunger affects the availability, access and utilization of learning opportunities and, conversely, how learning affects the availability, access and utilization of nutrients.

• Early childhood
Hunger both restricts learning opportunities for infants (i.e. access and utilization) and impairs their future capacity to learn (i.e. utilization of future learning opportunities). Reduced learning at this stage undermines the cognitive foundation for acquiring future skills and knowledge to address hunger (i.e. availability, access and utilization of nutrients in the future).

• School age
Hunger limits opportunities to learn by reducing attendance (i.e. access) and making it hard to concentrate (i.e. to utilize the opportunity afforded by school). It can also damage the future capacity of the child to learn (i.e. to utilize future learning opportunities) by preventing catch-up growth. Reduced learning at this stage further weakens the foundation for acquiring future skills and knowledge to address hunger (i.e. to improve the availability, access and utilization of nutrients). It also prevents children from acquiring some skills related to nutrition and health (i.e. utilization of nutrients) that can be applied immediately.

• Adulthood
At this stage, hunger increases the opportunity costs of learning courses (i.e. impedes access) and undermines concentration (i.e. prevents utilization) for those who do attend. And inadequate learning makes it difficult to acquire a range of specific skills and knowledge to address hunger: from agricultural extension (increasing production and availability) to income-generating activities (increasing resources and hence access) to health, sanitation and nutrition courses (improving utilization). This learning would benefit not just the adults, but also their children in the next generation.

To effectively address hunger and learning, it is important to examine all of these dimensions of the problem to determine where interventions are required to ensure a virtuous (rather than vicious) cycle.

Nutrition and learning at school age are also critical, since they help determine the outcomes for the future adults. As has been seen, improved nutrition and learning in adulthood are associated with new possibilities — to take on more fulfilling and productive work, to be able to read books, to participate in local council meetings, to protect loved ones from infections, to choose nutritious foods for a family, or to enjoy an evening free from worry. These returns improve prospects for the next generation, which grows up less hungry and more knowledgeable and has even greater potential to secure a better future for its children.

At an aggregate level, these improvements in nutrition and learning expand opportunities and choices for millions of people — national development, in the truest sense. But they also contribute to other processes associated with development — including economic growth — that further support the next generations and perpetuate the positive cycle.

5.2 Economic growth

The relationship between hunger and learning affects long-term economic growth along two pathways. First, reduced hunger increases learning, which improves human capital and leads to greater economic growth. Second, learning reduces hunger, which increases participation in the labour force and improves the efficiency of workers, thereby contributing to economic growth. This section looks at each of these relationships in more detail.

Hunger's impact on learning and economic growth

Between the mid 1960s and the early 1990s, a number of developing countries in East Asia (including South Korea) made remarkable economic progress — outperforming any other region in the world (World Bank 1993). The growth of GNP per capita in eight 'East Asian Tigers' averaged over 5 percent between 1965

Figure 5.2 — Vision diagram — seeing the future payoffs

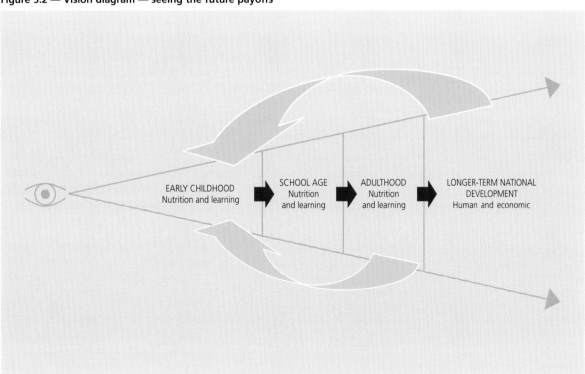

83

and 1990 (World Bank 1993). Numerous studies have been conducted in an attempt to understand the causes of their success and that of other countries with similar progress. While a number of factors appear to have contributed to the growth, human capital has been consistently identified as one of the most critical.

Human capital (Schultz 1971) refers to the skills and talents of the workforce. As the understanding of economic growth has developed, the role of human capital has become more clearly recognized. In endogenous growth theories, there are increasing returns to new ideas and technology in a country's economy (Barro 1998; Lucas 1988; Lucas 1990; Romer 1986; Romer 1993). Economies require an educated workforce with the skills to generate new technologies and put them to use. Economic growth can therefore result from investments in human capital, when part of a larger development strategy. Analyses of the economic successes in East Asia suggest that the level of primary education may have been the most important factor in the growth — even greater than the impact of physical investments (Mingat 1998).[25] The basic correlation is presented in Figure 5.3.[26]

This report demonstrates how hunger limits learning in two principal ways: its effect on basic cognitive capacity (brain structure) and its effect on the ability to make use of opportunities to learn (such as primary schooling). By limiting learning, it leads to a workforce with low human capital that does not have the skills or acumen to improve its output. Economic growth is therefore stymied. By contrast, good nutrition supports learning, the creation of human capital, and economic progress.

This positive process can be reinforced through several intergenerational effects. First, better educated parents with greater human capital have both the knowledge and resources to address hunger (Smith and Haddad 2000). This improves learning (and therefore human capital) in the next generation. Second, as we have seen, better educated parents will support the education of their children (UN Millennium Project 2005b).

Third, greater learning reduces fertility rates. In many developing countries, parents have a large number of children to increase the chance that at least a few will survive into adulthood and be able to contribute to the households' livelihoods. However, with education, women tend to have more opportunities and know better how to care for their children and protect them from fatal infection. As a result, the need to have large numbers of children decreases, and the fertility rate declines.[27]

This has several positive benefits for children's learning. The amount of resources available for each child increases, making it more likely that their parents will be able to properly nourish them and pay for the fees and uniforms needed to send the child to school. Parents also have more time to spend with them, helping the children with their homework or providing

Figure 5.3 — Level of schooling and gross domestic product are correlated in developing countries

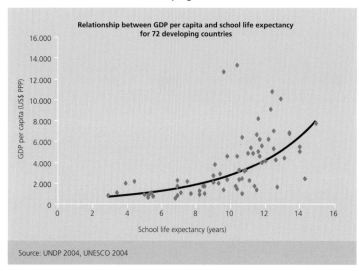

Source: UNDP 2004, UNESCO 2004

other support. As a result, these children will attend school for longer and increase the amount of human capital and — eventually — the rate of economic growth.

These intergenerational effects at the household level can be reinforced by government decisions. The economic growth generated through increased human capital provides a greater tax base and more resources for governments. Simultaneously, the improvements in learning and nutrition reduce the costs of governmental services: better nourished children require less health assistance and will not have to repeat as many grades at school.

Moreover, the demographic shift caused by steep declines in fertility leads to a population in which there are relatively more income-generating adults for each child.[28] Thus, not only will the absolute amount of resources available to the government increase (through greater taxes and lower costs), but that amount can be spent on fewer people, increasing the quality of nutrition and learning. If governments choose to reinvest the earnings, the potential returns over the long term are enormous.

Learning's impact on hunger and economic growth

Part of the evidence for hunger's direct impact on economic growth comes from veterans of the American Civil War. Examining records from Union Army veterans (who fought on the side of the north in the 1860s conflict), Nobel-prize winning economist Robert Fogel and colleagues recognized that the veterans' capacity for manual labour at later stages of life was far below current levels at a comparable age. Fogel suggested that this reflected a change over the centuries in the capacity of the 'human engine' (Fogel 2004). Put another way, the productivity of humans had increased over time with better nutrition — and with technological innovations (such as automobiles) that reduced health hazards (such as the bacteria-ridden horse manure on the streets of New York).

He identified three primary ways that nutrition affected economic growth. First, improved nutrition brought more people into the labour force, since they were physically capable of participating. With sufficient calories, a man could take on manual labour such as bricklaying or working on a factory assembly line.[29] It therefore contributed to the absolute increase in the labour force, leading to improved economic growth.

Second, it meant that more calories were available for any person in the labour force. The increased calories from a good meal would allow people to work harder and longer. Several studies have shown that protein-energy malnutrition and micronutrient deficiencies are associated with lower productivity due to physical effects (cf. Horton 1999; Horton and Ross 2003; cf. UN Millennium Project 2005a).[30]

Third, the body itself was more efficient at converting that energy into output, since there was less interference from disease (which increases metabolic requirements and causes the loss of nutrients).[31] Thus, improved nutrition contributed to the technical efficiency of the labour force, thereby contributing to economic growth. He suggests that at least half of the growth in the British economy since 1800 can be explained by these factors.

This report has shown how learning is essential to improving nutrition. Learning not only increases the basic mental capacity to address hunger, but can also provide the specific skills (e.g. agricultural extension, nutrition training) required to do so. As a result, learning strengthens nutrition and therefore the ability of people to participate in the economy effectively. There are also intergenerational effects. Decreased hunger in one generation leads to improved learning in the next, since children of better-nourished parents often have a greater capacity to learn.

At the governmental level, the effect of reduced hunger has an immediate benefit in the increase in the tax base and the resources available to reinvest. But it also lessens the economic burden, since fewer resources will be diverted to caring for the sick or providing social benefits for those in need. As with the other major pathway (from reduced hunger to increased learning and economic growth), government decisions can allow these additional resources to be reinvested, thus reinforcing, strengthening and perpetuating the cycle.

Key lessons

The impact of increased human capital and improved 'human engines' on economic growth is well-established in the literature. An analysis of the relationship between hunger and learning adds new dimensions to these understandings. It shows how addressing hunger is critical to learning and the formation of human capital; it also demonstrates that learning is central to the improvement of the 'human engine'. There are, of course, numerous other factors that influence growth, ranging from openness to trade to macroeconomic policy. And there is no single formula for success. But the discussion above does suggest several key lessons:

• These processes require time.

It takes a generation for the investments in learning and nutrition to fully show up in economic growth, as better nourished and stimulated children grow into productive adults. The intergenerational feedback will multiply these effects in succeeding generations.

• The pay-offs of investing in learning and better nutrition can be enormous.

The investments in hunger and learning are mutually reinforcing. The direct and intergenerational benefits build on each other, compounding like interest, over time. These improvements lead to long-term economic growth, as has been seen in the recent successes of the East Asian Tigers and Chile, and in the earlier economic transformations in Japan, Britain and the United States.

• Government decisions are critical.

These processes only take hold when governments make carefully thought-out choices and support them through appropriate investments and policies. In East Asia, for example, the governments not only spent more on education in absolute terms than elsewhere, but they focused on the most appropriate priorities for their context: for example, on improving primary education. Commitment to these strategies over the long run is what made the difference.

The next chapter turns to the challenges to making these political choices.

Intermezzo 5: Nutrition, learning and economic growth: The case of Chile

Chile dramatically decreased infant mortality, improved malnutrition rates and increased educational attainment — all while the country was still relatively poor and under-developed. In fact, the country attributes its current economic success to the investments made in nutrition, health, education and sanitation that began over 40 years ago.

Dramatic improvements

The situation in Chile today is quite different from that of the early 1960s. At that time, Chile had one of the highest infant mortality rates in Latin America (120 per thousand). This total decreased to 11 per thousand in 1994 and 7.8 per thousand in 2004, the lowest rate in the region (see Figure 5a below). A similar trend has been observed in preschool child mortality, which has declined from 14 per thousand in 1960 to 0.6 per thousand in 1994 and 0.4 per thousand in 2002.

In roughly the same period, the percentage of children with malnutrition has also been reduced dramatically, from 60 percent in 1950 to 1.7 percent in 2004. Moderate and severe malnutrition decreased from 5.2 percent and 2.2 percent respectively in 1950, to 0.1 percent in 2004. The percentage of newborns with low birthweight (below 2.5 kg) has diminished from 11.6 percent to 4.8 percent from 1975 to 2000. As an additional indicator of this change, the average 18 year old Chilean male is 11 centimetres taller than his homologue of 30 years ago.

During the past 40 years, a considerable improvement has simultaneously occurred in elementary education. In 1960, more than 30 percent of the population was illiterate; the rate now stands at less than 2 percent. Only 10 percent of the children in 1960 had completed elementary education. Today, close to 90 percent of children attend primary school.

A range of interventions

Successive governments, prodded and guided by academic researchers, designed and implemented a set of policies to protect children from the damaging effects of malnutrition from the time they were in the womb to adolescence. They focused in particular on interventions related to *health and nutrition, education* and *sanitation*.

Figure 5a — Dramatic reductions in early childhood mortality were achieved in Chile

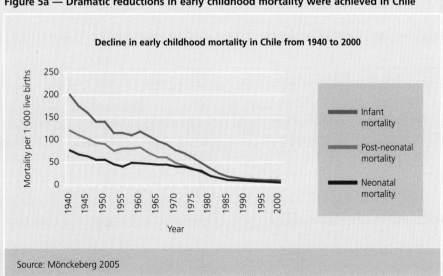

Source: Mönckeberg 2005

Health and nutrition interventions

The first step was to organize a national health infrastructure. In 1952, several organizations that provided health care were merged and transformed into the National Health Service (NHS). The NHS developed and scaled up several initiatives to foster mother and child health. Some of the key initiatives undertaken included:

• Breastfeeding campaign

Because a large share (85 percent) of Chile's population lives in urban areas, and perhaps as a result of a system of free milk distribution, there was an abrupt decline in the practice of breastfeeding. An extensive programme was introduced to promote breastfeeding, using both the mass media (e.g. radio, television, magazines) and formal education. More than 70 percent of mothers now exclusively breastfeed their children during the first 90 days, representing an 88 percent increase.

• Treatment of severely malnourished children

After a successful pilot, a private foundation took over this programme, which involved providing appropriate foods, stimulation and maternal training to severely malnourished children. The programme is estimated to be responsible for a 25 percent reduction in child mortality rates.

Other important interventions included a nationwide growth monitoring system, nutrition education, family planning, targeted food rations for poor households, immunizations and the provision of rural health care.

Education interventions

In the area of education, after developing infrastructure and increasing the numbers of trained teachers, the country focused on two principal interventions: school feeding and crèches.

• School feeding

The programme was principally aimed at stimulating enrolment and maintaining attendance. Delivery of service was transferred to private agencies, leaving the public foundation JUNAEB (Junta Nacional de Auxilio Escolar y Becas) with the role of evaluation and control. JUNAEB is an institution created by law to implement any interventions needed to promote equitable access to education. It focuses primarily on school feeding, but also works on related issues such as health care, housing and scholarships. The reorganization of the school feeding programme halved the cost and improved the quality of the service, while accomplishing the goal of combating school drop-out.

• Preschool programme

The preschool programme provides both food and stimulation to vulnerable children between the ages of two and six in poor urban areas.

Sanitation interventions

For many years, a high percentage of the population in Chile lived in extremely impoverished areas that lacked sanitation facilities. Chile developed a programme that emphasized the importance of sanitation in preventing early malnutrition. During the initial stage of this programme, a low cost, brick-and-timber sanitary unit was built on the plots of 300 or more families living in a slum area. In the past 15 years, 250,000 sanitary units have been built in different cities of the country. In 1960, only 40 percent of the population had drinking water in their homes, and only 35 had an adequate sewage system. At present, 99 percent of the population have drinking water at home, and 93 percent live in housing connected to a sewage system.

Achieving political support

The political decisions supporting a national health and nutrition policy did not happen spontaneously: they were induced. In the case of Chile, a university (Universidad de Chile) through an institute (Instituto de Nutrición y Tecnología de los Alimentos, INTA) has played a very significant role in both creating awareness of the problem and developing a strategy to address intersectoral challenges.

INTA recognized that, in order to obtain political support, malnutrition and health problems had to become visible political issues. It developed a defined communications strategy to create awareness of nutritional and health problems in the community. With this purpose in mind, INTA worked with the mass media, and even trained journalists, in an attempt to create awareness about the adverse effects of malnutrition and poor health on individuals and the whole society. Eventually, a stage was reached when practically all the candidates for public office had (and still have) programmes aimed at eradicating malnutrition and improving child health conditions.

Chile also understood that child development, child health and malnutrition are intersectoral challenges. To address them through a comprehensive approach, the Council for Food and Nutrition (Consejo Nacional para la Alimentación y Nutrición; CONPAN) was created. This was an autonomous, interministerial agency entrusted with the preparation and coordination of a nutritional policy for the country. But it soon became bogged down as a result of bureaucratic resistance and interministerial conflicts.

As a result, CONPAN was disbanded, and policymakers concentrated their efforts on specific interventions aimed at improving the nutritional condition of specific target groups, rather than on developing a comprehensive policy. The new strategy was much more effective — though it made the overall costs of the integrated programme less visible by spreading them among separate initiatives.

Economic growth *through* investments in nutrition and learning

The largest proportion of Chile's improvements in child mortality, malnutrition and education was achieved during a time when per capita Gross National Product (GNP) did not change substantially and while poverty persisted almost unchanged.

The programmes were funded through a combination of political commitment and innovative private sector financing. Political commitment was spurred by academics and others who created awareness and concern among the public by disseminating research and knowledge. Subsequently, the economy has grown at record rates — at least in part due to the improved human capital.

Source: Mönckeberg 2005

6. Political choices

There is a saying among the Hausa of northern Nigeria that "a bull will always manage to carry its own horns." The implication is that people, too, will take up activities if they see the purpose and value in them. Theory and empirical evidence suggest that investments in reduced hunger and enhanced learning can have important impacts on current and future national development by expanding the real opportunities of the population and strengthening economic growth.

Yet it is not always easy to convince policymakers to make these investments. There are many practical constraints to the successful implementation of the intervention packages discussed in the report, including: political priorities, resource limitations, institutional weaknesses, physical barriers and even discouragement from past experiences. But there are also ways to overcome these constraints and lessons to be learned from other countries.

6.1 Political will and priorities

"Frankly, we have other priorities"

The suggestion to focus resources on nutrition and learning may provoke an impatient retort from ministers that "We have other priorities." Despite the considerable body of literature on 'what works' in nutrition and learning, many well-tested interventions have not been implemented and remain a low priority for governments. In order to address this neglect or indifference, measures need to be taken to increase awareness, identify champions, and achieve and maintain commitment.

• Increasing awareness

Some policymakers are not aware of the damaging relationship between hunger and learning. One of the first steps in creating awareness is to gather information about the extent of the problem within the country. A nationwide survey provided the impetus for Thailand's long-term nutritional strategy.

In some places, academic institutions and non-governmental organizations can assist the government in obtaining the necessary data. A university-led study, conducted in conjunction with non-governmental organizations, helped provide the basis for the Fome Zero programme in Brazil. In Chile, a non-partisan national nutritional institute (INTA) gathered baseline data about the hunger situation within the country.

Once the extent of the problem is identified, information can be targeted to different audiences to raise awareness and generate commitment. For the public, media campaigns can sensitize people to the seriousness of the issue. Chile and Thailand both worked with the media in innovative ways to convey their messages (Box 6.1). The Government and NGOs in Mali used a combination of counselling sessions, role plays, village mobilization meetings and radio shows to reach a wider population (Parlato and Seidel 1998). For policymakers, more technical information on the likely impact of interventions — and the implications of doing nothing — can be more persuasive. PROFILES is a relatively recent technique to provide computer-generated scenarios that allow policymakers to assess the costs and benefits of various combinations of actions (AED 2006).

• Identifying champions

Many countries have found creative and effective ways to increase awareness, but progress often requires identifying champions who can offer high-level support and ensure that attention is given to these issues. Champions are often senior government officials who "build coalitions of interest … and steer policies and program[mes] through the planning and clearing process in an entrepreneurial way" (Heaver 2005: 27). Examples of national champions for nutrition and learning interventions range from the President in Brazil to senior officials in the Ministry of Education and Agriculture in Thailand to the President of Sierra Leone. In Kenya, an assistant minister for

6. Political choices

Box 6.1 — The media can help raise awareness

Both Chile and Thailand found effective ways to work with the media to raise awareness of nutrition issues. In Chile, the national nutrition institute created a fellowship programme for journalists that explained the damaging effects of malnutrition on mental development. After graduating, these journalists returned to television, print and radio, concerned about the issues and eager to prepare informed pieces on hunger. With their articles, they included emotionally-charged images showing the effects of undernutrition on the brain. This media attention contributed to a 'health culture' in Chile that forced politicians to take these issues seriously.

In Thailand, the Government teamed up with the private sector to create and repeatedly run a television advertisement, showing hungry Thai children eating dirt in a poor province in the northeast. The advertisement helped to inspire national indignation — and action.

Source: Mönckeberg 2005; Heaver 2005

education served as a champion by highlighting the importance of having a national policy on health and nutrition education (UCLA International Institute 2004).

Champions need to be supported to convince others. Within their country, they have to be able to draw on solid policy research and backing from academic institutions. However, a lesson from Chile is that institutes providing this information must retain professional independence from the government of the day. Otherwise, they risk losing credibility: "The crucial point ... is to reach an acceptable balance between political involvement and independence ... The whole team of experts participating in a health and nutrition programme have to be cautious not to get involved with contingent, changing, and short-lived issues. ... It is important for professionals to win support from all sides" (Mönckeberg 2005: 7).

Sometimes, support can come from champions at the regional level. The Sahel Alliance brought together education ministers from a number of different countries to share lessons and support joint action on food-for-education initiatives, such as school feeding. In Latin America, a school feeding network (LA-RAE) has been established to share information, progress and lessons learned on school feeding in the region (see Box 6.2).

In the absence of champions in national settings, UN and bilateral donors must take a more active role. The food, nutrition and education task forces operating in each UN Country Team should ensure that the Common Country Assessment and the resulting UN Development Assistance Framework adequately address hunger and learning issues.

• Achieving and maintaining commitment

Even if politicians recognize the importance of these investments, they may worry that the benefits will only be seen after five or ten years. By then, they may no longer be in power — and will have no opportunity to claim credit for the improvements. Several courses of action can be taken to address this concern (see Box 6.3).

One way to achieve sustained commitment at both the national and community level is to provide a means for leaders to know whether efforts are successful, even in the short term. National and local information systems reporting on child growth and development outcomes are critical for keeping governments and donor agencies informed of progress — and committed to action. In Zambia, an impact assessment of a school and nutrition programme helped persuade the Government to take it to scale and to incorporate school health and nutrition interventions into its long-term strategic plan (UCLA International Institute 2004). Local growth monitoring programmes can show results even within as little as two years (Heaver 2005).

Perhaps the most effective way to ensure long-term commitment is to legally mandate the interventions. The legal institutionalization of programmes protected Chile's interventions through successive regimes. India recently passed legislation mandating a hot midday meal for school children. Indonesia considered the school feeding programme an integral part of its national safety net, preserving it even during times of economic crisis.[32]

In Brazil there is a proposal aimed at modifying Article 6 of the Brazilian Constitution to include the right to food among the fundamental human rights (Belik and Del Grossi 2003). Other nations that have a constitutional guarantee of the right to food include South Africa and Nigeria (FAO 1998) — though of course a constitutional guarantee does not ensure that the right to food will always be enforced. Nutritional and learning goals should also be incorporated into national development plans and poverty reduction strategy papers. Government commitments to the Millennium Development Goals can also be used to focus more effort and resources on nutrition and learning outcomes.

A final means to create long-term commitment is to appeal to the judgement of history. Those leaders and policymakers who have initiated efforts to address hunger and improve learning have been acknowledged for their foresight and importance, even when the results were achieved years later. The architects of the Chilean and Thai successes are widely admired around the world, but above all within their own countries.

6.2 Resource constraints

"We cannot afford these kinds of interventions"

"We simply do not have the funds for these kinds of programmes" is another common response to the proposal to invest in reduced hunger and enhanced learning. But this view usually reflects a misunderstanding of the costs and benefits — or a lack of awareness of some of the ways to keep expenses down.

The kinds of nutrition interventions proposed for early childhood, for example, are some of the most cost-effective available (Jones and others 2003). When calculations are made comparing

---

Box 6.2 — Working regionally to build support for Food for Education

Two recent initiatives offer different (but as yet untested) approaches to building international support for sustaining food for education. The Sahel Alliance was formed in 2003 at a regional ministerial meeting in Dakar, Senegal. The alliance aims to create a regional strategy to promote food for education. It has endorsed two major steps: first, integrating school feeding activities in government strategies and action plans, as well as in Poverty Reduction Strategy Papers; and second, strengthening collaboration at the country level between central and local partners, as well as between the ministries of education and health.

The Latin American School Feeding Network (LA-RAE in Spanish) was officially launched on 22-26 March 2004 at a conference in Santiago, Chile. It seeks to strengthen and expand Latin American school feeding and child nutrition programmes by connecting stakeholders. Using a membership organization model — open to all interested parties, including parents, teachers, government officials, the food industry and nutrition and education groups — the network intends to provide a forum (including a website) for sharing information among Latin American countries and to help Latin American countries develop their own national school feeding associations, such as the one established in September 2003 in Colombia.

Box 6.3 — Some ideas for keeping politicians interested in nutrition programmes

"The following ideas for keeping nutrition high on the agenda of politicians might be tested through action research:

- Explain how improving nutrition benefits other programmes that are leading politicians' personal priorities — primary education or industrial development, for example.

- Stress that considerable improvement in child growth can be achieved within two years of a GMP [Growth Monitoring Programme] moving into a new area — well within the time horizon of a politician's time in office.

- Cut implementation into time-bound chunks with regular performance milestones, so politicians have regular achievements to announce to the public.

- Provide top politicians with regular performance information in a user-friendly format.

- Commission opinion research among clients, so politicians know that people care about the nutrition programme and votes may depend on it.

- Take politicians on field visits so they see this for themselves.

- Set up a programme oversight board, consisting of parliamentarians of different parties, senior finance and planning officials, NGOs and other civil society representatives, to review programme performance independently.

- Have a representative client 'service user group' report directly to this board about the quality of services they are getting.

- Ensure that regular reports about programme performance appear in the media.

- Ensure that, every time they meet a politician, senior donor officials ask, How are the children growing [and learning]?"

Source: Heaver 2005: 45

the future benefits with the costs, the returns greatly exceed the investment. Iodine supplementation for pregnant women, for instance, pays for itself from 15 to 250 times (Behrman and others 2004). Interventions to prevent low birthweight, promote exclusive breastfeeding for six months, and provide complementary feeding in infancy cost up to US $20 per capita per year. By comparison the productivity losses due to poor nutrition in developing country settings are conservatively estimated to be 2 percent to 3 percent of GDP a year (Horton 1999b). The arithmetic is not difficult to do; it is cheaper for a developing country to prevent hunger and malnutrition than to let it continue to exist.[33]

In some cases, programmes can be made more affordable through cost-saving measures. Take school feeding. Several possibilities exist for keeping costs down. For instance, the costs can be greatly lowered if the programme is targeted to the neediest provinces or districts, rather than providing universal coverage. Moreover, relatively expensive foods with relatively low nutritional content, such as milk, can be replaced with more cost-effective alternatives (Del Rosso 1999). Micronutrient-fortified high-energy biscuits in Bangladesh reduced the costs of the school feeding programme to US$18 per child per year — while achieving impressive results in terms of attendance and academic performance (Ahmed 2005). Involving the private sector in the provision of meals can also substantially reduce costs (Mönckeberg 2005; Del Rosso 1999).

Another possibility is to combine programmes through school-based initiatives such as FRESH and the Essential Package, to achieve multiple objectives using the same basic infrastructure. The UN Hunger Task Force and the New Partnership for African Development encourage the use of 'home-grown' school feeding, where the food is bought locally, reducing costs and supporting local farmers (UN Millennium Project 2005a). Some of these lessons can be applied to other interventions as well, such as mother-and-child nutrition, take-home rations and cash transfers.

6.3 Institutional capacities

"We do not have the institutional structures or expertise to deal with these issues"

Sometimes ministers throw up their hands and laugh, saying, "Yes, we should do all these things, but have you seriously considered our institutional capacity?" There are at least three major institutional challenges to implementing interventions for reducing hunger and improving learning, including the lack of intersectoral coordination, the difficulties of scaling up programmes, and the absence of sufficient local-level expertise.

• The lack of intersectoral coordination

The most successful countries in dealing with hunger have taken multi-sectoral approaches, involving food, health, sanitation and education. But such approaches require intersectoral coordination, which can be difficult to achieve. Many countries do not have an institutional home for hunger and nutrition. Moreover, donors increasingly support sector-wide approaches (SWAPs) in education, health and basic infrastructure. As a result, in some countries, the development of integrated packages of appropriate interventions becomes dominated by a single sector, such as health or education, which cannot address the intersectoral nature of a comprehensive strategy.

There are at least two approaches that can be implemented to overcome these challenges. One is to provide a home for hunger-related interventions, by establishing national nutritional councils. In Thailand a central food and nutrition planning committee was set up in the 1970s (see Intermezzo 6). It established a series of National Food and Nutrition Plans to be included in the country's larger five-year National Economic and Social Development Plan. In Brazil in the early 2000s, a National Food Security Council (Conselho de Segurança Alimentar Nutricional, CONSEA) was created to set guidelines for the federal Government's food and nutrition security policies. It is comprised of members of civil society (two-thirds) and government officials (one-third).

But other approaches can also be effective. Instead of creating a council, it is possible to demonstrate the relevance of programmes to each of the concerned ministers, so that they make it part of their own work (Heaver 2005). Comprehensive approaches that use school feeding, for example, help achieve the aims of the Ministry of Education by increasing enrolment and school attendance. They support the Ministry of Health by addressing childhood diseases, such as worms, and by offering a vital opportunity to inform children of how to prevent HIV/AIDS. They strengthen the quality of the 'human capital' of the workforce, thus serving the goals of the Ministry of Industry. And through their impact on education, they improve the productivity of farmers and their openness to new ideas, helping the Ministry of Agriculture to meet its targets. This approach has worked in several countries. In Chile, ministers of health, economy, education, agriculture, work, social welfare and planning, spurred on by academic champions, developed separate, but complementary programmes (Mönckeberg 2005). Such an approach has also been successful in bringing together the health and education sectors in a health-promoting schools project in rural China (Xu and others 2000).

• Scaling up

Another difficulty that governments face is the challenge of scaling up programmes to the national level. How can it be done with limited staff? Achieving universal coverage is possible, if it is based on strategies for community mobilization and support (Shrimpton 2002; see Box 6.4). Some external facilitation is usually required. In community-based nutrition programmes that have shown success — whether in Tanzania or Thailand — facilitators provide initial training and then continue to offer supervision to support community mobilizers. The community facilitators are usually paid, but the community mobilizers carry out these functions voluntarily, perhaps with some community-based compensation. In school feeding programmes, members of the local communities are expected to serve as cooks, kitchen helpers and guards, or to pay for people to fulfil these basic operational roles (WFP and others 1999).

Once the basic implementing mechanisms are established in a few locations, rapid expansion can occur by documenting and replicating interventions. With technical support, communities can assess their needs, select the appropriate mix of interventions, adapt the tools to local conditions and implement them in new settings. While the start-up costs of developing

---

Box 6.4 — Three approaches to scaling up nutrition programmes

There is no one blueprint for scaling up, and there are many ways of trying to achieve it, including scale by expansion, scale by explosion and scale by association. Expansion produces scale in a careful and controlled way, with small trials gradually expanding to cover larger and larger areas through a process of implementers learning to be more effective and efficient.

Going to scale by explosion is the 'big bang' approach, usually enacted because of a national policy to achieve maximum coverage in the shortest possible time. Explosion is sometimes at the expense of the quality and outcomes. It can, however, be suitable for a 'blueprint' approach to fixed patterns of interventions, such as a system for rapid and efficient delivery of emergency food supplies. It is less effective for more complex, comprehensive interventions.

Achieving scale by association occurs when different programmatic experiences in different localities 'grow together', with the support of a general set of national guidelines. The scaling up of nutrition and learning programmes is probably best suited to the models of systematic expansion or growth by association, or a combination of both.

Source: Myers 1984

new interventions and tools are high, adapting these intervention models for new areas is an efficient way to achieve wider coverage.

• Human resources

A third major institutional constraint is the lack of adequately trained human resources. Reducing hunger and enhancing learning requires decisions about the right mix of interventions to meet locally specific needs. Personnel at the district level need enough power and autonomy for decision-making and an adequate level of knowledge of appropriate programmes. In some districts, the problems may include insufficient adult learning about agricultural production. In others, it may be inadequate breastfeeding and complementary feeding practices during infancy because mothers have to return to work too soon after birth. In still others, poor attention spans of school-age children may pose the greatest challenge. In most cases, it will be a combination of problems, and the wrong decision will lead to the choice of an ineffective package of programmes.

What is needed is training — not university degrees but locally organized short-term courses, plus ongoing on-the-job training through supportive supervision. Several initiatives, from USAID's BASICS to the Integrated Management of Childhood Illnesses, demonstrate that training in relatively simple guidelines can create effective programmes that are scaleable within and across countries.

6.4 Physical and environmental constraints

"It is next to impossible to reach people in emergencies and in remote areas"

Natural disasters, such as floods and earthquakes, can create physical barriers that make it difficult to reach those in need. Civil strife and armed conflict may also disrupt government services and force populations to flee from areas of violence and become refugees or internally displaced persons. In most of these situations, the provision of food and nutrition services is among the highest priorities for humanitarian aid. The international community — including the International Federation of the Red Cross and the World Food Programme — are expert at working with governments to reach people affected by disaster. And recent work with Bhutanese refugees in Nepal demonstrates that interventions can be implemented effectively in relief settings (see Box 4.1).

Providing services to sparsely populated regions can be challenging, even without a disaster. Many people in need live in remote areas, where there is no easy access to government services. Physical impediments, such as mountainous terrain or insufficient roads, compound the problem. One way of reaching these groups is to create mobile service delivery units. A service along the border between Angola and Zambia shows the promise of this technique (see Box 6.5).

6.5 Past experience

"We tried that before; it didn't work."

Often policymakers are discouraged by past experience. Similar efforts have been made before, they point out, but the programmes did not achieve the expected results. Although there can be many reasons for past failures (including the challenges described above), some of the most important relate to sequencing and approach.

In developing adult learning programmes, for example, sequencing of interventions is critical. It is necessary to keep in mind not just the supply side (the provision of learning opportunities), but also

Box 6.5 — Mobile equipment helps address vitamin and mineral deficiencies in a Zambian refugee camp

At the outbreak of new fighting in the eastern and southern regions of Angola in 2000, thousands of people fled across the border to Zambia. A refugee camp was established to accommodate the growing numbers. By 2003, with a population of over 26,000 people, the camp had a number of small businesses, including blacksmiths, bakeries and shops. It also had a market, which sold leafy green vegetables, tomatoes, tobacco and other products, and was open seven days a week. But most of the population was reliant on food aid, and the staple provisions did not meet their micronutrient needs — a common problem in refugee settings. As a result, there were high levels of vitamin A and iron deficiencies.

A group of international agencies and government ministries had the idea of milling and fortifying maize from mobile equipment on site — something never tried before. The system was tested over a year. An evaluation survey suggests that the fortified milled maize is associated with a significant increase in the vitamin A and iron status of adolescents and a reduction in anaemia among children (Seals and others 2006).

There are limitations to the survey methodology, and further study is required to understand some of the results. But the experiment provides some of the first empirical evidence that camp-level fortification and milling may lead to substantial benefits for some refugees experiencing vitamin and mineral deficiencies.

Source: Seals and others 2006

Box 6.6 — Motivating the desire to learn: Farmers' Field Schools

The United Nations Food and Agriculture Organization and a number of international non-governmental organizations have been using an approach to addressing hunger that ensures a demand for learning new agricultural techniques: Farmers' Field Schools for Integrated Pest and Production Management. The Schools work with a group of farmers over the course of an agricultural season. In a small plot, they demonstrate methods that have been externally recommended for each stage of the production process, from soil preparation to the harvest and marketing.

Farmers need to be adequately numerate and literate to take the necessary measurements in the demonstration plot and to apply the new techniques themselves. Farmers are often willing to pay for literacy programmes so that they can participate in the schools. As one observer of Farmers' Field Schools in Senegal wrote: "The programme was a success in as far as it delivered what people needed at the point they needed it, hence questions of motivation and keeping groups going became irrelevant. Farmers needed the information and therefore kept coming" (Oxenham and others 2002: 32).

Source: Oxenham and others 2002

the demand side (the desire and need for the learning). Many adult literacy programmes aimed at addressing hunger have failed because of their exclusive focus on the supply of the training, offering courses in literacy or income-generation in places where there is no real opportunity to apply the knowledge to address hunger. The demand does not emerge unless there is something new to manage — unless the possibility of improved production, resource accumulation, or the assumption of new responsibilities is allowed to take shape at the local level. Adult education programmes make most sense when they build upon some degree of local economic empowerment, as the experience with Farmers' Field Schools demonstrates (see Box 6.6).

Sometimes the sequencing is correct, but the approach needs to be improved. A lesson from many successful countries is that they did not have the right approach at first, but eventually did find it because of a willingness to learn and change course. In Uganda (see Intermezzo 4), it took several attempts before an adult literacy programme was developed that truly met the needs of the population.

The Government of Bangladesh has experimented with different combinations of school feeding, take-home rations and cash transfers to improve enrolment and academic performance in its country (Ahmed 2004). In Chile, the Government attempted to establish a national nutrition council but it quickly became bogged down in interministerial disputes. Eventually, it was disbanded, and a much more effective approach was designed that targeted individual ministries (Mönckeberg 2005). In Thailand, the Government's initial centralized, top-down approach made little progress on the problem of undernutrition. Only after an overhaul of the programme was the astonishing success of the more community-based system achieved (see Intermezzo 6).

Intermezzo 6: Mobilizing communities to eradicate undernutrition in Thailand

Thailand, like several other Southeast Asian nations, has been remarkably successful in reducing the prevalence of undenutrition in its country. But its success was not immediate — it took several false starts to discover that a multi-sectoral approach involving communities offered the most effective way to address this problem.

In less than a decade, between 1986 and 1995, Thailand reduced the national prevalence of underweight children by over 10 percent and almost halved the rate of stunting (see Figure 6a). This progress occurred at twice the speed of countries that did not invest in nutrition programmes. How did Thailand achieve such impressive results? The process, which spanned over several decades, actually started in the 1960s but gained momentum in the 1980s — and involved adjusting course where necessary.

Getting started

In the 1960s, a first national nutrition survey showed that malnutrition was a serious and widespread problem, affecting around half of all children under 5. This led the country's first National Economic Development Plan (NEDP) to point out that it was absolutely necessary to identify "measures to cope with the malnutrition that occurs in quite a number of cases among the rural population as a result of ignorance and lack of a balanced diet".

Equipped with these findings and recommendations, non-governmental organizations, the private sector and the media took the lead in creating public awareness about undernutrition in the country. They had the support of the Thai Royal Family, though elected politicians took more time to convince. After a decade of awareness raising, the efforts seemed to finally pay off: the first National Food and Nutrition Plan (NFNP) of 1976 acknowledged that nutrition was a multi-sectoral issue that could not be adequately dealt with as part of the health sector alone. Instead, it needed a plan of its own — and dedicated resources.

An action plan was developed using a central government-led approach. But unfortunately, the results were not particularly impressive: 50 percent of preschool children continued to suffer from protein-energy malnutrition. The most positive result was that the plan further strengthened awareness of nutrition problems among public and private sectors and helped to generate the political commitment on the part of the nation's policymakers. Over time, there was something akin to a national consensus that addressing undernutrition was a critical investment in the future of individuals, communities and the nation. But there was also a recognition that the current approach was not working. With surprising openness

Figure 6a — Thailand has made rapid progress in reducing protein-energy malnutrition

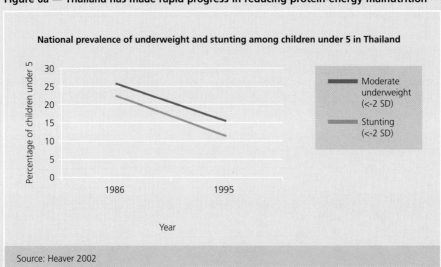

Source: Heaver 2002

and self-criticism, the Government abandoned that approach and developed a new strategy.

Finally on track

The new multi-sectoral strategy combined a bottom-up approach with a few critical top-down elements. On the one hand, communities were greatly empowered. They were deeply involved in the process of assessing their situation, implementing solutions and monitoring progress. An innovative 'Basic Minimum Needs' approach allowed villages to use an index to rate their current situation — and to identify appropriate interventions.

To achieve maximum reach with limited resources, volunteers were mobilized on a massive scale to assist in implementing the system. By 1989, the number of trained volunteers had reached 500,000. They were given a manageable caseload (of about 10 households per volunteer) which allowed them to fulfil their duties, while also maintaining their other jobs. Their rewards took the form of local recognition, rather than financial payments. Communities also contributed to the costs of almost all interventions.

At the same time, some elements of the programme were still run by the central government. It targeted resources to the most needy regions and ensured some consistency in approach (e.g. the use of volunteers and the Basic Minimum Needs approach). These centralized elements gave the programme a national coherence.

Technical support helped

As in Chile, universities played an important role in the success of the programme. In particular, the Institute of Nutrition at Mahidol University provided technical support for the interventions. Being accepted and relied upon by the Government, and having administrative and intellectual independence enabled the Institute to offer advice that was taken seriously. The universities also served another important function: they trained many of the officials who implemented the programmes.

The Government's earlier emphasis on primary and secondary education also benefited the programme. It made it possible to identify volunteers with the necessary background to implement the programme at the village and community levels.

Results can be achieved with limited external assistance

Thailand's achievement was particularly remarkable because the country was able to fund its national nutrition programme from domestic resources, without relying significantly on foreign aid. The emphasis was placed on ensuring that the country had access to necessary technical support, rather than on obtaining external financial resources for interventions. The country relied instead on low-cost programmes, implemented through heavy community involvement. When the successful programme began in the 1970s and early 1980s, Thailand was a relatively poor developing country with its subsequent economic growth still in its future.

Sources: Heaver and Kachondam 2002; Ismail and others 2003

7. The way forward

In Naguib Mahfouz's novella *The Journey of Ibn Fattouma*, the title character sets out with a caravan to visit neighbouring lands in search of answers to the problems that beset his country. After numerous tribulations, he arrives in the land of Halba, where he becomes acquainted with a local sheikh and his daughter. In one conversation, the sheikh lauds Ibn Fattouma's interest in recording his learning in notebooks but in another, the daughter questions his commitment to doing something for his people.[34] By the end of the story, as Ibn Fattouma journeys to further destinations, he is still protesting his intent to return to his homeland with the knowledge to improve it.

The preceding chapters of this report have tried to assemble the current knowledge about hunger and learning from the studies and experiences of countries around the world. But as the daughter's admonishment suggests, it is important not only to gather knowledge but also to apply it to achieve real progress. Both national governments and the international community need to take steps to address hunger and learning.

But how should they get started? Five basic steps are required to implement effective national strategies: situation analysis, strategy formulation, resource mobilization, implementation and monitoring. These steps provide an approach, not a blueprint. Each situation is different — requiring different solutions to different problems. But the basic approach should help policymakers identify strategies appropriate for their context.

Step 1: Situation analysis

National level

A situation analysis involves assessing the current conditions related to hunger and learning in the country.[35] As a starting point, policymakers can refer to the figures for their countries in the Data Compendium to this report. But these national figures only represent a beginning. Analysis must determine where hunger and inadequate learning — and future vulnerability — exist at the subnational level, information critical for setting priorities. Several techniques can be useful for conducting these kinds of assessments. Many governments have used mapping tools, which allow countries to identify the areas most in need. Successful mapping has been carried out in Burundi, Ghana, India, Indonesia, Sierra Leone and Viet Nam among many other countries. With subnational data for these indicators, it is possible to determine which age groups and problems need particular attention in each area.

As a simplified example, Map 7.1 shows how the technique can be applied in Burundi. Stunting figures (an indicator of growth faltering and therefore mental impairment) are superimposed on school life expectancy figures (a proxy indicator for enrolment). The map shows areas needing interventions for growth faltering and poor attendance, and provinces where hunger is likely a factor in lowering attendance rates — that is, where stunting is high and enrolment low. The technique can also be used to examine much smaller geographic and administrative units.

It is also necessary to analyse the programmes and services already addressing these problems. One way to begin this process is to conduct an inventory of the main programmes and initiatives related to hunger and learning in the country. The inventory would have to consider the geographic coverage of the programmes and the main implementers. Once the inventory has been made, it is important to assess the ability of the current response to meet the demand to a minimally acceptable standard.

International level

At the international level, the situation across various countries can be compared in terms of their progress on the two indicators

Map 7.1 — High stunting, low enrolment trouble-spots in Burundi

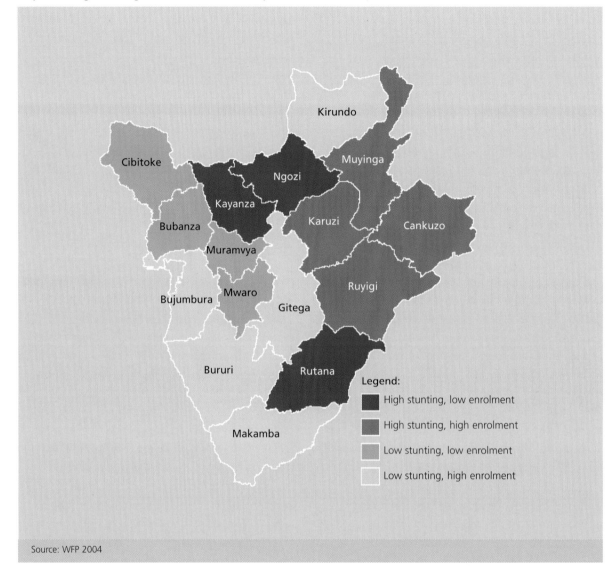

Source: WFP 2004

(underweight and undernourishment) for the Hunger Target for Millennium Development Goal 1. It is possible to identify 22 high need countries — with too slow or reversing trends for both underweight and undernourishment. Of these, eight (including Burundi, Tanzania and Yemen) are falling behind on both hunger indicators. This implies that appropriate policies and considerable financial resources need to be invested for there to be a hope of them meeting the Hunger Target of Millennium Development Goal 1.

Step 2: Strategic planning

National level

The next step at the national level involves developing a comprehensive strategy for dealing with problems. In many cases, plans will already exist, but it will be necessary to modify them based on a more comprehensive view of the issues. The 'knowledge tree' summarizes the possible interventions for each problem area discussed in previous chapters (Figure 7.1).

Figure 7.1 — Knowledge tree: Identifying the right interventions for hunger and learning

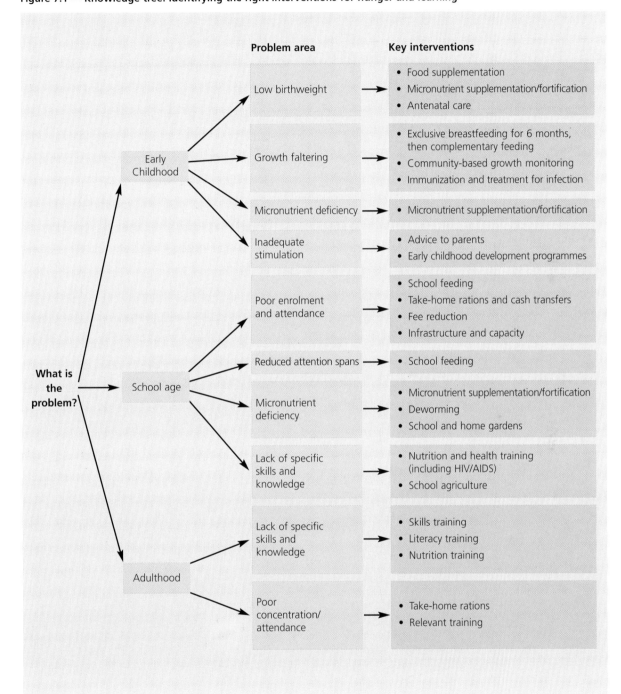

In most cases, policymakers will want to create packages of interventions that work together to meet the needs of a particular area — or, if the problems are widespread, packages that can form the basis of a national programme.

Principles for Action

But what should guide policymakers as they develop an implementation strategy for these interventions? Some principles for effective action are listed below:

7. The way forward

- **Take a lifecycle approach, but give priority to early interventions**

Interventions should be guided by the needs of a particular area. But in some cases, there will be a range of needs and insufficient resources to cover all of them. It has been shown that the most effective time to intervene is early in the lifecycle. Pregnancy and early childhood are the periods when hunger has its greatest impact on future learning capacity. At this stage, the young individual is growing rapidly and easily damaged if not given proper nutrition, care and stimulation. While these findings make sense in human development terms, the approach also holds true from a cost-benefit perspective (cf. Heckman and Carniero 2003). This does not mean that, in economic terms, investments should be made only in early childhood and the beginning of school-age years. Instead priority should go to those years, since they have the highest returns if investment is equal across all ages.

- **Identify clear objectives**

Many strategies fail because they are not clear about what they want to achieve and who they want to reach. The Results-Based Management approach identifies three levels of expected results that should be specified in any planning process:

❏ Outputs, or the immediate result of activities (e.g. 2,000 children received iron supplements);

❏ Outcomes, or medium-term changes in the situation based on the outputs (e.g. child anaemia rates decreased 10 percent); and

❏ Impacts, or the broader goals (e.g the learning capacity of children improved).

Realistic targets and meaningful indicators should be identified.

- **Take care to sequence programmes**

Early childhood interventions are less effective if they do not build on pre-existing primary health services. School feeding and comprehensive approaches require sufficient educational infrastructure and capacity. Adult learning needs to respond to pre-existing demand for the knowledge and skills. Without sequencing, well-intentioned programmes can fail.

- **Scale up effective programmes, where possible**

In many countries, effective projects reach only a small number of villages, where, say, a specific NGO works. Single projects can be quite useful for piloting new interventions, but if the projects are successful, it is important to replicate them in a larger area (Heaver 2005). Scaling up ensures the maximum return on investments (see Box 6.5).

- **Consider the broader context**

In almost all the cases examined in the previous chapters, the interventions focusing on hunger and learning were developed as part of comprehensive national poverty alleviation strategies. In many countries, a national poverty reduction strategy will already exist. Such countries can revise poverty reduction strategies with an integrated, multi-sectoral approach to meet the goals for hunger and learning. The strategy should be developed with broad stakeholder participation. Key actors include relevant ministries of the national government, grass-roots leaders and women. At the local level, strategies should consider the communities' particular needs. If interventions are not part of a larger complementary strategy, they will be less successful or even counterproductive.

- **Demonstrate political commitment**

Effective strategies depend on national governments making hunger and learning priorities. In some countries, programmes are legally mandated. Sometimes, a country's leader will declare fighting hunger a top priority — as in Sierra Leone or Brazil. All these signals of commitment (Box 7.1) must be followed with action.

1. "Politicians emphasize the need to tackle nutrition in their speeches.

2. Government sponsors public campaigns to raise awareness about the causes and consequences of malnutrition and about the benefits of investing in nutrition.

3. Governments hold workshops within and between departments to explain how improving nutrition is central to achieving their development goals.

4. Commitments to international goals (such as the MDGs) are translated into national policies for nutrition.

5. Nutrition policies are translated into specific national and regional targets.

6. Targets are translated into concrete investment plans and budgets, and donor support is sought where necessary.

7. The size of the budget request for nutrition reflects its priority in policy statements.

8. The budget actually sanctioned for nutrition is close to the budget requested.

9. What is actually spent on nutrition is close to the budget sanctioned.

10. The coverage and quality of the different nutrition interventions relate to what has been spent.

11. Politicians regularly review the performance of nutrition programmes.

12. Senior civil servants regularly review the performance of nutrition programmes."

Source: Heaver 2005

International level

For the international community, the identification of country needs (based on the Hunger Target indicators) permits the segmentation of intervention strategies.

• Low-need countries

Appropriate strategies might include topping up support to help the country reach the goals. It might also involve helping to transfer success stories to other countries that are struggling. Finally, international recognition for their efforts should be an additional incentive to continue their progress.

• Medium-need countries

Donors should support national strategies for addressing hunger and learning that are consistent with the interventions identified in the previous chapters for pregnant mothers and infants, school-aged children and adults. This may involve assisting with the start-up costs, piloting projects or providing technical advice.

• High-need countries

In these countries, a two-pronged strategy will be necessary. On the one hand, donors need to devote substantial resources to assist governments in making the necessary investments consistent with the suggestions laid out in this report. On the other hand, donors have to place political pressure for better governance to ensure that the funds are properly used and that a sustained commitment is made to hunger and learning.

Step 3: Resource mobilization and allocation

National level

This step involves identifying and securing the resources necessary to implement the strategies. Based on the packages of interventions identified and the objectives agreed on, the costs for the programmes should be estimated.[36] To meet these costs, three basic funding sources can be identified (Sachs and others 2004):

1. Domestic government resources

Maps 7.2 and 7.3 provide an overview of government expenditures on health (where nutrition initiatives are often housed) and education. Of course, expenditures must translate into improved services, and the amount required in each country will differ. Nevertheless, the map offers a way for governments to contextualize their own current levels of expenditures in these areas.

2. External finance

In some cases, external finance, or international donor assistance, is necessary, especially to cover the initial investments for large programmes. The Data Compendium to this report offers an initial way to assess the amount of aid currently available from national and international sources.

3. Out-of-pocket expenditures by beneficiaries

In many of the poorest areas, user fees should not be significant, at least at the outset, or they might act as a barrier to participation. So, only minimal cost recovery can be expected from beneficiary out-of-pocket expenditures.

International level

The long-term commitment of donors, local governments and implementing agencies — combined with a predictable financial commitment to education and hunger priorities — is especially important for the poorest countries and those whose health and education budgets rely on significant external support. To provide the country with more decision-making power, donor commitments should be untied and include an exit strategy if a country meets agreed and monitored performance targets.

To ensure sufficient financing, changes are needed in the international system, some of which are already under way: debt cancellation for highly indebted poor countries, scaled up and better quality development assistance, trade reform that levels the playing field and greater domestic resource mobilization. Innovative funding solutions, such as those proposed by the Quintet Against Hunger, must also be considered (Box 7.2).

Step 4: Implementation

National level

This step involves taking the actions to carry out the identified programmes and activities at a community or local level. Several actions are important for creating a community-based implementation framework (Ndure and others 1999). First, it is necessary to identify key partners for programme implementation. These key partners may be from the government, community and private sector. It may help to agree on principles for making intersectoral collaboration work. Second, an institutional framework for action should be developed. This involves defining the different roles of partners. Third, an appropriate action plan should be designed and implemented, and a timeframe for the implementation of activities developed. And fourth, a conscious effort should be made to learn from others with experience in these areas.

International level

A global partnership — bringing together governments, NGOs, firms and bilateral and multilateral agencies — is required to turn the vicious cycle of hunger and inadequate learning into a virtuous cycle that would allow millions of households to begin to escape the hunger trap. The partnership would have

The Quintet Against Hunger and Walk the World are two innovative international approaches for raising funds to address hunger.

Led by the Presidents of Brazil, Chile, France, Spain and more recently Germany, the Quintet is targeting other government leaders. With the support of the United Nations Secretary-General, the Quintet has pushed forward a campaign to generate the additional funds needed to achieve the Millennium Development Goals by 2015 through a series of innovative financing mechanisms estimated to generate US$50 billion a year. They include: taxing of financial transactions, taxing of the arms trade, creating an International Financial Facility for states to securitize their increases in future official development assistances in bond markets, and creating 'ethical funds' that provide opportunities for socially responsible investing.

Walk the World (co-sponsored by WFP) is creating a grass-roots campaign to raise awareness and funds for the fight against hunger. For the past two years, people around the world have walked on a selected day in May or June in a sign of global solidarity with those experiencing hunger. In 2005, more than 200,000 people walked in 269 cities in 91 countries in all 24 time zones. Individual walkers identify sponsors, who offer a donation based on completion of the walk. Private companies have contributed by offering funds for everyone who goes on the website. Walk the World will likely grow as an event in the coming years.

to focus on activities such as: assisting governments to mainstream nutrition and learning; providing technical support for interventions; and helping to mobilize resources for these efforts. To be successful, the partnership must be based on close coordination and harmonization of efforts among the major stakeholders over a sustained period of up to a decade.

Step 5: Monitoring and accountability

National level

Once the programme is implemented, monitoring and evaluation can strengthen multi-sectoral responses. Under a Results-Based Management approach, they provide policymakers, programme managers and implementers with current information on the progress of programme activities and on the key issues of their effectiveness, efficiency and continuing relevance. They help to determine if the objectives are realistic or if they need to be revised — and to identify problems so that group members can take steps to avoid or solve them (FAO 2001). The findings of the monitoring and evaluation will be based on the indicators developed for the situation analysis (and

linked to the Millennium Development Goal for hunger). At the end of an implementation phase, it should therefore be possible to make a new situation analysis and to begin the steps again.

Ultimately, accountability for implementing projects in accordance with plans (and achieving larger goals such as the Hunger Target for Millennium Development Goal 1) comes from democratic elections where voters can express discontent with or approval for the progress. A strong media and civil society (including academics and NGOs) can help ensure that the public is kept aware of the current situation. Innovative approaches for helping to achieve accountability should also be considered. The New Partnership for African Development's (NEPAD) African Peer Review Mechanism, for example, is a voluntary system based on the principles of technical competence, credibility and freedom from political manipulation. Although not primarily focused on nutrition and learning, the mechanism could be adapted to provide credible external reviews of government performance in these areas, thereby giving hungry people greater confidence in the findings and providing a standard for governments to meet.

Map 7.2 — Where health is — and is *not* — a priority

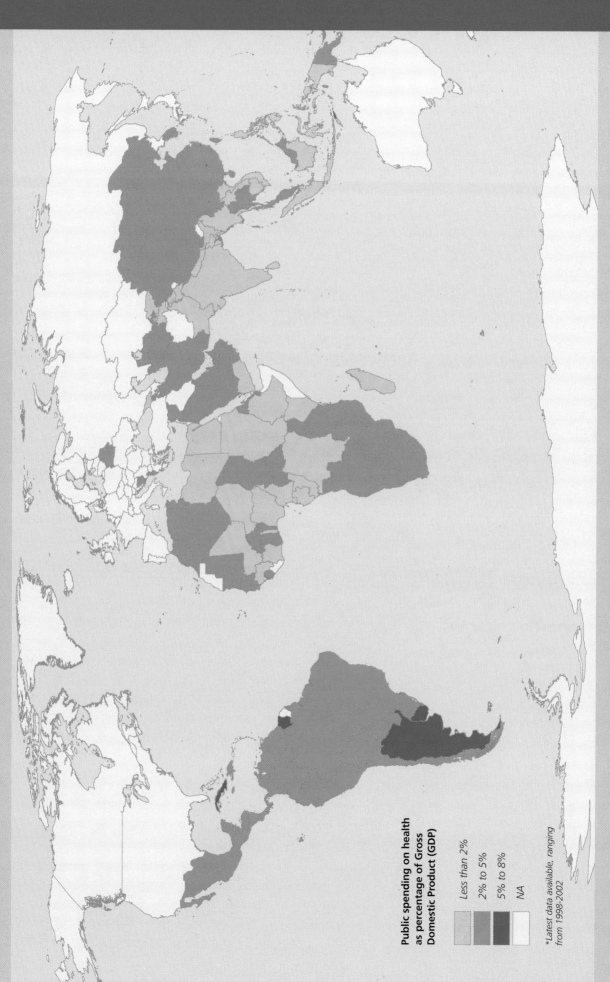

Public spending on health as percentage of Gross Domestic Product (GDP)

Less than 2%

2% to 5%

5% to 8%

NA

*Latest data available, ranging from 1998-2002

The boundaries and the designations used on this map do not imply any official endorsement or acceptance by the United Nations. Map produced by WFP VAM.

Data source: UNDP

Map 7.3 — Where education is — and is *not* — a priority

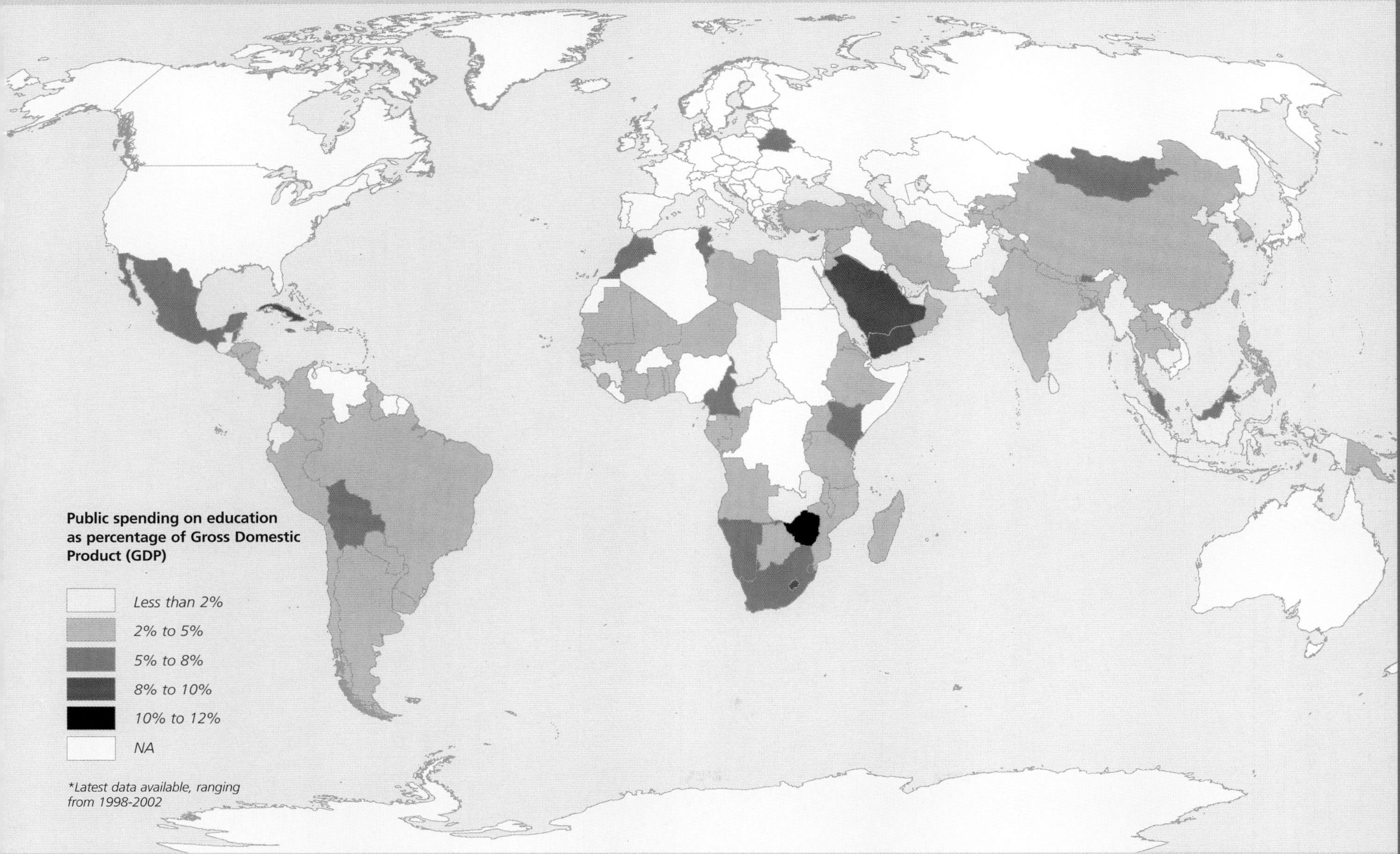

Public spending on education as percentage of Gross Domestic Product (GDP)

Less than 2%

2% to 5%

5% to 8%

8% to 10%

10% to 12%

NA

*Latest data available, ranging from 1998-2002

The boundaries and the designations used on this map do not imply any official endorsement or acceptance by the United Nations. Map produced by WFP VAM.

Data source: UNDP

7. The way forward

International level

The Hunger Target of Millennium Development Goal 1 provides a means of tracking not only national progress but also the adequacy of the efforts by the international community. Assessing needs based on this target can help donor nations to evaluate progress and perhaps change approaches. For instance, a country in the high-need category but with a history of poor governance may be offered more limited assistance initially, but with the promise of increases if the funds are invested properly. However, donor nations must also be held to account if they do not provide sufficient support for these efforts.

Conclusion

At the end of November 2005, representatives of government, aid agencies and donor nations gathered in Niamey, Niger, to learn lessons from the severe food crisis that had occurred in that country. Earlier in the year, images of emaciated mothers and infants had disturbed the world and prompted calls for urgent action. While the attention given to the crisis was critical, this report has suggested the importance of seeing beyond the immediate images. The affected children are not just experiencing short-term physical suffering; once their lives are out of danger, they will still suffer long-term mental damage that could lower their intellectual ability for life. This will limit their ability to create better livelihoods and address hunger for themselves and the next generation. The children in the pictures also represent only a small percentage of those whose lives are being damaged by hunger. Less visible and less dramatic hunger compromises the intellects of millions every day. Unless the problems of this wider group of hungry people are addressed with a long-term perspective, the lost potential will limit the development prospects of the nation.

This report has argued that understanding the relationship between hunger and learning is critical for achieving both individual and national development. Several key messages emerge:

- Hungry children must be reached as early as possible: hunger has its most damaging and long-lasting impacts on learning when it occurs in early childhood and, to a less extent, at school age.

- To be sustainable, targeted interventions in nutrition and learning are needed at appropriate points throughout life, creating a virtuous cycle of good nutrition and learning through the generations.

- Where these investments have been made as part of a larger development strategy, the improvements in human and economic terms have been enormous.

- National governments must take the lead with far-sighted actions, but they require the full support of the international community.

In the end, the decision to act is political. We began this report with the lines of the Chilean poet, Pablo Neruda. They suggested that hunger is often neglected, since many of its most serious consequences are not readily apparent. The report has brought to light how hunger damages mental capacity and prevents individuals from ever reaching their intellectual potential. It may therefore be appropriate to close with the last lines of that oft-quoted excerpt from Neruda's work, *The Great Tablecloth*, which conveys in simple language a plea for action:

> **For now I ask no more**
> **Than the justice of eating.**

PART IV: Resource Compendium

"How large is the undernutrition problem in my country?"

This part of the report offers resources for the reader.
The Technical Compendium elaborates on key technical points in the text.
The Data Compendium offers essential data for policymakers dealing with hunger issues.

A. Technical Compendium

The Poverty and Hunger Index (PHI)

In 2000, 189 countries endorsed the Millennium Declaration, which contained the Millennium Development Goals (MDGs). In 2001, the same countries adopted UN resolution A/56/326 that set a roadmap for the eight MDGs, identifying 18 targets and 48 official indicators.

The first MDG calls for halving the proportion of people suffering from poverty and hunger by the year 2015. Five official indicators have been employed for tracking progress towards this goal:

- Proportion of population living on less than US$1 a day

- Poverty gap

- Share of the poorest quintile in national income or consumption

- Proportion of population undernourished

- Prevalence of underweight children

The resolution did not envisage a particular hierarchy among those measures.

The PHI is a composite indicator that measures countries' average achievements in reducing poverty and hunger using the five official indicators for measuring progress towards MDG 1 (Gentilini and Webb 2005).

Following the UNDP Human Development Index (HDI) statistical methodology, before the PHI itself is calculated, an index needs to be created for each of these dimensions. The following diagram illustrates this process.

Figure IIA — Process for preparing the PHI

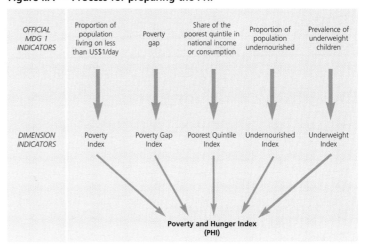

To calculate these five 'dimension indicators', minimum and maximum values (goalposts) are chosen for each underlying indicator.

Figure IIB — Goalposts for calculating the PHI

Official MDG 1 Indicators	Maximum value	Minimum value
Proportion of population living on less than US$1 a day	100	0
Poverty Gap	100	0
Share of the poorest quintile in national income or consumption	20	0
Proportion of population undernourished	100	0
Prevalence of underweight children	100	0

Performance in each dimension is expressed as a value between 0 and 1 by applying the following general formula:

$$\text{Dimension index value } Di = 1 - \left(\frac{\text{actual value} - \text{minimum value}}{\text{maximum value} - \text{minimum value}} \right)$$

Note that in order to be consistent with the HDI methodology of 'more is better', an additional operation had to be undertaken for all indexes but the poorest quintile dimensional index — i.e. the ratio had to be subtracted from 1 so that better values tend to 1, and the worse ones tend to zero.

The PHI is then calculated as a simple average of the dimension indices (i).

$$PHI = \sum_{i=1}^{5} [Di] \cdot 1/5$$

For example, the following illustration of the calculation of the PHI uses data for Brazil:

1. Calculating the poverty dimensional index

The poverty index measures the relative achievement of a country in reducing income poverty as measured by the international US$1/day poverty line (1993 PPP). For Brazil, with the latest available figures showing a poverty rate of 8 percent, the poverty index is 0.920.

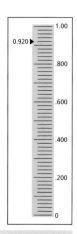

$$\text{Poverty index} = 1 - \left(\frac{8-0}{100-0}\right) = 0.920$$

2. Calculating the poverty gap dimensional index

The poverty gap index expresses countries performance in reducing the poverty gap (the average distance of the poor from the poverty line). Given that the most recent poverty gap figure for Brazil is 2.1 percent, the poverty gap index is 0.979.

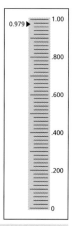

$$\text{Poverty gap index} = 1 - \left(\frac{2.1-0}{100-0}\right) = 0.979$$

3. Calculating the poorest quintile dimensional index

The share of the poorest quintile in national income or consumption represents a measure of inequality. In particular, it signals the inequality among the poorest 20 percent of the population — i.e. what the share of the bottom quintile is in national income or consumption. The share of Brazil's bottom quintile is 2.4 percent, and the corresponding poorest quintile index is 0.120. Note that in order to express value 1 as the optimum and 0 as the worse value, in this case we do not need to subtract the ratio from 1.

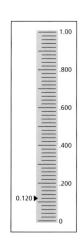

$$\text{Poorest quintile index} = \left(\frac{2.4-0}{20-0}\right) = 0.120$$

4. Calculating the undernourishment dimensional index

Undernourishment indicates the proportion of people in a country who do not consume an adequate amount of food. The most recent data shows that undernourishment affects 9 percent of the Brazilian population. Therefore, the corresponding undernourishment dimensional index is 0.910.

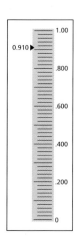

$$\text{Undernourishment index} = 1 - \left(\frac{9-0}{100-0}\right) = 0.910$$

5. Calculating the underweight dimensional index.

The fifth official MDG 1 indicator is the prevalence of underweight among preschool children in a country. This indicator expresses the low weight-for-age of children under 5 as compared to the WHO/NCHS standards. Underweight in Brazil is quite low, only 5.7 percent. Hence, the dimensional index is high, 0.943.

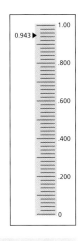

$$\text{Undernourishment index} = 1 - \left(\frac{5.7 - 0}{100 - 0}\right) = 0.943$$

6. Calculating the PHI

Once the dimension indicators have been calculated, determining the PHI is straightforward. It is a simple average of the five dimension indicators. In the case of Brazil, the PHI is:

$$\text{PHI} = [(0.920) + (0.979) + (0.120) + (0.910) + (0.943)] / 5 = 0.774$$

Therefore, the final PHI value for Brazil is **0.774**.

Figure IIC — PHI values for Brazil

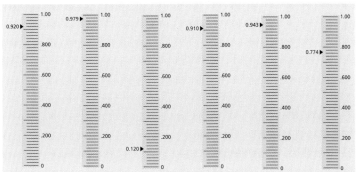

7. Calculating the Measure of Progress (MoP)

This step involves normalizing the five PHI dimensions in order to quantify the achievement of MDG 1 in a single number — the MoP. The normalization of dimension i (Ni) is derived by applying the usual formula involving an observation rate (2000i), and maximum and minimum rates (2015i and 1990i respectively):

$$Ni = (2000i - 1990i) / (2015i - 1990i)$$

While '1990' refers to data closest to year 1990 for all the five dimensions, '2000' stands for 'latest available data' in those dimensions (i.e. the data used to construct the PHI). Values range from 1 to -∞, where reaching 1 means reaching the dimensional goal (e.g. halving poverty according to 1990 levels by 2015), 0.5 indicates being on track with the dimensional goal, 0 is equal having made no progress, and negative numbers indicate a reversing trend. Note that value 1 represents an artificial limit: in the few cases where the dimensional value exceed 1 (i.e. when a country halved the rate already in 2000), manual corrections were made to equalize it to 1. In other words, a value of 1 represents reaching the dimensional goal, no matter if just reached or exceeded.[37] For any given country, the corresponding MoP is calculated as the average of the normalized dimensions:

$$MoP = \sum_{i=1}^{5} [Ni] \cdot 1/5$$

Thus, progress towards reaching MDG 1 is quantified in the form of a single number — value '1' of the MoP. That value is attained when — and only when — all five dimensional indexes are met. A MoP value of 0.5 indicates being on track to meet MDG 1 (or that 50 percent of the path towards MDG 1 has been completed); a 0 represents no progress at all; finally, a negative number indicates a reversing trend (a situation today that is making it even more difficult to reach the MDG goal).

Figure IID — Classifying progress

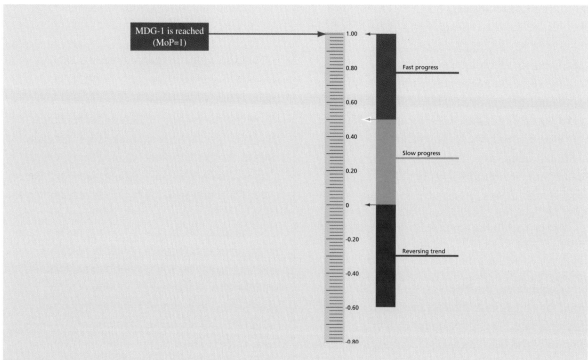

8. Example: Is Brazil on track with MDG 1?

The 1990 and 2000 rates for Brazil and the corresponding dimension indicators are the following:

	Poverty		Poverty Gap		Share of the poorest 20th		Undernourishment		Underweight	
	Rate	Dimension indicator	Rate	Dimension indicator	Rate	Dimension indicator	Rate	Dimension indicator	Rate	Dimension indicator
1990	14	0.860	4.3	0.957	2.1	0.105	12	0.880	7	0.930
2000	8	0.920	2.1	0.979	2.4	0.120	9	0.910	5.7	0.943
2015	7	0.930	2.15	0.978	3.15	0.158	6	0.940	3.5	0.965

Then, the values for the normalized dimensions are:

$$N \ (poverty = (0.920 - 0.860) / (0.930 - 0.860)) = 0.857$$
$$N \ (poverty \ gap) = (0.979 - 0.957) / (0.978 - 0.957) = 1$$
$$N \ (poorest \ quintile) = (0.120 - 0.105) / (0.158 - 0.105) = 0.285$$
$$N \ (undernourishment) = (0.910 - 0.880) / (0.940 - 0.880) = 0.500$$
$$N \ (underweight) = = (0.943 - 0.930) / (0.965 - 0.930) = 0.371$$

Then Brazil's progress towards the goal is calculated as follows:

$$\textbf{MoP} = [(0.857) + (1) + (0285) + (0.500) + (0.371)] / 5 = 0.603$$

Therefore, Brazil has shown fast progress towards the goal.

9. Priority Country Matrix

In order to better assess countries performance towards MDG 1, it is also important to combine the progress in reducing poverty and hunger over the 90s (as measured by the MoP) with the level of poverty and hunger (as measured by the PHI), which allows us to identify the set of countries that require priority actions. The figure below shows the set of countries that have fallen furthest behind meeting MDG 1 in the form of a matrix which identified high, medium and low priorities (see the corresponding red, orange and yellow cells). Both the ranking and the progress rating matter in defining
a) which countries are likely to meet the MDG goals,
b) which countries are making progress on some indicators, but not all, and
c) which nations are heading in the wrong direction, and therefore needing priority attention.

The level of the PHI has been divided into low (less than 0.700), medium (between 0.700 and 0.800) and high (more than 0.800). The three MoP categories of progress follow the already mentioned fast, slow and reversing trend distinction.
Therefore, with a PHI of 0.774 and an MoP of 0.603 Brazil is performing quite well. This does not mean that Brazil has resolved poverty and hunger-related problems, but it does mean that the country is implementing appropriate policies and programmes to fight these problems and that it is on the right track to reach MDG 1 by 2015.

This methodology has been replicated for the 57 countries for which data for all five official MDG 1 domains are available for two observation points. For these countries, accounting for 85 percent of the population of the developing world, we were able to provide insight on their performance towards reaching MDG 1. Nevertheless, data available for just one observation point allowed for the construction only of the PHI. In this case, the number of countries for which the PHI is available is 83, accounting for more than 90 percent of the population of the developing world.

PLEASE NOTE:
The designations employed and the presentation of country or area names in the World Hunger Series do not imply the expression of any opinion whatsoever on the part of the United Nations World Food Programme concerning the legal status of any country, territory, city or area or of its authorities, or concerning the delimitation of its frontiers or boundaries.

There is no established convention for the designation of 'developed' and 'developing' countries or areas in the United Nations system. In common practice, Japan in Asia, Canada and the United States in northern America, Australia and New Zealand in Oceania, and Europe are considered 'developed' regions.[38]

Figure IIE — Priority matrix

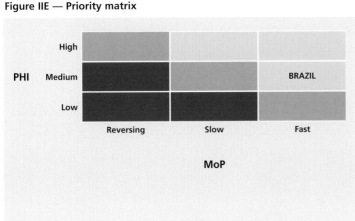

B. Data Compendium

B1. Overview

The data compendium is structured in four sections and nine tables, which pose and answer some of the principal questions that policymakers might ask in dealing with hunger issues:

Section I. How large is the undernutrition problem in the country?

Table 1. How many mothers and children suffer from undernutrition?

Table 2. How many people suffer from different forms of vitamin and mineral deficiencies?

Table 3. Where does the country stand on meeting the MDG for poverty and hunger?

Table 4. How many mothers, infants and children are lost each year?

Section II. What are the main causes of hunger in the country?

Table 5. Is food available and accessible to all?

Table 6. How vulnerable is the country to external risks such as man-made disasters, natural catastrophes and disease?

Table 7. Does lack of learning contribute to hunger in the country?

Section III. Is the country doing its best to fight hunger?

Table 8. Is a sufficient level of basic nutritional, educational and health services provided?

Section IV. How much does the international community contribute to the fight against hunger?

Table 9. How much help does the country receive, and how much of it is food aid?

The tables should serve as a starting point for assessing how well a country is doing on the given indicators.

B2. Data sources and methodology

Data presented in the compendium are from several sources: the World Food Programme's primary sources, international organizations such as the United Nations and its specialized agencies, and research institutes. Whenever possible, data have been collected from the original source or the institution mandated to collect them. Where data were available from different sources, the more recent source has been used when the quality of the data appeared equal. Unless otherwise indicated, the data are from the most recent year available from the indicated source. Data have not been broken down to sub-national level, even if they may be available from the given sources. Please note that many factors affect data availability, comparability and reliability. For this reason, data should be used with care.

Table structure

In general, tables start with a title, posing the question that will be answered by the data. The table header is divided into groups of indicators, followed by a short description of the specific indicators within those groups, and an indication of the year that data were collected. If a year-span is followed by an asterisk (e.g. 1995-2003*), this means that the data refers to the most recent year available during the indicated period. Headings in blue identify indicators that are used to measure progress on the Millennium Development Goals. Please note that some indicator names may have been modified from their conventional form in order to give greater emphasis to a point. Definitions of the indicators, as well as the sources and explanation of the notes in the table, are given after every table.

Terminology of the indicators

Descriptions of the indicators have been kept as short as possible without changing the meaning of the indicator given by the source. This may cause certain inconsistencies in the table headers, as different sources use different wordings.

B3. Classification of countries

The tables present data from 147 selected countries. These countries constitute 137 developing countries (DEV) as defined by the 2004 UNDP classification, combined with 84 Low-income, food-deficit (LIFD) countries as identified by FAO. These designations do not necessarily express a judgment about the development of a particular country. The term 'country' does not imply political independence but may refer to any territory for which authorities report separate statistics.

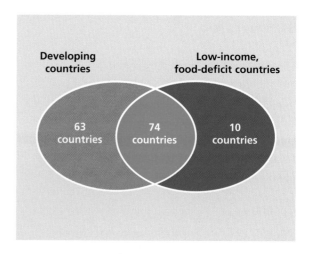

Sub-Saharan Africa					
Angola	DEV	LIFD	Liberia	DEV	LIFD
Benin	DEV	LIFD	Madagascar	DEV	LIFD
Botswana	DEV		Malawi	DEV	LIFD
Burkina Faso	DEV	LIFD	Mali	DEV	LIFD
Burundi	DEV	LIFD	Mauritania	DEV	LIFD
Cameroon	DEV	LIFD	Mauritius	DEV	
Cape Verde	DEV	LIFD	Mozambique	DEV	LIFD
Central African Republic	DEV	LIFD	Namibia	DEV	
Chad	DEV	LIFD	Niger	DEV	LIFD
Comoros	DEV	LIFD	Nigeria	DEV	LIFD
Congo, Republic of	DEV	LIFD	Rwanda	DEV	LIFD
Congo, Dem. Republic of	DEV	LIFD	Sao Tome and Principe	DEV	LIFD
Côte d'Ivoire	DEV	LIFD	Senegal	DEV	LIFD
Djibouti	DEV	LIFD	Seychelles	DEV	
Equatorial Guinea	DEV	LIFD	Sierra Leone	DEV	LIFD
Eritrea	DEV	LIFD	Somalia	DEV	LIFD
Ethiopia	DEV	LIFD	South Africa	DEV	
Gabon	DEV		Sudan	DEV	LIFD
Gambia	DEV	LIFD	Swaziland	DEV	LIFD
Ghana	DEV	LIFD	Tanzania, United Republic of	DEV	LIFD
Guinea	DEV	LIFD	Togo	DEV	LIFD
Guinea-Bissau	DEV	LIFD	Uganda	DEV	LIFD
Kenya	DEV	LIFD	Zambia	DEV	LIFD
Lesotho	DEV	LIFD	Zimbabwe	DEV	LIFD

Asia & Oceania

Afghanistan	DEV	LIFD	Mongolia	DEV	LIFD
Bangladesh	DEV	LIFD	Myanmar	DEV	
Bhutan	DEV	LIFD	Nauru	DEV	
Brunei Darussalam	DEV		Nepal	DEV	LIFD
Cambodia	DEV	LIFD	Pakistan	DEV	LIFD
China	DEV	LIFD	Palau	DEV	
Fiji	DEV		Papua New Guinea	DEV	LIFD
Hong Kong, China (SAR)	DEV		Philippines	DEV	LIFD
India	DEV	LIFD	Samoa	DEV	LIFD
Indonesia	DEV	LIFD	Singapore	DEV	
Kiribati	DEV	LIFD	Solomon Islands	DEV	LIFD
Korea, Dem. People's Rep. of	DEV	LIFD	Sri Lanka	DEV	LIFD
Korea, Republic of	DEV		Thailand	DEV	
Laos	DEV	LIFD	Timor-Leste	DEV	LIFD
Malaysia	DEV		Tonga	DEV	LIFD
Maldives	DEV	LIFD	Tuvalu	DEV	LIFD
Marshall Islands	DEV		Vanuatu	DEV	LIFD
Micronesia	DEV		Viet Nam	DEV	

Eastern and Southern Europe & CIS

Albania		LIFD	Georgia		LIFD
Armenia		LIFD	Kyrgyzstan		LIFD
Azerbaijan		LIFD	Tajikistan		LIFD
Belarus		LIFD	Turkey	DEV	
Bosnia and Herzegovina		LIFD	Turkmenistan		LIFD
Cyprus	DEV		Uzbekistan		LIFD

Middle East & North Africa

Algeria	DEV		Morocco	DEV	LIFD
Bahrain	DEV		Occupied Palestinian Territories	DEV	
Egypt	DEV	LIFD	Oman	DEV	
Iran	DEV		Qatar	DEV	
Iraq	DEV	LIFD	Saudi Arabia	DEV	
Jordan	DEV		Syria	DEV	LIFD
Kuwait	DEV		Tunisia	DEV	
Lebanon	DEV		United Arab Emirates	DEV	
Libyan Arab Jamahiriya	DEV		Yemen	DEV	LIFD

Latin America & Caribbean

Antigua and Barbuda	DEV		Guyana	DEV	
Argentina	DEV		Haiti	DEV	LIFD
Bahamas	DEV		Honduras	DEV	LIFD
Barbados	DEV		Jamaica	DEV	
Belize	DEV		Mexico	DEV	
Bolivia	DEV		Nicaragua	DEV	LIFD
Brazil	DEV		Panama	DEV	
Chile	DEV		Paraguay	DEV	
Colombia	DEV		Peru	DEV	
Costa Rica	DEV		Saint Kitts and Nevis	DEV	
Cuba	DEV		Saint Lucia	DEV	
Dominica	DEV		St. Vincent and the Grenadines	DEV	
Dominican Republic	DEV		Suriname	DEV	
Ecuador	DEV	LIFD	Trinidad and Tobago	DEV	
El Salvador	DEV		Uruguay	DEV	
Grenada	DEV		Venezuela	DEV	
Guatemala	DEV				

B4. Data tables — Section I. How large is the undernutrition problem in the country?

Table 1.   How many women and children suffer from undernutrition?

	Malnourished mothers and infants			Malnourished children under 5 years of age					
	Proportion of women with low body mass index (%)	Proportion of infants with low birth-weight (%)	Proportion of infants **not** exclusively breastfed up to the age of 6 months (%)	Prevalence of moderately and severely underweight children (%)		Estimated number of moderately and severely underweight children ('000)	Prevalence of severely underweight children (%)	Prevalence of wasted children (%)	Prevalence of stunted children (%)
	1992-2002*	1998-2003*	1995-2003*	~1990	1995-2003*	1995-2003*	1992-2003*	1995-2003*	1995-2003*
Sub-Saharan Africa									
Angola	-	12	89	40.6	30.5	825	8	6.3	45.2
Benin	10.5	16	62	-	22.9	267	5	7.5	30.7
Botswana	-	10	66	-	12.5	31	2	5	23.1
Burkina Faso	13.2	19	94	32.7	34.3	878	12	13.2	36.8
Burundi	-	16	38	37.7	45.1	541	13	7.5	56.8
Cameroon	7.9	11	88	15.1	22.2	542	4	5.9	29.3
Cape Verde	-	13	43[k]	-	-	-	2[x]	5.6[x]	16.2[x]
Central African Republic	15.3	14	83	27.3	24.3	150	6	6.4	28.4
Chad	21	17[x]	90	38.8	28	461	9	11.2	29.1
Comoros	10.3	25	79	18.5	25.4	31	9	11.5	42.3
Congo, Republic of	-	-	96[k]	23.9	-	-	3	5.5[x]	27.5[x]
Congo, Democratic Republic of	-	12	76	34.4	31	3 168	9	13.4	38.1
Côte d'Ivoire	7.4	17	90	23.8	21.2	528	5	7.8	25.1
Djibouti	-	-	-	22.9	18.2	21	6	12.9	25.7
Equatorial Guinea	-	13	76	-	-	-	4	-	-
Eritrea	40.6	21[y]	48	41	39.6	284	12	12.6	37.6
Ethiopia	26	15	45	46.2	47.2	5 878	16	10.5	51.5
Gabon	6.6	14	94	-	11.9	23	2	2.7	20.7
Gambia	-	17	74	26.2	17	38	4	8.2	19.1
Ghana	11.2	11	69	27.3	24.9	742	5	9.5	25.9
Guinea	11.9	12	89	-	23.2	341	5	9.1	26.1
Guinea-Bissau	-	22	63	-	25	73	7	10.3	30.4
Kenya	11.9	11	87	22.6	19.9	1 026	4	6.1	33
Lesotho	-	14	85	15.8	17.9	44	4	5.4	45.4
Liberia	-	-	65	-	26.5	170	8	6	39.5
Madagascar	20.6	14	59	40.9	40	1 222	11	7.4[y]	48.3
Malawi	6.5	16	56	23.9	25.4	572	-	5.5	49
Mali	-	23	75	-	33.2	857	11	10.6	38.2
Mauritania	8.6	-	80	47.6	31.8	159	10	12.8	34.5
Mauritius	-	13	84[x,k]	23.9	14.9	15	2	13.7	9.7
Mozambique	10.9	14[x]	70	27	26.1	819	6	7.9[y]	35.9
Namibia	13.8	14	81	-	-	-	5	8.6[x]	28.5[x]
Niger	20.7	17	99	42.6	40.1	1 022	14	13.6	39.7
Nigeria	16.2	14	83	35.5	30.7	6 408	9	15.6	33.5
Rwanda	5.9	9	16	29.4	24.3	367	7	6.8	42.6
Sao Tome and Principe	-	-	44	-	12.9	3	2	3.6	28.9
Senegal	-	18	76[k]	21.6	22.7	370	6	8.4	25.4
Seychelles	-	-	-	5.7	-	-	0	2[x]	5.1[x]
Sierra Leone	-	-	96	-	27.2	246	9	9.9	33.8
Somalia	-	-	91	-	25.8	521	7	17.2	23.3
South Africa	-	15	93	-	9.2	440	2	2.5[x]	22.8[x]
Sudan	-	31	84	33.9	40.7	1 994	7	13.1[x]	34.3[x]
Swaziland	-	9	76	-	10.3	17	2	1.3	30.2
Tanzania, United Republic of	-	13	68	28.9	29.4	1 820	7	5.4	43.8

Table 1. How many women and children suffer from undernutrition?

	Malnourished mothers and infants			Malnourished children under 5 years of age					
	Proportion of women with low body mass index (%)	Proportion of infants with low birth-weight (%)	Proportion of infants **not** exclusively breastfed up to the age of 6 months (%)	Prevalence of moderately and severely underweight children (%)		Estimated number of moderately and severely underweight children ('000)	Prevalence of severely underweight children (%)	Prevalence of wasted children (%)	Prevalence of stunted children (%)
	1992-2002*	1998-2003*	1995-2003*	~1990	1995-2003*	1995-2003*	1992-2003*	1995-2003*	1995-2003*
Togo	10.9	15	82	-	25.1	204	7	12.3	21.7
Uganda	9.4	12	37	23	22.8	1 222	5	4.1	39.1
Zambia	13	12	60	20.5	25	480	7	5	46.8
Zimbabwe	4.5	11	67	11.5	13	246	2	6.4	26.5
Asia & Oceania									
Afghanistan	-	-	-	-	49.3	2 062	-	16.1[y]	47.6
Bangladesh	45.4	30	54	65.8	47.7	9 258	13	10.3	44.7
Bhutan	-	15	-	37.9	18.7	65	3	2.6	40
Brunei Darussalam	-	10	-	-	-	-	-	-	-
Cambodia	21.2	11	88	47.4	45.2	952	13	15	44.6
China	-	6	33[k]	17.4	10	9 256	1	2.2	14.2
Fiji	-	10	53[k]	-	-	-	1	8.2[x]	2.7[x]
Hong Kong, China (SAR)	-	-	-	-	-	-	-	-	-
India	41.2	30	63[k]	56.1	46.7	55 371	18	15.7	44.9
Indonesia	-	9	60	35.5	27.3	5 907	6	-	-
Kiribati	-	5	20[x,k]	-	-	-	-	10.8[x]	28.3[x]
Korea, Dem. People's Rep. of	-	7	30	-	27.9	508	-	10.4	45.2
Korea, Republic of	-	4	-	-	-	-	-	-	-
Laos	-	14	77	44	40	347	13	15.4	40.7
Malaysia	-	10	71[k]	25	12.4	337	1	-	-
Maldives	-	22	90	39	45	23	7	20[y]	36
Marshall Islands	-	12	37[x,k]	-	-	-	-	-	-
Micronesia	-	18	40[k]	-	-	-	-	-	-
Mongolia	-	8	49	12.3	12.7	34	3	3.6[y]	24.6
Myanmar	-	15	89	32.4	35.3	1 880	8	8.2	41.6
Nauru	-	-	-	-	-	-	-	-	-
Nepal	26.6	21	32	48.5	48.3	1 781	13	9.6	50.5
Pakistan	-	19[x]	84[k]	40.2	37.4	8 799	12	14.2[x]	36.3[x]
Palau	-	9	41[k]	-	-	-	-	-	-
Papua New Guinea	-	11[x]	41	-	-	-	-	5.5[x]	43.2[x]
Philippines	-	20	66	33.5	31.8	3 103	-	6.5	32.1
Samoa	-	4[x]	-	-	-	-	-	-	-
Singapore	-	8	-	14.4	-	-	-	4.2[x]	10.6[x]
Solomon Islands	-	13[x]	35[k]	-	-	-	4	6.6[x]	27.3[x]
Sri Lanka	-	22	16	37.3	32.9	498	-	13.3	20.4
Thailand	-	9	96[k]	25.3	17.6	931	-	5.4	13.4
Timor-Leste	-	10	56	-	42.6	34	13	-	-
Tonga	-	0	38[k]	-	-	-	-	0.9[x]	1.3[x]
Tuvalu	-	5	-	-	-	-	-	-	-
Vanuatu	-	6	50[k]	-	-	-	-	5.5	20.1
Viet Nam	-	9	85	45	33.8	2 598	6	8.6	36.5
Eastern and Southern Europe & CIS									
Albania	-	3	94	8.1	14.3	39	4	11.1	31.7
Armenia	5	7	70	3.3	2.6	4	0	1.9	12.9
Azerbaijan	-	11	93	10.1	6.8	47	1	8[y]	19.6

129

Table 1. How many women and children suffer from undernutrition?

	Malnourished mothers and infants			Malnourished children under 5 years of age					
	Proportion of women with low body mass index (%)	Proportion of infants with low birth-weight (%)	Proportion of infants **not** exclusively breastfed up to the age of 6 months (%)	Prevalence of moderately and severely underweight children (%)		Estimated number of moderately and severely underweight children ('000)	Prevalence of severely underweight children (%)	Prevalence of wasted children (%)	Prevalence of stunted children (%)
	1992-2002*	1998-2003*	1995-2003*	~1990	1995-2003*	1995-2003*	1992-2003*	1995-2003*	1995-2003*
Belarus	-	5	-	-	-	-	-	-	-
Bosnia and Herzegovina	-	4	94	-	4.1	8	1	6.3	9.7
Cyprus	-	-	-	-	-	-	-	-	-
Georgia	-	6	82[k]	-	3.1	8	0	2.3	11.7
Kyrgyzstan	6.2	7[x]	76	-	11	58	2	3.4	24.8
Tajikistan	-	15	86	-	-	-	-	4.9	30.9
Turkey	2.6	16	93	10.4	8.3	589	1	1.9	16
Turkmenistan	10.1	6	87	-	12	60	2	5.7	22.3
Uzbekistan	9.8	7	81	-	7.9	213	2	11.6[y]	31.3
Middle East & North Africa									
Algeria	-	7	87	9.1	6	201	1	2.7	18
Bahrain	-	8	66[k]	7.2	8.7	6	2	5.3	9.7
Egypt	0.6	12	70	10.4	8.6	748	1	5.1	20.6
Iran	-	7[x]	56	-	10.9	676	2	4.9	15.4
Iraq	-	15	88	11.9	15.9	610	2	5.9	22.1
Jordan	2.3	10[x]	73	6.4	4.4	32	1	1.9	7.8
Kuwait	-	7	88[k]	10.5	10.5	26	3	1.2[y]	3.2[y]
Lebanon	-	6	73[k]	-	3	10	0	2.9	12.2
Libyan Arab Jamahiriya	-	7[x]	-	-	4.7	28	1	2.7	15.1
Morocco	3.9	11[x]	34[k]	9.5	9	296	2	2.2[x,y]	24.2[x,y]
Occupied Palestinian Territories	-	9	71[k]	-	-	-	1	-	-
Oman	-	8	-	24.3	17.8	73	4	7.2[y]	10.4[y]
Qatar	-	10	88	-	5.5	3	-	1.5	8.1
Saudi Arabia	-	11[x]	69[k]	-	-	-	3	-	-
Syria	-	6	19[k]	12.1	6.9	160	1	3.8	18.8
Tunisia	-	7	54	9	4	32	1	2.2	12.3
United Arab Emirates	-	15[x]	66[k]	-	-	-	3	-	-
Yemen	25.2	32[x]	82	30	46.1	1 756	-	12.9	51.7
Latin America & Caribbean									
Antigua and Barbuda	-	8	-	-	-	-	-	-	-
Argentina	-	7	-	1.9	5.4	191	1	3.2	12.4
Bahamas	-	7	-	-	-	-	-	-	-
Barbados	-	10[x]	-	-	-	-	1[x]	4.9[x]	7[x]
Belize	-	6	76[k]	-	-	-	1[x]	-	-
Bolivia	0.9	9	46	11.3	7.6	113	1	1.3	26.8
Brazil	6.2	10[x]	-	7	5.7	950	1	2.3	10.5
Chile	-	5	37	2.5	0.8	11	-	0.3	1.5
Colombia	3.1	9	74	10.1	6.7	317	1	0.8	13.5
Costa Rica	-	7	65[x,k]	2.8	5.1	20	0	2.3	6.1
Cuba	-	6	59	-	3.9	26	0	2	4.6
Dominica	-	-	-	-	-	-	-	-	-
Dominican Republic	-	11	90	10.3	4.6	44	1	1.5	6.1
Ecuador	-	16	65	16.5	14.3	203	-	2.4	26.4
El Salvador	-	13	84	15.2	10.3	75	-	1.4	18.9
Grenada	-	9	61[k]	-	-	-	-	-	-

Table 1. How many women and children suffer from undernutrition?

	Malnourished mothers and infants			Malnourished children under 5 years of age					
	Proportion of women with low body mass index (%)	Proportion of infants with low birth-weight (%)	Proportion of infants **not** exclusively breastfed up to the age of 6 months (%)	Prevalence of moderately and severely underweight children (%)		Estimated number of moderately and severely underweight children ('000)	Prevalence of severely underweight children (%)	Prevalence of wasted children (%)	Prevalence of stunted children (%)
	1992-2002*	1998-2003*	1995-2003*	~1990	1995-2003*	1995-2003*	1992-2003*	1995-2003*	1995-2003*
Guatemala	2	13	49	33.2	22.7	439	4	2.5	46.4
Guyana	-	12	89	18.3	13.6	11	3	11.4	10
Haiti	-	21	76	26.8	17.3	195	4	4.5	22.7
Honduras	-	14	65	18	16.6	163	-	1.1	29.2
Jamaica	-	9	-	4.6	3.8	10	-	3.8^y	4.4
Mexico	-	9	62^{x,k}	14.2	7.5	836	1	2	17.7
Nicaragua	3.8	12	69	11	9.6	78	2	2	20.2
Panama	-	10^x	75^x	15.8	8.1	27	-	1	18.2
Paraguay	-	9^x	93^k	-	-	-	-	0.3^x	13.9^x
Peru	0.7	11^x	29	10.7	7.1	215	1	0.9	25.4
Saint Kitts and Nevis	-	9	44^k	-	-	-	-	-	-
Saint Lucia	-	8	-	-	13.8	2	-	6.1^x	10.8^x
Saint Vincent and the Grenadines	-	10	-	-	-	-	-	-	-
Suriname	-	13	91	-	13.2	6	2	6.5	9.8
Trinidad and Tobago	-	23	98	6.7	5.9	5	0	4.4	3.6
Uruguay	-	8	-	7.4	-	-	1	1.4^x	9.5^x
Venezuela	-	7	93^k	7.7	4.4	125	1	3	12.8

Definitions of the Indicators:

Low body mass index: Proportion of women whose weight (in kg) divided by the squared height (in m²) is smaller than 18.5 kg/m².

Low birthweight: Proportion of infants who weigh less than 2 500 grams at birth.

Underweight: Proportion of children below minus two (moderate) or three (severe) standard deviations from median weight for age of the reference population.

Wasting: Proportion of children below minus two standard deviations from median weight for height of the reference population.

Stunting: Proportion of children below minus two standard deviations from median height for age of the reference population.

Main Sources:

Low body mass index, stunting, wasting: SCN, 5th Report on the World Nutrition Situation 2004.

Birthweight, breastfeeding, severe underweight: UNICEF, State of the World's Children Report 2005.

Underweight: WHO, Global Database on Child Growth and Malnutrition (http://www.who.int/nutgrowthdb). The number of underweight children is calculated from this source.

Severity of malnutrition by prevalence ranges (percentage of children under 5)

Indicator:	Low	Medium	High	Very High
Stunting:	<20	20-29	30-39	>40
Underweight:	<10	10-19	20-29	>30
Wasting:	<5	5-9	10-15	>15

Notes:

*: Data refer to the most recent year available during the period specified in the table heading.

x: Data refer to years or periods other than those specified in the column heading, differ from the standard definition, or refer only to part of a country.

y: Data from different sources vary significantly (>33%) for these countries.

k: Data refer to exclusive breastfeeding for less than four months.

Table 2. How many people suffer from different forms of vitamin and mineral deficiencies?

	Iodine deficiency			Vitamin A deficiency			Iron deficiency		Economic impact
	Proportion of population affected by goitre (%)	Estimated annual number of children born mentally impaired ('000)	Estimated proportion of households **not** consuming iodised salt (%)	Estimated proportion of children under 6 with sub-clinical vitamin A deficiency (%)	Estimated annual number of child deaths due to vitamin A deficiency ('000)	Estimated proportion of children receiving **no** dose of vitamin A per year (%)	Estimated prevalence of iron deficiency anaemia in children under 5 years (%)	Estimated prevalence of iron deficiency anaemia in women aged 15-49 (%)	Estimated annual loss to all forms of vitamin-micronutrient deficiency as % of GDP
	2000#	2000#	2000#	2000#	2000#	2000#	2000#	2000#	2000#
Sub-Saharan Africa									
Angola	33	235	65	55	34	25	72	59	2.1
Benin	<5	10	28	70	9	5	82	65	1.1
Botswana	17	9	33	30	0.5	15	37	31	0.6
Burkina Faso	29	180	78	46	20	3	83	48	2
Burundi	42	125	4	44	9	5	82	60	2.5
Cameroon	12	65	16	36	11	1	58	32	0.8
Central African Republic	11	16	14	68	5	10	74	49	-
Chad	24	100	42	45	13	9	76	56	1.2
Congo, Republic of	36	59	-	32	2	0	55	48	1.9
Congo, Democratic Republic of	-	-	7	58	96	20	58	54	0.8
Eritrea	10	16	3	30	2	33	75	53	1.1
Ethiopia	23	685	72	30	51	84	85	58	1.7
Gabon	27	12	85	41	0.45	11	43	32	1.1
Gambia	20	10	92	64	1	9	75	53	1.3
Ghana	18	120	50	60	12	0	65	40	1.1
Guinea	23	83	40	40	8	7	73	43	1.4
Guinea-Bissau	17	13	99	31	2	0	83	53	1.5
Kenya	10	105	9	70	24	10	60	43	0.8
Lesotho	19	11	31	54	1	-	51	43	0.8
Liberia	18	29	-	38	5	0	69	44	1.2
Madagascar	6	43	48	42	13	17	73	42	0.8
Malawi	22	115	64	59	18	25	80	27	1.4
Mali	42	270	26	47	24	20	77	47	2.7
Mauritania	21	24	98	17	2	2	74	42	1.3
Mozambique	17	134	38	26	14	29	80	54	1.2
Namibia	18	12	36	59	0.5	16	42	35	0.8
Niger	20	130	85	41	26	11	57	47	1.7
Nigeria	8	370	2	25	82	23	69	47	0.7
Rwanda	13	46	10	39	10	6	69	43	1.1
Senegal	23	86	84	61	10	15	71	43	1.3
Sierra Leone	16	40	77	47	13	9	86	68	1.4
South Africa	16	160	38	33	6	-	37	26	0.4
Swaziland	12	4	41	38	0.6	-	47	32	0.6
Tanzania, United Republic of	16	-	33	37	-	7	65	45	-
Togo	14	25	33	35	3	23	72	45	1
Uganda	9	111	5	66	29	63	64	30	1
Zambia	25	115	32	66	19	17	63	46	1.3
Zimbabwe	9	35	7	28	5	-	53	44	0.7
Asia & Oceania									
Afghanistan	48	535	85	53	50	16	65	61	2.3
Bangladesh	18	750	30	28	28	10	55	36	0.9
Bhutan	-	-	5	32	0.6	-	81	55	1.6
Cambodia	18	85	86	42	8	43	63	58	1.4
China	5	940	7	12	23	-	8	21	0.2
India	26	6 600	50	57	330	76	75	51	1
Indonesia	10	445	35	26	14	39	48	26	0.5
Laos	14	27	25	42	2	30	54	48	1.1

Table 2. How many people suffer from different forms of vitamin and mineral deficiencies?

	Iodine deficiency			Vitamin A deficiency			Iron deficiency		Economic impact
	Proportion of population affected by goitre (%)	Estimated annual number of children born mentally impaired ('000)	Estimated proportion of households **not** consuming iodised salt (%)	Estimated proportion of children under 6 with sub-clinical vitamin A deficiency (%)	Estimated annual number of child deaths due to vitamin A deficiency ('000)	Estimated proportion of children receiving **no** dose of vitamin A per year (%)	Estimated prevalence of iron deficiency anaemia in children under 5 years (%)	Estimated prevalence of iron deficiency anaemia in women aged 15-49 (%)	Estimated annual loss to all forms of vitamin-micronutrient deficiency as % of GDP
	2000#	2000#	2000#	2000#	2000#	2000#	2000#	2000#	2000#
Mongolia	15	9	55	29	0.3	7	37	18	0.6
Myanmar	17	205	52	35	13	3	48	45	0.7
Nepal	24	200	37	33	7	2	65	62	1.5
Pakistan	38	2 100	83	35	56	0	56	59	1.7
Papua New Guinea	-	-	-	37	2	-	40	43	0.5
Philippines	15	300	76	23	5	16	29	35	0.7
Thailand	13	140	26	22	1	-	22	27	0.4
Viet Nam	11	180	23	12	2	41	39	33	0.6
Eastern and Southern Europe & CIS									
Armenia	12	4	17	12	-	-	24	12	0.3
Azerbaijan	15	22	74	23	1	-	33	35	0.7
Georgia	21	11	92	11	-	-	33	31	0.5
Kyrgyzstan	21	24	73	18	0.3	-	42	31	0.9
Tajikistan	28	43	80	18	0.6	-	45	42	1.2
Turkey	23	335	36	18	3	-	23	33	0.7
Turkmenistan	11	11	25	18	0.55	-	36	46	0.7
Uzbekistan	24	136	81	40	4	-	33	63	1.2
Middle East & North Africa									
Egypt	12	225	20	7	1	-	31	28	0.5
Iran	9	125	6	23	3	-	32	29	0.3
Lebanon	11	8	13	20	0.1	-	21	24	0.4
Morocco	-	-	59	29	2	-	45	34	0.2
Syria	8	40	20	8	0.3	-	40	30	0.5
Yemen	16	143	61	40	10	0	59	49	1.3
Latin America & Caribbean									
Bolivia	<5	13	15	23	1	56	59	30	0.5
Brazil	<5	50	13	15	4	-	45	21	-
Dominican Republic	11	23	82	18	0.35	65	25	31	0.4
El Salvador	11	17	9	17	0.25	-	28	34	0.5
Guatemala	16	67	51	21	2	40	34	20	0.8
Haiti	12	29	88	32	3	70	66	54	0.8
Honduras	12	25	20	15	0.3	38	34	31	0.7
Nicaragua	4	7	4	9	0.15	-	47	40	0.6
Paraguay	13	22	17	13	0.15	-	52	25	0.7
Peru	10	60	7	17	1	94	50	32	0.5
Venezuela	10	60	10	5	0.15	-	41	38	0.5

Definitions of the Indicators:

Goitre: The swelling of the thyroid gland.

Sub-clinical Vitamin A deficiency: Retinol level in serum is <0.7 μmol/l.

Anaemia: Hb < 120 g/l in non-pregnant women of >15 years of age, Hb < 110 g/l in pregnant women of any age, Hb < 110 g/l in children 6-60 months of age.

Notes:

#: Where no recent data were available, prevalences were projected into the year 2000.

Main Sources:

All indicators: The Micronutrient Initiative and UNICEF, Vitamin & Mineral Deficiency: A Global Progress Report 2004.

Note by the sources: "Data on vitamin and mineral deficiency are imperfect. The figures given in this table are drawn from the best information currently available. Prevalence data are based on a global review of existing surveys of vitamin and mineral deficiencies. Functional consequences of VM deficiency are calculated using a specially-designed 'Profiles module'."

Table 3.   Where does the country stand on meeting the MDG for poverty and hunger?

	Poverty			Inequality			Performance on MDG 1	
	Population below international poverty line (%)	Poverty gap ratio (%)	Population below national poverty line (%)	Poorest quintile's share in consumption (%)	Richest 10% to poorest 10%	Gini index	Poverty Hunger Index (PHI)	Measure of Progress towards MDG 1
	1995-2003*	1995-2003*	1990-2002*	1995-2003*	1995 -2003*	1995 -2003*	2004	1990-2003*
Sub-Saharan Africa								
Angola	-	-	-	-	-	-	-	-
Benin	-	-	33.0	-	-	-	-	-
Botswana	-	-	-	-	77.6y	63.0y	0.65	-
Burkina Faso	45	14.4	45.3	4.5	26.2	48.2	0.66	0.35
Burundi	55	22.7	-	5.1	19.3	33.3	0.47	-0.73
Cameroon	17	4.1	40.2	5.6	15.7	44.6	0.72	0.38
Cape Verde	-	-	-	-	-	-	-	-
Central African Republic	-	-	-	-	69.2y	61.3y	0.47	-
Chad	-	-	64.0	-	-	-	-	-
Comoros	-	-	-	-	-	-	-	-
Congo, Republic of	-	-	-	-	-	-	-	-
Congo, Democratic Republic of	-	-	-	-	-	-	-	-
Côte d'Ivoire	11	1.9	36.8	5.2	16.6	44.6	0.75	-0.58
Djibouti	-	-	45.1	-	-	-	-	-
Equatorial Guinea	-	-	-	-	-	-	-	-
Eritrea	-	-	53.0	-	-	-	-	-
Ethiopia	23	4.8	44.2	9.1	6.6	30.0	0.65	0.46
Gabon	-	-	-	-	-	-	-	-
Gambia	-	-	64.0	4.8	20.2	47.5	0.68	0.41
Ghana	45	17.3	39.5	5.6	14.1	40.8	0.66	-1.90
Guinea	-	-	40.0	-	12.3y	40.3y	-	-
Guinea-Bissau	-	-	48.7	-	19.0y	47.0y	-	-
Kenya	23	5.9	42.0	6.0	15.6	42.5	0.69	0.68
Lesotho	36	19.0	-	1.5	105.0	63.2	0.64	-0.03
Liberia	-	-	-	-	-	-	-	-
Madagascar	61	27.9	71.3	4.9	19.2	47.5	0.54	-0.22
Malawi	42	14.8	65.3	4.9	22.7	50.3	0.62	-
Mali	-	-	63.8	-	23.1y	50.5y	0.50	-
Mauritania	26	7.6	46.3	6.2	12.0	39.0	0.71	0.85
Mauritius	-	-	10.6	-	-	-	-	-
Mozambique	38	12.0	69.4	6.5	12.5	39.6	0.62	-
Namibia	-	-	-	-	128.8y	70.7y	0.62	-
Niger	-	-	63.0y	2.6	46.0	50.5	0.49	-1.04
Nigeria	70	34.9	34.1	4.4	24.9	50.6	0.56	0.08
Rwanda	52	20.0	51.2	-	-	-	0.63	-
Sao Tome and Principe	-	-	-	-	-	-	-	-
Senegal	-	-	33.4	6.4	12.8	41.3	0.72	0.56
Seychelles	-	-	-	-	-	-	-	-
Sierra Leone	-	-	68.0	-	-	-	0.46	-
Somalia	-	-	-	-	-	-	-	-
South Africa	11	1.7	-	3.5y	33.1	57.8	-	-
Sudan	-	-	-	-	-	-	-	-
Swaziland	-	-	40.0	-	49.7y	60.9y	0.75	-
Tanzania, United Republic of	-	-	35.7	-	10.8y	38.2y	0.57	-
Togo	-	-	32.3y	-	-	-	-	-
Uganda	85	45.6	55.0	5.9	14.9	43.0	0.51	0.06
Zambia	64	32.6	72.9	3.3	36.6	52.6	0.49	-0.15
Zimbabwe	56	24.2	34.9	4.6	22.0	56.8	0.57	-0.82

Table 3. Where does the country stand on meeting the MDG for poverty and hunger?

	Poverty			Inequality			Performance on MDG 1	
	Population below international poverty line (%)	Poverty gap ratio (%)	Population below national poverty line (%)	Poorest quintile's share in consumption (%)	Richest 10% to poorest 10%	Gini index	Poverty Hunger Index (PHI)	Measure of Progress towards MDG 1
	1995-2003*	1995-2003*	1990-2002*	1995-2003*	1995-2003*	1995-2003*	2004	1990-2003*
Asia & Oceania								
Afghanistan	-	-	-	-	-	-	-	-
Bangladesh	36	8.1	49.8	9.0	6.8	31.8	0.64	0.20
Bhutan	-	-	-	-	-	-	-	-
Brunei Darussalam	-	-	-	-	-	-	-	-
Cambodia	34	9.7	36.1	6.9	11.6	40.4	0.63	-
China	17	3.9	4.6	4.7	18.4	44.7	0.76	0.63
Fiji	-	-	-	-	-	-	-	-
Hong Kong, China (SAR)	-	-	-	-	17.8	43.4	-	-
India	35	7.2	28.6	8.9	7.3	32.5	0.67	0.30
Indonesia	8	0.9	27.1	8.4	7.8	34.3	0.80	0.61
Kiribati	-	-	-	-	-	-	-	-
Korea, Dem. People's Rep. of	-	-	-	-	-	-	-	-
Korea, Republic of	2^t	-	-	7.9	7.8	31.6	-	-
Laos	26	6.3	38.6	7.6	9.7	37.0	0.69	-2.97
Malaysia	2^t	0.5^t	15.5^y	4.4	22.1	49.2	0.81	0.68
Maldives	-	-	-	-	-	-	-	-
Marshall Islands	-	-	-	-	-	-	-	-
Micronesia	-	-	-	-	-	-	-	-
Mongolia	27	8.1	36.3	5.6	17.8	30.3	0.70	-1.05
Myanmar	-	-	-	-	-	-	-	-
Nauru	-	-	-	-	-	-	-	-
Nepal	39	11.0	42.0	7.6	9.3	36.7	0.65	-
Pakistan	13	2.4	32.6	8.8	7.6	33.0	0.75	0.54
Palau	-	-	-	-	-	-	-	-
Papua New Guinea	-	-	37.5	4.5	23.8	50.9	-	-
Philippines	15	3.0	36.8	5.4	16.5	46.1	0.71	0.26
Samoa	-	-	-	-	-	-	-	-
Singapore	-	-	-	5.0	17.7	42.5	-	-
Solomon Islands	-	-	-	-	-	-	-	-
Sri Lanka	8	1.5	25.0	8.3^y	8.1	33.2	0.75	-0.38
Thailand	2^t	0.5^t	13.1	6.1	13.4	43.2	0.79	0.57
Timor-Leste	-	-	-	-	-	-	-	-
Tonga	-	-	-	-	-	-	-	-
Tuvalu	-	-	-	-	-	-	-	-
Vanuatu	-	-	-	-	-	-	-	-
Viet Nam	2^t	0.5^t	50.9	7.5^y	9.4	37.0	0.77	0.63
Eastern and Southern Europe & CIS								
Albania	2^t	0.5^t	-	9.1	5.9	28.2	0.85	-
Armenia	13	3.3	-	6.7	11.5	37.9	0.76	-0.51
Azerbaijan	4	0.6	-	7.4	9.7	36.5	0.82	0.76
Belarus	0	0.1	-	8.4	6.9	30.4	-	-
Bosnia and Herzegovina	-	-	-	9.5	5.4	26.2	-	-
Cyprus	-	-	-	-	-	-	-	-
Georgia	3	0.9	-	6.4	12.0	36.9	0.80	-
Kyrgyzstan	2^t	0.5^t	-	7.7^y	8.6	34.8	0.86	-
Tajikistan	7	1.3	-	7.9^y	7.8	32.6	-	-
Turkey	2^t	0.5^t	-	6.1	13.3	40.0	0.84	0.50
Turkmenistan	10	2.0	-	6.1	12.3	40.8	0.79	-
Uzbekistan	14	3.5	-	9.2	6.1	26.8	0.78	-5.51

Table 3.   Where does the country stand on meeting the MDG for poverty and hunger?

	Poverty			Inequality			Performance on MDG 1	
	Population below international poverty line (%)	Poverty gap ratio (%)	Population below national poverty line (%)	Poorest quintile's share in consumption (%)	Richest 10% to poorest 10%	Gini index	Poverty Hunger Index (PHI)	Measure of Progress towards MDG 1
	1995-2003*	1995-2003*	1990-2002*	1995-2003*	1995 -2003*	1995 -2003*	2004	1990-2003*
Middle East & North Africa								
Algeria	2ᵗ	0.5ᵗ	12.2	7.0	9.6	35.3	0.85	-
Bahrain	-	-	-	-	-	-	-	-
Egypt	3	0.5ᵗ	16.7	8.6ʸ	8.0	34.4	0.86	0.46
Iran	2ᵗ	0.5ᵗ	-	5.1	17.2	43.0	0.82	-
Iraq	-	-	-	-	-	-	-	-
Jordan	2ᵗ	0.5ᵗ	11.7	7.6	9.1	36.4	0.85	0.34
Kuwait	-	-	-	-	-	-	-	-
Lebanon	-	-	-	-	-	-	-	-
Libyan Arab Jamahiriya	-	-	-	-	-	-	-	-
Morocco	2ᵗ	0.5ᵗ	19.0	6.5	11.7	39.5	0.83	0.35
Occupied Palestinian Territories	-	-	-	-	-	-	-	-
Oman	-	-	-	-	-	-	-	-
Qatar	-	-	-	-	-	-	-	-
Saudi Arabia	-	-	-	-	-	-	-	-
Syria	-	-	-	-	-	-	-	-
Tunisia	2ᵗ	0.5ᵗ	7.6	6.0	13.4	39.8	0.85	0.81
United Arab Emirates	-	-	-	-	-	-	-	-
Yemen	16	4.5	41.8	7.4	8.6	33.4	0.69	-1.19
Latin America & Caribbean								
Antigua and Barbuda	-	-	-	-	-	-	-	-
Argentina	3	0.5ᵗ	-	3.1	39.1	52.2	0.81	-
Bahamas	-	-	-	-	-	-	-	-
Barbados	-	-	-	-	-	-	-	-
Belize	-	-	-	-	-	-	-	-
Bolivia	14	5.3	62.7	4.0	24.6	44.7	0.74	-2.67
Brazil	8	2.1	17.4	2.4	68.0	59.3	0.77	0.60
Chile	2	0.5	17.0	3.3	40.6	57.1	0.82	0.78
Colombia	8	2.2	64.0	2.7	57.8	57.6	0.77	-1.24
Costa Rica	2	0.7	22.0	4.2	25.1	46.5	0.82	0.21
Cuba	-	-	-	-	-	-	-	-
Dominica	-	-	-	-	-	-	-	-
Dominican Republic	2ᵗ	0.5ᵗ	28.6	5.1	17.7	47.4	0.79	0.71
Ecuador	18	7.1	35.0	3.3	44.9	43.7	0.75	0.05
El Salvador	31	14.1	48.3	2.9	47.4	53.2	0.70	-0.15
Grenada	-	-	-	-	-	-	-	-
Guatemala	16	4.6	56.2	2.6	55.1	59.9	0.69	0.35
Guyana	3	0.6	35.0	4.5	-	-	0.79	-
Haiti	-	-	65.0ʸ	-	-	-	-	-
Honduras	21	7.5	53.0	2.7	49.1	55.0	0.69	0.26
Jamaica	2ᵗ	0.5ᵗ	18.7	6.7	11.4	37.9	0.84	0.65
Mexico	10	3.7	10.1ʸ	3.1	45.0	54.6	0.78	0.28
Nicaragua	45	16.7	47.9	5.6	15.5	43.1	0.64	0.13
Panama	7	2.3	37.3	2.4	62.3	56.4	0.74	0.29
Paraguay	16	7.4	21.8	2.2	73.4	57.8	0.74	-
Peru	18	9.1	49.0	2.9	49.9	49.8	0.73	-1.65
Saint Kitts and Nevis	-	-	-	-	-	-	-	-
Saint Lucia	25	8.5	-	5.2	-	-	-	-
Saint Vincent and the Grenadines	-	-	-	-	-	-	-	-
Suriname	-	-	-	-	-	-	-	-

Table 3. Where does the country stand on meeting the MDG for poverty and hunger?

	Poverty			Inequality			Performance on MDG 1	
	Population below international poverty line (%)	Poverty gap ratio (%)	Population below national poverty line	Poorest quintile's share in consumption (%)	Richest 10% to poorest 10%	Gini index	Poverty Hunger Index (PHI)	Measure of Progress towards MDG 1
	1995-2003*	1995-2003*	1990-2002*	1995-2003*	1995 -2003*	1995 -2003*	2004	1990-2003*
Trinidad and Tobago	-	-	21.0	-	14.4^y	40.3^y	0.81	-
Uruguay	2^t	0.5^t	-	4.8	18.9	44.6	0.83	-
Venezuela	14	6.6	31.3^y	3.0	62.9	49.1	0.75	-5.58

Definitions of the Indicators:

Population below international poverty line: Percentage of population below US$1 per day consumption using purchasing power parity (PPP) rates.

Poverty gap ratio: Mean distance below the poverty line as a proportion of the poverty line where the mean is taken over the whole population, counting the non-poor as having zero poverty gap.

Population below national poverty line: Proportion of the national population whose incomes are below the official threshold set by the national government.

Poorest quintile's share: Share of poorest quintile in national consumption.

Richest 10% to poorest 10%: Ratio of the income or consumption share of the richest group to that of the poorest.

Gini index: The Gini index measures inequality over the entire distribution of income or consumption. A value of 0 represents perfect equality, and a value of 100 perfect inequality.

PHI: A composite index measuring poverty and hunger in a country. For more information, please see the Technical Annex Compendium.

Measure of Progress towards MDG 1: A composite index measured by the progress in the five indicators for MDG 1 between the 1990 value (or the nearest available) and the latest value available. For more information, please see the Technical Annex Compendium.

Main Sources:

Poverty indicators, poorest quintile's share: United Nations Statistics Division, Millennium Indicators Database (http://millenniumindicators.un.org).

Population below national poverty line, inequality measures: UNDP, Human Development Report 2005.

PHI, Measure of Progress towards MDG 1: Gentilini and Webb 2005. The data used to calculate the indicator may differ from the data in these tables.

Notes:

*: Data refer to the most recent year available during the period specified in the table heading.

t: All 0.5% poverty gap estimates indicate that actual values are less than or equal to 0.5% and should be treated with caution.

v: Refers to expenditure shares by percentiles of population, ranked by per capita expenditure.

y: Data refer to a period other than that specified.

Table 4. How many mothers, infants and children are lost each year?

	Mothers			Infants			Children					
	Maternal mortality rate^a (per 100 000)		Births **not** attended by skilled health personnel (%)	Life expectancy at birth (in years)	Infant (under 1 year) mortality rate (per 1000)		Under 5 mortality rate (per 1000)			Proportion of 1 year old children **not** immunized against measles (%)	Children (0-17) orphaned by HIV/AIDS ('000)	Children (0-17) orphaned due to all causes ('000)
	1985-2003 reported*	2000 adjusted	1995-2003*	2003	1960	2003	1990	2003	Progress 1990-2003 (%)	2003	2003	2003
Sub-Saharan Africa												
Angola	-	1 700	55	40	208	154	260	260	0	38	110	1 000
Benin	500	850	34	53	176	91	185	154	17	17	34	340
Botswana	330	100	6	36	118	82	58	112	-93	10	120	160
Burkina Faso	480	1 000	69	45	181	107	210	207	1	24	260	830
Burundi	-	1 000	75	42	148	114	190	190	0	25	200	660
Cameroon	430	730	40	48	151	95	139	166	-19	39	240	930
Cape Verde	76	150	11	70	-	26	60	35	42	32	-	-
Central African Republic	1 100	1 100	56	42	187	115	180	180	0	65	110	290
Chad	830	1 100	84	46	-	117	203	200	1	39	96	500
Comoros	520	480	38	64	200	54	120	73	39	37	-	-
Congo, Republic of	-	510	-	54	143	81	110	108	2	50	97	260
Congo, Democratic Republic of	950	990	39	44	174	129	205	205	0	46	770	4 200
Côte d'Ivoire	600	690	37	45	195	117	157	192	-22	44	310	940
Djibouti	74	730	39	55	186	97	175	138	21	34	5	33
Equatorial Guinea	-	880	35	51	188	97	206	146	29	49	-	24
Eritrea	1 000	630	72	59	-	45	147	85	42	16	39	230
Ethiopia	870	850	94	50	180	112	204	169	17	48	720	3 900
Gabon	520	420	14	58	-	60	92	91	1	45	14	57
Gambia	730	540	45	57	207	90	154	123	20	10	2	45
Ghana	210^x	540	56	58	127	59	125	95	24	20	170	1 000
Guinea	530	740	65	52	215	104	240	160	33	48	35	420
Guinea-Bissau	910	1 100	65	47	-	126	253	204	19	39	-	81
Kenya	590	1 000	59	50	122	79	97	123	-27	28	650	1 700
Lesotho	-	550	40	38	136	63	120	84	30	30	100	180
Liberia	580	760	49	41	190	157	235	235	0	47	36	230
Madagascar	490	550	54	57	112	78	168	126	25	45	30	1 000
Malawi	1 100	1 800	39	42	205	112	241	178	26	23	500	1 000
Mali	580	1 200	59	45	285	122	250	220	12	32	75	730
Mauritania	750	1 000	43	51	180	120	183	183	0	29	2	140
Mauritius	21	24	1	72	67	16	25	18	28	6	-	-
Mozambique	1 100	1 000	52	45	180	109	235	158	33	23	470	1 500
Namibia	270	300	22	51	102	48	86	65	24	30	57	120
Niger	590	1 600	84	41	211	154	320	262	18	36	24	680
Nigeria	-	800	65	45	165	98	235	198	16	65	1 800	7 000
Rwanda	1 100	1 400	69	45	122	118	173	203	-17	10	160	810
Sao Tome and Principe	100	-	21	59	-	75	118	118	0	13	-	-
Senegal	560	690	42	56	173	78	148	137	7	40	17	460
Seychelles	-	-	-	72	-	11	21	15	29	1	-	-
Sierra Leone	1 800	2 000	58	38	220	166	302	284	6	27	-	350
Somalia	-	1 100	66	44	-	133	225	225	0	60	-	770
South Africa	150	230	16	49	-	53	60	66	-10	17	1 100	2 200
Sudan	550	590	14^x	59	123	63	120	93	23	43	91	1 300
Swaziland	230	370	30	35	150	105	110	153	-39	6	65	100
Tanzania, United Republic of	530	1 500	64	45	142	104	163	165	-1	3	980	2 500
Togo	480	570	51	52	158	78	152	140	8	42	54	240

Table 4. How many mothers, infants and children are lost each year?

	Mothers			Infants			Children					
	Maternal mortality rate' (per 100 000)		Births **not** attended by skilled health personnel (%)	Life expectancy at birth (in years)	Infant (under 1 year) mortality rate (per 1000)		Under 5 mortality rate (per 1000)			Proportion of 1 year old children **not** immunized against measles (%)	Children (0-17) orphaned by HIV/AIDS ('000)	Children (0-17) orphaned due to all causes ('000)
	1985-2003 reported*	2000 adjusted	1995-2003*	2003	1960	2003	1990	2003	Progress 1990-2003 (%)	2003	2003	2003
Uganda	510	880	61	49	133	81	160	140	13	18	940	2 000
Zambia	730	750	57	39	126	102	180	182	-1	16	630	1 100
Zimbabwe	700	1 100	27	37	97	78	80	126	-58	20	980	1 300
Asia & Oceania												
Afghanistan	1 600	1 900	86	42	245	165	260	257	1	50	-	1 600
Bangladesh	380	380	86	63	149	46	144	69	52	23	-	5 300
Bhutan	260	420	76	63	175	70	166	85	49	12	-	90
Brunei Darussalam	0	37	1	77	63	5	11	6	45	1	-	4
Cambodia	440	450	68	54	-	97	115	140	-22	35	-	670
China	50	56	3	71	150	30	49	37	24	16	-	20 600
Fiji	38	75	0	68	71	16	31	20	35	9	-	25
Hong Kong, China (SAR)	-	-	-	-	-	-	-	-	-	-	-	-
India	540	540	57	62	146	63	123	87	29	33	-	35 000
Indonesia	310	230	32	67	128	31	91	41	55	28	-	6 100
Kiribati	-	-	15	65	-	49	88	66	25	12	-	-
Korea, Dem. People's Rep. of	110	67	3	66	85	42	55	55	0	5	-	710
Korea, Republic of	20	20	0	76	90	5	9	5	44	4	-	630
Laos	530	650	81	59	155	82	163	91	44	58	-	290
Malaysia	50	41	3	72	73	7	21	7	67	8	-	480
Maldives	140	110	30	65	180	55	115	72	37	4	-	-
Marshall Islands	-	-	5	61	-	53	92	61	34	10	-	-
Micronesia	120	-	7	70	-	19	31	23	26	9	-	-
Mongolia	110	110	1	65	-	56	104	68	35	2	-	78
Myanmar	230	360	44	59	169	76	130	107	18	25	-	1 900
Nauru	-	-	-	61	-	25	-	30	60	-	-	-
Nepal	540	740	89	61	212	61	145	82	43	25	-	1 000
Pakistan	530	500	77	62	139	81	130	103	21	39	-	4 800
Palau	0	-	0	68	-	23	34	28	18	1	-	-
Papua New Guinea	370ˣ	300	47	60	143	69	101	93	8	51	-	220
Philippines	170	200	40	68	80	27	63	36	43	20	-	2 100
Samoa	-	130	0	68	134	19	42	24	43	1	-	-
Singapore	6	30	0	80	31	3	8	3	63	12	-	-
Solomon Islands	550ˣ	130	15	70	120	19	36	22	39	22	-	-
Sri Lanka	92	92	3	71	83	13	32	15	53	1	-	340
Thailand	36	44	1	70	103	23	40	26	35	6	-	1 400
Timor-Leste	-	660	76	58	-	87	160	124	23	40	-	-
Tonga	-	-	8	71	-	15	27	19	30	1	-	-
Tuvalu	-	-	1	61	-	37	56	51	9	5	-	-
Vanuatu	68	130	11	68	141	31	70	38	46	52	-	-
Viet Nam	95	130	15	71	70	19	53	23	57	7	-	2 100
Eastern and Southern Europe & CIS												
Albania	20	55	6	72	105	18	45	21	53	7	-	-
Armenia	22	55	3	68	-	30	60	33	45	6	-	-
Azerbaijan	25	94	16	65	-	75	105	91	13	2	-	-
Belarus	18	35	0	68	37	13	17	17	0	1	-	-

139

Table 4. How many mothers, infants and children are lost each year?

| | Mothers | | | Infants | | | Children | | | | | |
| | Maternal mortality rate[a] (per 100 000) | | Births **not** attended by skilled health personnel (%) | Life expectancy at birth (in years) | Infant (under 1 year) mortality rate (per 1000) | | Under 5 mortality rate (per 1000) | | | Proportion of 1 year old children **not** immunized against measles (%) | Children (0-17) orphaned by HIV/AIDS ('000) | Children (0-17) orphaned due to all causes ('000) |
	1985-2003 reported*	2000 adjusted	1995-2003*	2003	1960	2003	1990	2003	Progress 1990-2003 (%)	2003	2003	2003
Bosnia and Herzegovina	10	31	0	73	105	14	22	17	23	16	-	-
Cyprus	0	47	0[x]	78	30	4	12	5	58	14	-	-
Georgia	67	32	4	71	-	41	47	45	4	27	-	-
Kyrgyzstan	44	110	2	63	-	59	80	68	15	1	-	-
Tajikistan	45	100	29	61	-	92	128	118	8	11	-	-
Turkey	130[x]	70	19	70	163	33	78	39	50	25	-	-
Turkmenistan	9	31	3	60	-	79	97	102	-5	3	-	-
Uzbekistan	34	24	4	66	-	57	79	69	13	1	-	-
Middle East & North Africa												
Algeria	140	140	8	70	164	35	69	41	41	16	-	-
Bahrain	46	28	2	74	110	12	19	15	21	1	-	-
Egypt	84	84	31	67	186	33	104	39	63	2	-	-
Iran	37	76	10	69	164	33	72	39	46	1	-	2 100
Iraq	290	250	28	55	117	102	50	125	-150	10	-	-
Jordan	41	41	0	71	97	23	40	28	30	4	-	-
Kuwait	5	5	2	77	89	8	16	9	44	3	-	-
Lebanon	100[x]	150	11	70	65	27	37	31	16	4	-	-
Libyan Arab Jamahiriya	77	97	6	73	159	13	42	16	62	9	-	-
Morocco	230	220	60	71	132	36	85	39	54	10	-	-
Occupied Palestinian Territories	-	100	3	-	-	22	40	24	40	1	-	-
Oman	23	87	5	74	164	10	30	12	60	2	-	-
Qatar	10	140	2	74	94	11	25	15	40	7	-	-
Saudi Arabia	-	23	9	71	170	22	44	26	41	4	-	-
Syria	65	160	24[x]	72	134	16	44	18	59	2	-	-
Tunisia	69	120	10	72	170	19	52	24	54	10	-	-
United Arab Emirates	3	54	4	73	149	7	14	8	43	6	-	-
Yemen	350	570	78	59	225	82	142	113	20	34	-	-
Latin America & Caribbean												
Antigua and Barbuda	65	-	0	72	-	11	-	12	1	-	-	-
Argentina	46	82	1	74	60	17	28	20	29	3	-	750
Bahamas	-	60	1[x]	72	51	11	29	14	52	10	-	8
Barbados	0	95	9	75	74	11	16	13	19	10	-	4
Belize	140	140	17	68	74	33	49	39	20	4	-	6
Bolivia	390	420	35	65	152	53	120	66	45	36	-	340
Brazil	75	260	12	69	115	33	60	35	42	1	-	4 300
Chile	17	31	0	77	118	8	19	9	53	1	-	230
Colombia	78	130	14	72	79	18	36	21	42	8	-	910
Costa Rica	29	43	2	77	87	8	17	10	41	11	-	50
Cuba	34	33	0	77	39	6	13	8	38	1	-	130
Dominica	67	-	0	73	-	12	23	14	39	1	-	-
Dominican Republic	180	150	1	68	102	29	65	35	46	21	-	260
Ecuador	80	130	31	71	107	24	57	27	53	1	-	290
El Salvador	170	150	31	70	130	32	60	36	40	1	-	180
Grenada	1	-	1	67	-	18	37	23	38	1	-	-
Guatemala	150	240	59	66	136	35	82	47	43	25	-	510

Table 4. How many mothers, infants and children are lost each year?

	Mothers			Infants			Children					
	Maternal mortality rate# (per 100 000)		Births **not** attended by skilled health personnel (%)	Life expectancy at birth (in years)	Infant (under 1 year) mortality rate (per 1000)		Under 5 mortality rate (per 1000)			Proportion of 1 year old children **not** immunized against measles (%)	Children (0-17) orphaned by HIV/AIDS ('000)	Children (0-17) orphaned due to all causes ('000)
	1985-2003 reported*	2000 adjusted	1995-2003*	2003	1960	2003	1990	2003	Progress 1990-2003 (%)	2003	2003	2003
Guyana	190	170	14	62	100	52	90	69	23	11	-	33
Haiti	520	680	76	53	169	76	150	118	21	47	-	610
Honduras	110	110	44	67	137	32	59	41	31	5	-	180
Jamaica	110	87	5	73	56	17	20	20	0	22	-	45
Mexico	63	83	14	74	94	23	46	28	39	4	-	1 900
Nicaragua	97	230	33	70	130	30	68	38	44	7	-	150
Panama	70	160	10	75	58	18	34	24	29	17	-	48
Paraguay	180	170	29	72	66	25	37	29	22	9	-	150
Peru	190	410	41	70	142	26	80	34	58	5	-	720
Saint Kitts and Nevis	250	-	1	70	-	19	36	22	39	2	-	-
Saint Lucia	35	-	0	72	-	16	24	18	25	10	-	-
Saint Vincent and the Grenadines	93	-	0	70	-	23	26	27	-4	6	-	-
Suriname	150	110	15	66	-	30	48	39	19	29	-	13
Trinidad and Tobago	45	160	4	70	61	17	24	20	17	12	-	28
Uruguay	26	27	0	75	48	12	24	14	42	5	-	62
Venezuela	60	96	6	74	56	18	27	21	22	18	-	460

Definitions of the Indicators:

Maternal mortality rate: Annual number of deaths of women from pregnancy-related causes per 100 000 live births.

Skilled health personnel: Doctors, nurses or midwives.

Life expectancy: Number of years newborn children would live if subject to the mortality risks prevailing for the cross-section of population at the time of their birth.

Infant mortality rate: Probability of dying between birth and exactly one year of age expressed per 1000 live births.

Under 5 mortality rate: Probability of dying between birth and exactly five years of age expressed per 1000 live births.

Progress in under 5 mortality rate: Percentage change between the 1990 and the 2003 values.

Measles: A highly contagious acute disease of childhood. Overcrowding and disaster conditions are conducive to outbreaks, with high mortality, especially among the malnourished.

Orphans (by HIV/AIDS): Children, whose mother and/or father have died (due to AIDS).

Main Sources:

Mortality rates, attended births, measles: UNICEF, State of the World's Children Report 2005.

Life expectancy: WHO, World Health Report 2005.

Orphans: UNICEF, Children on the Brink 2004.

Notes

*: Data refer to the most recent year available during the period specified in the table heading.

#: The maternal mortality data in the column headed 'reported' are those reported by national authorities. Periodically, UNICEF, WHO and UNFPA evaluate these data and make adjustments. The column with 'adjusted' estimates for 2000 reflects the most recent of these reviews.

x: Data refer to years or periods other than those specified in the column heading, differ from the standard definition, or refer only to part of a country.

Section II. What are the main causes of hunger in the country?

Table 5. Is food available and accessible to all?

| | Undernourishment | | | | | Food consumption vs. needs | | | | Food Availability | |
	Prevalence of undernourishment in total population (%)		Number of undernourished persons (million)		Change in prevalence of undernourish-ment (%)	Dietary energy consumption (kcal/person/day)		Minimum dietary energy requirement (kcal/person/day)	Difference between consumption and requirement	Nutrition food gap ('000 tons)	Distribution food gap ('000 tons)
	1990-92	2000-02	1990-92	2000-02	1990-2000	1990-92	2000-02	2000-02	2000-02	2004	2004
Sub-Saharan Africa											
Angola	58	40	5.6	5.1	-31.0	1 783	2 042	1 800	242	0	51
Benin	20	15	1	0.9	-25.0	2 338	2 516	1 800	716	0	13
Botswana	23	32	0.3	0.6	39.1	2 263	2 155	1 860	295	-	-
Burkina Faso	21	19	1.9	2.3	-9.5	2 354	2 409	1 800	609	9	423
Burundi	48	68	2.7	4.4	41.7	1 896	1 636	1 790	-154	429	511
Cameroon	33	25	4	3.9	-24.2	2 115	2 267	1 860	407	0	80
Cape Verde	< 2.5	< 2.5	0	0	-	3 012	3 209	1 860	1 349	0	0
Central African Republic	50	43	1.5	1.6	-14.0	1 874	1 977	1 800	177	79	220
Chad	58	34	3.5	2.7	-41.4	1 784	2 146	1 810	336	335	469
Comoros	47	62	0.3	0.4	31.9	1 915	1 748	1 820	-72	-	-
Congo, Republic of	54	37	1.4	1.3	-31.5	1 861	2 087	1 840	247	-	-
Congo, Democratic Republic of	32	71	12.2	35.5	121.9	2 172	1 627	1 830	-203	3 595	4 063
Côte d'Ivoire	18	14	2.3	2.2	-22.2	2 472	2 620	1 850	770	0	100
Djibouti	53	27	0.3	0.2	-49.1	1 802	2 202	1 760	442	-	-
Equatorial Guinea	-	-	-	-	-	-	-	-	-	-	-
Eritrea	-	73	-	2.8	-	-	1 524	1 730	-206	302	335
Ethiopia	-	46	-	31.3	-	2 637	1 844	1 720	124	4 311	4 657
Gabon	10	6	0.1	0.1	-40.0	-	2 614	1 850	764	-	-
Gambia	22	27	0.2	0.4	22.7	2 365	2 269	1 850	419	10	45
Ghana	37	13	5.8	2.5	-64.9	2 077	2 620	1 860	760	0	63
Guinea	39	26	2.5	2.1	-33.3	2 108	2 382	1 830	552	0	82
Guinea-Bissau	24	35	0.3	0.5	45.8	2 301	2 100	1 800	300	7	43
Kenya	44	33	10.7	10.3	-25.0	1 921	2 107	1 830	277	0	38
Lesotho	17	12	0.3	0.2	-29.4	2 446	2 617	1 850	767	0	75
Liberia	34	46	0.7	1.4	35.3	2 210	1 993	1 820	173	63	132
Madagascar	35	37	4.3	6	5.7	2 083	2 060	1 800	260	505	799
Malawi	50	33	4.8	3.8	-34.0	1 880	2 155	1 790	365	0	192
Mali	29	29	2.7	3.6	0.0	2 215	2 199	1 800	399	348	618
Mauritania	15	10	0.3	0.3	-33.3	2 556	2 771	1 840	931	0	11
Mauritius	6	6	0.1	0.1	0.0	2 887	2 955	1 910	1 045	-	-
Mozambique	66	47	9.2	8.5	-28.8	1 733	2 034	1 890	144	0	132
Namibia	35	22	0.5	0.4	-37.1	2 061	2 269	1 820	449	-	-
Niger	41	34	3.2	3.8	-17.1	2 018	2 130	1 800	330	162	596
Nigeria	13	9	11.8	11	-30.8	2 540	2 705	1 820	885	0	251
Rwanda	44	37	2.8	3	-15.9	1 945	2 049	1 750	299	0	33
Sao Tome and Principe	18	13	0	0	-27.8	2 272	2 391	1 770	621	-	-
Senegal	23	24	1.8	2.3	4.3	2 275	2 280	1 850	430	0	25
Seychelles	14	9	0	0	-35.7	2 311	2 452	1 800	652	-	-
Sierra Leone	46	50	1.9	2.3	8.7	1 991	1 926	1 820	106	211	451
Somalia	-	-	-	-	-	-	-	-	-	1 419	1 447
South Africa	-	-	-	-	-	-	-	-	-	-	-
Sudan	32	27	8	8.5	-15.6	2 160	2 260	1 840	420	0	155
Swaziland	14	19	0.1	0.2	35.7	2 455	2 360	1 840	520	0	15
Tanzania, United Republic of	37	44	9.9	15.6	18.9	2 049	1 959	1 810	149	1 034	1 455
Togo	33	26	1.2	1.2	-21.2	2 150	2 297	1 830	467	0	78
Uganda	24	19	4.2	4.6	-20.8	2 274	2 364	1 770	594	0	176

Table 5. Is food available and accessible to all?

| | Undernourishment | | | | | Food consumption vs. needs | | | | Food Availability | |
	Prevalence of undernourishment in total population (%)		Number of undernourished persons (million)		Change in prevalence of undernourishment (%)	Dietary energy consumption (kcal/person/day)		Minimum dietary energy requirement (kcal/person/day)	Difference between consumption and requirement	Nutrition food gap ('000 tons)	Distribution food gap ('000 tons)
	1990-92	2000-02	1990-92	2000-02	1990-2000	1990-92	2000-02	2000-02	2000-02	2004	2004
Zambia	48	49	4	5.2	2.1	1 929	1 904	1 820	84	191	487
Zimbabwe	45	44	4.9	5.6	-2.2	1 974	2 024	1 840	184	382	576

Asia & Oceania

Afghanistan	-	-	-	-		-	-	-	-	0	305
Bangladesh	35	30	39.2	42.5	-14.3	2 070	2 190	1 770	420	52	1 744
Bhutan	-	-	-	-		-	-	-	-	-	-
Brunei Darussalam	4	3	0	0	-25.0	2 798	2 855	1 910	945	-	-
Cambodia	43	33	4.3	4.4	-23.3	1 871	2 058	1 760	298	-	-
China	16	11	193.5	142.1	-31.3	2 707	2 958	1 930	1 028	-	-
Fiji	10	5	0.1	0	-50.0	2 456	2 895	1 910	985	-	-
Hong Kong, China (SAR)	-	-	-	-		-	-	-	-	-	-
India	25	21	215.8	221.1	-16.0	2 366	2 420	1 810	610	0	4 133
Indonesia	9	6	16.4	12.6	-33.3	2 699	2 912	1 840	1 072	0	67
Kiribati	9	6	0	0	-33.3	2 653	2 852	1 800	1 052	-	-
Korea, Dem. People's Rep. of	18	36	3.7	8.1	100.0	2 451	2 137	1 900	237	0	120
Korea, Republic of	< 2.5	< 2.5	0.8	0.7	-	2 999	3 059	1 930	1 129	-	-
Laos	29	22	1.2	1.2	-24.1	2 111	2 286	1 720	566	-	-
Malaysia	3	< 2.5	0.5	0.6	-	2 823	2 891	1 840	1 051	-	-
Maldives	17	11	0	0	-35.3	2 378	2 542	1 830	712	-	-
Marshall Islands	-	-	-	-		-	-	-	-	-	-
Micronesia	-	-	-	-		-	-	-	-	-	-
Mongolia	34	28	0.8	0.7	-17.6	2 063	2 236	1 860	376	-	-
Myanmar	10	6	4	2.8	-40.0	2 634	2 880	1 810	1 070	-	-
Nauru	-	-	-	-		-	-	-	-	-	-
Nepal	20	17	3.9	4	-15.0	2 345	2 444	1 810	634	0	308
Pakistan	24	20	27.7	29.3	-16.7	2 305	2 430	1 760	670	0	1 680
Palau	-	-	-	-		-	-	-	-	-	-
Papua New Guinea	15	13	0.6	0.7	-13.3	2 410	2 463	1 780	683	-	-
Philippines	26	22	16.2	17.2	-15.4	2 262	2 375	1 800	575	0	206
Samoa	11	4	0	0	-63.6	-	-	-	-	-	-
Singapore	-	-	-	-		-	-	-	-	-	-
Solomon Islands	33	20	0.1	0.1	-39.4	2 015	2 239	1 770	469	-	-
Sri Lanka	28	22	4.8	4.1	-21.4	2 229	2 388	1 860	528	-	-
Thailand	28	20	15.2	12.2	-28.6	2 252	2 453	1 860	593	-	-
Timor-Leste	11	7	0.1	0.1	-36.4	-	-	-	-	-	-
Tonga	-	-	-	-		-	-	-	-	-	-
Tuvalu	-	-	-	-		-	-	-	-	-	-
Vanuatu	13	12	0	0	-7.7	2 525	2 572	1 780	792	-	-
Viet Nam	31	19	20.6	14.7	-38.7	2 178	2 534	1 830	704	-	-

Eastern and Southern Europe & CIS

Albania	-	6	-	0.2	-	-	2 861	1 980	881	-	-
Armenia	-	34	-	1.1	-	-	2 190	1 970	220	0	0
Azerbaijan	-	15	-	1.2	-	-	2 482	1 940	542	0	0
Belarus	-	< 2.5	-	0.2	-	-	3 006	1 970	1 036	-	-
Bosnia and Herzegovina	-	8	-	0.3	-	-	2 764	2 000	764	-	-
Cyprus	< 2.5	< 2.5	0	0	-	3 123	3 251	1 980	1 271	-	-
Georgia	-	27	-	1.4	-	-	2 275	1 960	315	-	-
Kyrgyzstan	-	6	-	0.3	-	-	2 951	1 920	1 031	0	0

143

Table 5. Is food available and accessible to all?

	Undernourishment						Food consumption vs. needs				Food Availability	
	Prevalence of undernourishment in total population (%)		Number of undernourished persons (million)		Change in prevalence of undernourish-ment (%)	Dietary energy consumption (kcal/person/day)		Minimum dietary energy requirement (kcal/person /day)	Difference between consumption and requirement	Nutrition food gap ('000 tons)	Distribution food gap ('000 tons)
	1990-92	2000-02	1990-92	2000-02	1990-2000	1990-92	2000-02	2000-02	2000-02	2004	2004
Tajikistan	-	61	-	3.7	-	-	1 835	1 900	-65	0	15
Turkey	< 2.5	3	1	1.8	-	3 494	3 358	1 970	1 388	-	-
Turkmenistan	-	9	-	0.4	-	-	2 719	1 920	799	0	0
Uzbekistan	-	26	-	6.6	-	-	2 269	1 920	349	0	0
Middle East & North Africa											
Algeria	5	5	1.3	1.7	0.0	2 922	2 991	1 860	1 131	0	0
Bahrain	-	-	-	-	-	-	-	-	-	-	-
Egypt	4	3	2.5	2.4	-25.0	3 200	3 341	1 900	1 441	0	0
Iran	4	4	2.1	2.7	0.0	2 979	3 075	1 840	1 235	-	-
Iraq	-	-	-	-	-	-	-	-	-	-	-
Jordan	4	7	0.1	0.4	75.0	2 817	2 668	1 800	868	-	-
Kuwait	23	5	0.5	0.1	-78.3	1 420	3 051	1 980	1 071	-	-
Lebanon	< 2.5	3	0.1	0.1	-	3 165	3 181	1 920	1 261	-	-
Libyan Arab Jamahiriya	< 2.5	< 2.5	0	0	0.0	3 277	3 324	1 900	1 424	-	-
Morocco	6	7	1.5	2	16.7	3 028	3 042	1 860	1 182	0	0
Occupied Palestinian Territories	-	19	-	0.6	-	-	-	1 740	-	-	-
Oman	-	-	-	-	-	-	-	-	-	-	-
Qatar	-	-	-	-	-	-	-	-	-	-	-
Saudi Arabia	4	3	0.7	0.8	-25.0	2 771	2 844	1 860	984	-	-
Syria	5	4	0.7	0.6	-20.0	2 832	3 038	1 840	1 198	-	-
Tunisia	< 2.5	< 2.5	0.1	0.1	-	3 152	3 271	1 880	1 391	0	0
United Arab Emirates	4	< 2.5	0.1	0.1	-	2 928	3 199	2 030	1 169	-	-
Yemen	34	36	4.2	6.7	5.9	2 037	2 037	1 770	267	-	-
Latin America & Caribbean											
Antigua and Barbuda	17	24	0	0	41.2	2 460	2 342	1 940	402	-	-
Argentina	< 2.5	< 2.5	0.7	0.6	-	2 994	3 074	1 940	1 134	-	-
Bahamas	9	6	0	0	-33.3	2 617	2 753	1 940	813	-	-
Barbados	< 2.5	< 2.5	0	0	-	3 080	3 059	1 980	1 079	-	-
Belize	7	4	0	0	-42.9	2 653	2 844	1 800	1 044	-	-
Bolivia	28	21	1.9	1.8	-25.0	2 112	2 250	1 780	470	0	110
Brazil	12	9	18.5	15.6	-25.0	2 812	3 010	1 900	1 110	-	-
Chile	8	4	1.1	0.6	-50.0	2 612	2 845	1 920	925	-	-
Colombia	17	13	6.1	5.7	-23.5	2 435	2 579	1 820	759	0	562
Costa Rica	6	4	0.2	0.2	-33.3	2 714	2 858	1 930	928	-	-
Cuba	8	3	0.8	0.4	-62.5	2 716	2 998	1 960	1 038	-	-
Dominica	4	8	0	0	100.0	2 941	2 752	1 930	822	-	-
Dominican Republic	27	25	1.9	2.1	-7.4	2 262	2 323	1 920	403	0	96
Ecuador	8	4	0.9	0.6	-50.0	2 509	2 737	1 820	917	0	315
El Salvador	12	11	0.6	0.7	-8.3	2 493	2 549	1 800	749	0	94
Grenada	9	8	0	0	-11.1	2 830	2 867	1 910	957	-	-
Guatemala	16	24	1.4	2.8	50.0	2 351	2 187	1 750	437	0	352
Guyana	21	9	0.2	0.1	-57.1	2 347	2 709	1 880	829	-	-
Haiti	65	47	4.6	3.8	-27.7	1 780	2 083	1 930	153	71	305
Honduras	23	22	1.1	1.5	-4.3	2 313	2 353	1 770	583	234	374
Jamaica	14	10	0.3	0.3	-28.6	2 503	2 675	1 920	755	0	0
Mexico	5	5	4.6	5.2	0.0	3 101	3 155	1 890	1 265	-	-
Nicaragua	30	27	1.2	1.4	-10.0	2 215	2 283	1 810	473	160	270
Panama	21	26	0.5	0.8	23.8	2 316	2 237	1 830	407	-	-

Table 5. Is food available and accessible to all?

	Undernourishment						Food consumption vs. needs				Food Availability	
	Prevalence of undernourishment in total population (%)		Number of undernourished persons (million)		Change in prevalence of undernourish-ment (%)		Dietary energy consumption (kcal/person/day)		Minimum dietary energy requirement (kcal/person/day)	Difference between consumption and requirement	Nutrition food gap ('000 tons)	Distribution food gap ('000 tons)
	1990-92	2000-02	1990-92	2000-02	1990-2000		1990-92	2000-02	2000-02	2000-02	2004	2004
Paraguay	18	14	0.8	0.8	-22.2		2 402	2 556	1 840	716	-	-
Peru	42	13	9.3	3.4	-69.0		1 962	2 550	1 810	740	0	543
Saint Kitts and Nevis	13	12	0	0	-7.7		2 576	2 636	1 910	726	-	-
Saint Lucia	8	5	0	0	-37.5		2 736	2 936	1 900	1 036	-	-
Saint Vincent and the Grenadines	22	13	0	0	-40.9		2 299	2 534	1 900	634	-	-
Suriname	13	11	0.1	0	-15.4		2 528	2 628	1 910	718	-	-
Trinidad and Tobago	13	12	0.2	0.2	-7.7		2 635	2 735	1 940	795	-	-
Uruguay	6	4	0.2	0.1	-33.3		2 662	2 828	1 910	918	-	-
Venezuela	11	17	2.3	4.3	54.5		2 465	2 352	1 850	502	-	-

Definitions of the Indicators:

Undernourishment: The condition of people whose dietary energy consumption is continuously below a minimum dietary energy requirement for maintaining a healthy life and carrying out light physical activity.

Change in prevalence in undernourishement: Percentage change between the 1990-92 and the 2000-02 values.

Dietary energy consumption per person: Amount of food, in kcal per day, for each individual in the total population.

Minimum dietary energy requirement: Amount of dietary energy per person considered adequate to meet the energy needs for maintaining a healthy life and carrying out light physical activity.

Nutrition food gap: Amount of food needed to raise food consumption of entire population to the minimum nutritional requirement disregarding different income groups.

Distribution food gap: Amount of food needed to raise consumption in each income group to the nutritional target.

Main Sources:

Undernourishment, food consumption and needs: FAO Statistics Division, Food Security Statistics: (www.fao.org/faostat/foodsecurity/index_en.htm).

Food availability: USDA, Food Security Assessment Report GFA-16, 2005.

Table 6. How vulnerable is the country to external risks such as man-made disasters, natural catastrophes and disease?

	Impact of diseases					Natural Disasters		Man-made disasters			
	Proportion of adults (15-49) living with HIV (%)	Number of adults (15-49) living with HIV ('000)	Number of children (0-14) living with HIV ('000)	Malaria death rate (per 100 000)	Tuberculosis death rate (per 100 000)	Total number of people affected in natural disasters (annual average '000)		Population of concern to UNHCR by country of asylum ('000)		Refugee population ('000)	Est. number of internally displaced persons ('000)
	2003	2003	2003	2000	2003	1990-1999	2000-2004	2003	1999-2003 (average)	2004	2000-2005*
Sub-Saharan Africa											
Angola	3.9	220	23	354	20	99	95	147	198	14	40-340
Benin	1.9	62	6	177	12	84	2	6	5	5	-
Botswana	37.3	330	25	15	34	11	29	4	3	-	-
Burkina Faso	4.2	270	31	292	33	282	9	1	1	0	-
Burundi	6	220	27	143	59	26	338	136	132	-	170
Cameroon	6.9	520	43	108	21	81	1	64	53	59	-
Cape Verde	-	-	-	22	39	2	6	-	-	-	-
Central African Republic	13.5	240	21	137	54	8	4	53	54	29	-
Chad	4.8	180	18	207	48	93	67	147	49	-	-
Comoros	-	-	-	80	8	0	0	-	0	-	-
Congo, Republic of	4.9	80	10	78	57	8	11	96	111	69	-
Congo, Democratic Republic of	4.2	1 000	110	224	59	15	146	238	323	211	-
Côte d'Ivoire	7	530	40	76	68	0	1	132	134	-	500
Djibouti	2.9	8	1	119	98	35	69	29	24	-	-
Equatorial Guinea	-	-	-	152	39	-	-	-	-	-	-
Eritrea	2.7	55	6	74	52	162	856	14	246	-	59
Ethiopia	4.4	1 400	120	198	60	3 478	8 239	130	178	118	132
Gabon	8.1	45	3	80	23	0	0	19	19	14	-
Gambia	1.2	6	1	52	39	4	3	8	11	-	-
Ghana	3.1	320	24	70	41	104	29	48	26	-	-
Guinea	3.2	130	9	200	43	3	44	187	296	156	82
Guinea-Bissau	-	-	-	150	34	4	20	8	52	8	-
Kenya	6.7	1 100	100	63	89	1 324	2 003	242	236	-	360
Lesotho	28.9	300	22	84	46	50	155	-	0	-	-
Liberia	5.9	96	8	201	53	101	4	602	364	-	215
Madagascar	1.7	130	9	184	36	272	819	-	0	-	-
Malawi	14.2	810	83	275	52	1 919	760	12	8	-	-
Mali	1.9	120	13	454	64	32	8	11	11	11	-
Mauritania	0.6	9	-	108	73	75	110	30	30	0	-
Mauritius	-	-	-	0	11	1	0	-	0	-	-
Mozambique	12.2	1 200	99	232	62	724	802	10	5	-	-
Namibia	21.3	200	15	52	52	44	208	22	23	9	-
Niger	1.2	64	6	469	30	194	743	0	0	0	-
Nigeria	5.4	3 300	290	141	57	86	69	10	8	-	200
Rwanda	5.1	230	22	200	69	98	68	63	190	43	-
Sao Tome and Principe	-	-	-	80	28	-	-	-	-	-	-
Senegal	0.8	41	3	72	47	44	95	23	24	21	64
Seychelles	-	-	-	4	5	0	1	-	-	0	-
Sierra Leone	-	-	-	312	88	20	0	95	279	-	-
Somalia	-	-	-	81	118	165	578	11	37	-	370
South Africa	21.5	5 100	230	0	28	37	3 043	111	56	-	-
Sudan	2.3	380	21	70	54	1 575	647	161	335	-	6 000
Swaziland	38.8	200	16	0	83	53	154	1	1	-	-
Tanzania, United Republic of	8.8	1 500	140	130	52	786	678	650	669	580	-
Togo	4.1	96	9	47	74	29	1	13	12	12	-
Uganda	4.1	450	84	152	71	115	165	236	223	0	1 400
Zambia	16.5	830	85	141	61	429	967	227	243	202	-
Zimbabwe	24.6	1 600	120	1	61	2 016	1 404	13	8	-	150

Table 6. How vulnerable is the country to external risks such as man-made disasters, natural catastrophes and disease?

	Impact of diseases					Natural Disasters		Man-made disasters			
	Proportion of adults (15-49) living with HIV (%)	Number of adults (15-49) living with HIV ('000)	Number of children (0-14) living with HIV ('000)	Malaria death rate (per 100 000)	Tuberculosis death rate (per 100 000)	Total number of people affected in natural disasters (annual average '000)		Population of concern to UNHCR by country of asylum ('000)		Refugee population ('000)	Est. number of internally displaced persons ('000)
	2003	2003	2003	2000	2003	1990-1999	2000-2004	2003	1999-2003 (average)	2004	2000-2005*
Asia & Oceania											
Afghanistan	-	-	-	8	93	60	1 382	912	1 416	-	167
Bangladesh	-	-	-	1	57	9 152	7 906	20	22	20	500
Bhutan	-	-	-	5	21	7	0	-	-	-	-
Brunei Darussalam	<0.1	<0.2	-	0	5	-	-	-	-	-	-
Cambodia	2.6	170	7	14	81	920	1 507	0	8	0	-
China	0.1	830	-	0	18	116 057	138 598	299	296	299	-
Fiji	0.1	1	-	7	4	44	8	-	-	-	-
Hong Kong, China (SAR)	-	-	-	-	7	1	1	2	-	-	-
India	0.9	-	120	3	31	30 903	104 213	165	171	159	600
Indonesia	0.1	110	-	1	65	637	415	17	81	0	342-600
Kiribati	-	-	-	17	4	8	0	-	-	-	-
Korea, Dem. People's Rep. of	-	-	-	0	16	1 468	1 196	-	-	-	-
Korea, Republic of	<0.1	8	-	0	10	87	121	0	0	0	-
Laos	0.1	2	-	28	26	287	213	-	-	-	-
Malaysia	0.4	51	-	1	16	5	26	79	57	19	-
Maldives	-	-	-	3	2	2	4	-	-	-	-
Marshall Islands	-	-	-	15	4	1	0	-	-	-	-
Micronesia	-	-	-	10	6	3	1	-	-	-	-
Mongolia	<0.1	<0.5	-	0	32	61	473	-	-	-	-
Myanmar	1.2	320	8	20	24	67	15	3	1	-	-
Nauru	-	-	-	13	4	-	-	-	-	-	-
Nepal	0.5	60	-	8	28	97	206	135	131	125	100-200
Pakistan	0.1	73	-	4	43	2 400	829	1 130	1 553	967	-
Palau	-	-	-	6	8	-	-	-	-	-	-
Papua New Guinea	0.6	16	-	28	47	113	9	8	-	7	-
Philippines	<0.1	9	-	2	49	4 101	1 762	2	1	0	60
Samoa	-	-	-	6	5	28	0	-	-	-	-
Singapore	0.2	4	-	0	5	0	0	0	0	0	-
Solomon Islands	-	-	-	8	4	9	0	-	-	-	-
Sri Lanka	<0.1	4	-	9	9	343	830	468	650	0	352
Thailand	1.5	560	12	8	17	2 205	2 571	122	111	-	-
Timor-Leste	-	-	-	-	95	0	1	1	-	0	-
Tonga	-	-	-	9	5	1	3	-	-	-	-
Tuvalu	-	-	-	14	6	0	0	-	-	-	-
Vanuatu	-	-	-	11	8	3	13	-	-	-	-
Viet Nam	0.4	200	-	9	22	2 211	1 972	15	-	2	-
Eastern and Southern Europe & CIS											
Albania	-	-	-	0	4	325	38	0	1	-	-
Armenia	0.1	3	-	0	11	132	59	239	266	236	8
Azerbaijan	<0.1	1	-	0	11	244	7	585	636	-	575
Belarus	-	-	-	0	7	6	0	17	79	1	-
Bosnia and Herzegovina	<0.1	1	-	0	8	0	69	405	614	-	-
Cyprus	-	-	-	0	0	0	0	5	2	0	210
Georgia	0.1	3	-	0	13	26	248	265	274	3	240
Kyrgyzstan	0.1	4	-	0	18	20	0	6	12	-	-
Tajikistan	<0.1	<0.2	-	0	32	40	619	4	11	-	-
Turkey	-	-	-	0	4	174	30	6	7	-	230-1.000

147

Table 6. How vulnerable is the country to external risks such as man-made disasters, natural catastrophes and disease?

	Impact of diseases					Natural Disasters		Man-made disasters			
	Proportion of adults (15-49) living with HIV (%)	Number of adults (15-49) living with HIV ('000)	Number of children (0-14) living with HIV ('000)	Malaria death rate (per 100000)	Tuberculosis death rate (per 100000)	Total number of people affected in natural disasters (annual average '000)		Population of concern to UNHCR by country of asylum ('000)		Refugee population ('000)	Est. number of internally displaced persons ('000)
	2003	2003	2003	2000	2003	1990-1999	2000-2004	2003	1999-2003 (average)	2004	2000-2005*
Turkmenistan	<0.1	<0.2	-	0	10	0	0	14	15	13	-
Uzbekistan	0.1	11	-	0	16	5	220	46	35	44	3
Middle East & North Africa											
Algeria	0.1	-	-	22	2	7	57	169	169	169	1 000
Bahrain	0.2	<0.6	-	0	5	-	-	-	-	-	-
Egypt	<0.1	12	-	0	3	26	0	94	48	90	-
Iran	0.1	31	-	0	3	179	12 782	989	1 576	1 080	-
Iraq	<0.1	<0.5	-	15	33	81	2	190	148	-	>1.000
Jordan	<0.1	<0.5	-	0	0	20	30	8	7	-	-
Kuwait	-	--	-	0	3	0	0	103	133	2	-
Lebanon	0.1	3	-	0	1	10	4	3	6	-	50-600
Libyan Arab Jamahiriya	0.3	10	-	0	1	0	0	12	12	12	-
Morocco	0.1	15	-	8	10	37	9	2	2	-	-
Occupied Palestinian Territories	-	-	-	-	4	-	-	-	-	-	-
Oman	0.1	1	-	0	1	0	0	0	0	-	-
Qatar	-	-	-	0	7	-	-	-	-	-	-
Saudi Arabia	-	-	-	0	5	0	3	-	-	241	-
Syria	<0.1	<0.5	-	0	5	33	66	10	7	-	-
Tunisia	<0.1	1	-	0	2	10	5	0	0	-	-
United Arab Emirates	-	-	-	0	2	-	-	-	-	-	-
Yemen	0.1	12	-	24	12	35	0	63	70	64	-
Latin America & Caribbean											
Antigua and Barbuda	-	-	-	0	1	8	0	-	-	-	-
Argentina	0.7	120	-	0	6	58	96	4	4	3	-
Bahamas	3	5	<0.2	0	6	0	2	-	0	-	-
Barbados	1.5	3	<0.2	0	2	0	1	-	-	-	-
Belize	2.4	4	<0.2	0	4	6	17	1	7	1	-
Bolivia	0.1	5	-	1	33	77	108	1	0	1	-
Brazil	0.7	650	-	0	8	1 119	325	4	3	3	-
Chile	0.3	26	-	0	1	34	95	1	0	1	-
Colombia	0.7	180	-	0	8	193	133	1 244	688	0	1580-3410
Costa Rica	0.6	12	-	0	1	103	21	14	13	-	-
Cuba	0.1	3	-	0	1	237	1 302	1	1	1	-
Dominica	-	-	-	0	3	0	0	-	-	-	-
Dominican Republic	1.7	85	2	0	15	103	23	-	-	-	-
Ecuador	0.3	20	-	0	27	45	74	9	4	8	-
El Salvador	0.7	28	-	0	9	12	412	0	0	0	-
Grenada	-	-	-	0	1	0	12	-	-	-	-
Guatemala	1.1	74	-	1	12	18	50	1	1	1	242
Guyana	2.5	11	1	4	21	65	0	-	-	-	-
Haiti	5.6	260	19	1	50	260	119	0	0	-	-
Honduras	1.8	59	4	1	12	288	221	0	0	0	-
Jamaica	1.2	21	<0.5	0	1	56	75	-	0	-	-
Mexico	0.3	160	-	0	5	236	82	6	16	6	10-12
Nicaragua	0.2	6	-	0	8	195	53	0	0	0	-
Panama	0.9	15	-	0	4	5	11	2	2	-	-
Paraguay	0.5	15	-	0	12	53	14	0	0	0	-

Table 6. How vulnerable is the country to external risks such as man-made disasters, natural catastrophes and disease?

	Impact of diseases					Natural Disasters		Man-made disasters			
	Proportion of adults (15-49) living with HIV (%)	Number of adults (15-49) living with HIV ('000)	Number of children (0-14) living with HIV ('000)	Malaria death rate (per 100 000)	Tuberculosis death rate (per 100 000)	Total number of people affected in natural disasters (annual average '000)		Population of concern to UNHCR by country of asylum ('000)		Refugee population ('000)	Est. number of internally displaced persons ('000)
	2003	2003	2003	2000	2003	1990-1999	2000-2004	2003	1999-2003 (average)	2004	2000-2005*
Peru	0.5	80	-	1	22	531	918	1	1	-	60
Saint Kitts and Nevis	-	-	-	0	2	1	0	-	-	-	-
Saint Lucia	-	-	-	0	2	0	0	-	-	-	-
Saint Vincent and the Grenadines	-	-	-	0	4	0	0	-	-	-	-
Suriname	1.7	5	<0.2	1	12	-	-	-	-	-	-
Trinidad and Tobago	3.2	28	1	0	1	0	0	-	-	-	-
Uruguay	-	6	-	0	3	2	3	0	0	-	-
Venezuela	0.7	100	-	0	5	65	17	29	16	0	-

Definitions of the Indicators:

HIV prevalence rate: Proportion of population infected with HIV expressed in percentage.

Malaria and tuberculosis death rates: Proportion of people of all age groups who died due to malaria or tuberculosis in a given year.

People affected in natural disasters: Injured, homeless and people requiring immediate assistance during a period of emergency due to a natural disaster (drought; earthquake; epidemic; extreme temperature; famine; flood; insect infestation; landslide; volcanic eruption; tsunami; wildfire; windstorm).

Population of concern to the UNHCR: Refugees, returnees, asylum-seekers and others of concern (selected IDPs, groups of war victims, etc.).

Internally displaced persons: Persons or groups of persons who have been forced or obliged to flee or to leave their homes and who have not crossed an internationally recognized State border.

Main Sources:

HIV prevalence: United Nations Statistics Division, Millennium Indicators Database (http://millenniumindicators.un.org).

Number of persons living with HIV: UNAIDS, Report on the Global AIDS Epidemic, fouth global report, 2004.

Malaria and tuberculosis: United Nations Statistics Division, Millennium Indicators Database.

People affected in disasters: CRED, EM-DAT Emergency Disasters Database (http://www.em-dat.net).

Population of concern to UNHCR: UNHCR, Statistical Yearbook 2003.

Refugee population: UNHCR, Refugee Trends 1 Jan - 30 Sept 2004.

Internally displaced persons: Internal displacement monitoring centre, Global Statistics (www.idpproject.org).

Table 7. Does lack of learning contribute to hunger in the country?

	Overall performance		Input		Participation					Outcomes	
	Education for All Development Index, rank	Gender-related EFA Index, rank	Pupil/ teacher ratio	Percentage of **untrained** teachers (%)	Net rate of **non-** enrolment to primary school (%)		Out-of-school children ('000)	Girls to boys ratio in primary schools	School life expectancy (years)	Adult **Illiteracy** rate (%)	Share of females among Illiterates (%)
	2001	2001	2001	2001	1990	2001	2001	2001	2001	2000-2004	2000-2004
Sub-Saharan Africa											
Angola	-	-	35	-	42.0[x]	38.7	-	0.86	4.4[x,y]	-	-
Benin	116	125	53	-	55.2[x]	28.7[x]	308[x,y]	0.70	7.1[x,y]	60.2	64
Botswana	83	58	27	11	15.1	19.1	61	1.00	11.6[x]	21.1	45
Burkina Faso	127	122	47	-	73.8	65.0[x]	1 383[x]	0.71	3.4[x]	87.2	56
Burundi	117	109	49	-	46.8[x]	46.6[x]	537[x]	0.79	5.2[x]	49.6	60
Cameroon	-	-	61	-	26.4[x]	-	-	0.86	9.3[x]	32.1	64
Cape Verde	73	88	29	33	6.2[x]	0.6	0	0.96	11.6[x]	24.3	72
Central African Republic	-	-	74	-	46.5	-	-	0.67	-	51.4	67
Chad	124	126	71	-	63.5[x]	41.7[x]	578[x]	0.63	5.3[x,y]	54.2	59
Comoros	109	102	39	-	43.3[x]	45.3[x]	-	0.82	6.9[x,y]	43.8	58
Congo, Republic of	-	-	56	-	20.7[x]	-	-	0.93	7.7[x]	17.2	68
Congo, Democratic Republic of	-	-	-	-	45.5	65.4	-	0.90	-	-	-
Côte d'Ivoire	114	120	44	-	54.4	37.4	958	0.74	-	-	-
Djibouti	112	114	34	-	68.7	66.0[x]	73[x]	0.76	3.9[x]	-	-
Equatorial Guinea	106	107	43	-	9.5[x]	15.4	10	0.91	9[x,y]	-	-
Eritrea	113	113	44	27	83.9[x]	57.5	314	0.81	5[x]	-	-
Ethiopia	122	116	57	31	76.7[x]	53.8	6 076	0.71	5.2[x]	58.5	57
Gabon	-	-	49	-	14.0[x]	21.7[x]	45[x,z]	0.99	-	-	-
Gambia	111	105	38	-	52.0[x]	27.1[x]	55[x]	0.92	-	-	-
Ghana	103	98	32	35	47.6[x]	39.8	1 265	0.91	7.5[x]	26.2	66
Guinea	-	-	47	-	74.5[x]	38.5	498	0.75	-	-	-
Guinea-Bissau	125	124	44	65	62.0[x]	54.8	118[y]	0.67	5.5[x,y]	-	-
Kenya	-	-	32	2	25.7[x]	30.1[x]	1 826[x]	0.98	8.5[x]	15.7	69
Lesotho	93	97	47	25	27.0	15.6	52	1.02	10.7	18.6	32
Liberia	120	117	38	-	-	30.1	142[y]	0.73	10.3[y]	44.1	69
Madagascar	-	-	48	-	35.2[x]	31.4	726	0.96	-	-	-
Malawi	108	103	63	49	50.2	19.0[x]	371[x]	0.96	-	38.2	69
Mali	-	-	56	-	79.6	61.7[x]	-	0.75	-	81	56
Mauritania	118	104	39	-	64.7[x]	33.3[x]	145[x]	0.96	6.9[x]	58.8	60
Mauritius	53	60	25	0	5.1	6.8	9	1.00	12.4[x]	15.7	63
Mozambique	121	118	66	40	55.3	40.3	1 042	0.79	5.4[x,y]	53.5	68
Namibia	78	65	32	63	16.8[x]	21.8	82	1.01	11.7[x]	16.7	54
Niger	126	123	41	27	76.0	65.8	1 250	0.68	2.9[x]	82.9	55
Nigeria	-	-	40	-	40.1[x]	-	-	0.80	-	33.2	61
Rwanda	104	87	59	19	32.6	16.0	210	0.99	8.2[x]	30.8	64
Sao Tome and Principe	-	-	33	-	-	2.9	1[x]	0.94	9.6[x]	-	-
Senegal	119	112	49	10	52.9[x]	42.1	669	0.91	-	60.7	59
Seychelles	22	31	14	22	-	0.9	0	0.99	13.7[x]	8	-
Sierra Leone	-	-	37	21	59.0[x]	-	-	0.70	6.8[x,z]	-	-
Somalia	-	-	-	-	91.8[x]	-	-	-	-	-	-
South Africa	87	64	37	32	12.1[x]	10.5	738	0.96	12.9[x]	14	54
Sudan	-	-	-	-	56.7[x]	54.2[x]	-	0.85	-	40.1	64
Swaziland	89	35	32	-	22.8	23.3	49	0.95	9.8[x]	19.1	57
Tanzania, United Republic of	-	-	46	-	50.4	45.6	3 184	0.98	-	22.9	68
Togo	99	121	35	20	24.8	8.2	64	0.82	10.4[x,y]	40.4	69
Uganda	-	-	54	-	47.3[x]	-	-	0.96	11.5[x]	31.1	67
Zambia	94	96	45	0	20.9[x]	34.0[x]	702[x]	0.94	6.9[x,z]	20.1	66
Zimbabwe	84	81	38	5	14.3[x]	17.3	443	0.97	9.8[x]	10	69

Table 7. Does lack of learning contribute to hunger in the country?

	Overall performance		Input		Participation					Outcomes	
	Education for All Development Index, rank	Gender-related EFA Index, rank	Pupil/ teacher ratio	Percentage of **untrained** teachers (%)	Net rate of **non-** enrolment to primary school (%)		Out-of-school children ('000)	Girls to boys ratio in primary schools	School life expectancy (years)	Adult **Illiteracy** rate (%)	Share of females among Illiterates (%)
	2001	2001	2001	2001	1990	2001	2001	2001	2001	2000-2004	2000-2004
Asia & Oceania											
Afghanistan	-	-	43	-	73.5^x	-	-	0.08	-	-	-
Bangladesh	107	100	55	34	28.8	13.4	2 425	1.02	8.4	58.9	57
Bhutan	-	-	40	8	86.1^x	-	-	-	7.5^x	-	-
Brunei Darussalam	-	-	14	-	10.3^x	-	-	0.99	13.2^x	6.1	68
Cambodia	96	111	56	4	33.4^x	13.8^x	306^x	0.89	9^x	30.6	70
China	54	92	20	3	2.6	5.4^x	5 820^x	1.00	10.4^x	9.1	73
Fiji	41	44	28	-	0.4^x	0.2	0^x	1.00	-	7.1	60
Hong Kong, China (SAR)	-	-	-	-	-	2.4^x	-	1.00	-	-	-
India	105	110	40	-	-	17.2^t	20 549	0.85	9^x	38.7	-
Indonesia	65	61	21	-	3.3	7.9	2 049	0.98	10.9	12.1	69
Kiribati	-	-	-	-	-	-	-	1.02	-	-	-
Korea, Dem. People's Rep. of	-	-	-	-	-	-	-	-	-	-	-
Korea, Republic of	-	-	32	-	0.3	0.1	5	1.00	15.7^x	-	-
Laos	-	-	30	24	37.4^x	17.2	128	0.86	8.5^x	33.6	67
Malaysia	-	-	20	-	6.3^x	4.8	154	1.00	12.3^{x,z}	11.3	64
Maldives	20	37	23	33	13.3^x	3.8	2	0.99	12.3^x	2.8	50
Marshall Islands	-	-	17	-	-	4.2^x	-	0.83	-	-	-
Micronesia	-	-	-	-	-	-	-	-	-	-	-
Mongolia	62	77	32	-	9.9^x	13.4	33	1.03	10.3^x	2.2	56
Myanmar	91	67	33	-	2.2	18.1	968	1.00	7.4^{x,z}	14.7	64
Nauru	-	-	-	-	-	19.0^x	-	1.04	-	-	-
Nepal	110	115	40	-	18.8	29.5	918^{x,z}	0.87	9.6^x	56	65
Pakistan	123	119	44	-	65.3^x	40.9^x	8 145^{x,z}	0.74	-	58.5	60
Palau	-	-	18	-	-	3.4^x	0^{x,z}	0.93	-	-	-
Papua New Guinea	101	100	36	0	34.0^x	27.0^x	193^x	0.90	-	-	-
Philippines	70	46	35	-	3.5^x	7.0	803	0.99	12^x	7.4	50
Samoa	55	59	25	-	-	5.1	1	0.98	11.8^x	1.3	58
Singapore	-	-	-	-	3.6^x	-	-	-	-	7.5	77
Solomon Islands	-	-	-	-	16.8^x	-	-	-	-	-	-
Sri Lanka	-	-	-	-	10.1^x	0.2	2	0.97	-	7.9	64
Thailand	60	63	19	-	24.1^x	13.7^x	873^x	0.96	12.5^{x,z}	7.4	66
Timor-Leste	-	-	51	-	-	-	-	-	11.4^x	-	-
Tonga	45	62	21	0	8.2	0.3	0	0.98	13.4^x	1	48
Tuvalu	-	-	26	-	-	-	-	0.96	-	-	-
Vanuatu	-	-	29	0	29.4^x	6.8	2	0.99	9.4^x	-	-
Viet Nam	64	82	26	13	9.5^x	6.0^x	544^x	0.93	10.5^x	9.7	69
Eastern and Southern Europe & CIS											
Albania	33	13	22	-	4.9^x	2.8	7^z	1.00	11.3^{x,z}	1.3	67
Armenia	47	40	19	-	-	-	23	0.98	10.8^x	0.6	73
Azerbaijan	56	39	16	0	-	20.2	146	0.98	10.5	-	-
Belarus	25	30	17	2	13.8^x	5.8	27^x	0.98	14	0.3	67
Bosnia and Herzegovina	-	-	-	-	-	-	-	-	-	5	85
Cyprus	19	25	-	-	13.1	4.1	3	1.00	13	-	-
Georgia	40	36	14	23	2.9^x	9.3	26	1.00	11.1^x	-	-
Kyrgyzstan	46	24	24	51	7.7^x	10.0	45	0.97	12.7	-	-
Tajikistan	31	83	22	18	23.3^x	2.8	16	0.95	10.7^x	0.5	68
Turkey	-	-	-	-	10.5	12.1^x	1 049^x	0.92	10.7^x	13.5	79

151

Table 7. Does lack of learning contribute to hunger in the country?

	Overall performance		Input		Participation					Outcomes	
	Education for All Development Index, rank	Gender-related EFA Index, rank	Pupil/ teacher ratio	Percentage of **untrained** teachers (%)	Net rate of **non-**enrolment to primary school (%)		Out-of-school children ('000)	Girls to boys ratio in primary schools	School life expectancy (years)	Adult **Illiteracy** rate (%)	Share of females among Illiterates (%)
	2001	2001	2001	2001	1990	2001	2001	2001	2001	2000-2004	2000-2004
Turkmenistan	-	-	-	-	-	-	-	-	-	1	73
Uzbekistan	-	-	-	-	21.8^x	-	-	0.99	11.4^x	0.7	74
Middle East & North Africa											
Algeria	82	94	28	3	6.8	4.9	213	0.93	-	31.1	65
Bahrain	52	73	16	-	1.0	9.0^x	7^x	0.99	-	11.5	55
Egypt	90	99	23	-	16.3^x	9.7^x	786^x	0.94	-	44.4	64
Iran	-	-	24	4	7.7^x	13.5	1 097	0.96	11.5^x	-	64
Iraq	-	-	21	0	-	9.5	349^y	0.82	9^{x,y}	-	-
Jordan	51	56	20	-	5.9	8.7	68	1.00	12.6^x	9.1	74
Kuwait	67	50	14	-	51.0^x	15.4	24	0.99	-	17.1	42
Lebanon	68	86	17	85	22.2^x	10.2^x	45^x	0.96	13.1^x	-	-
Libyan Arab Jamahiriya	-	-	8	-	3.9^x	-	-	1.00	16.5^x	18.3	77
Morocco	97	108	28	-	43.2	11.6	437	0.89	9.1^{x,z}	49.3	63
Occupied Palestinian Territories	-	-	-	-	-	4.9	19	1.01	12.7	-	-
Oman	85	84	23	0	30.7	25.5	97	0.98	10.4^x	25.6	55
Qatar	69	54	12	-	10.6	5.5	3	0.96	12.9^x	15.8	35
Saudi Arabia	92	89	12	-	41.3	41.1	1 415	0.97	9.6^x	22.1	61
Syria	71	93	24	4	7.7	2.5	65	0.93	-	17.1	74
Tunisia	75	90	22	-	6.1	3.1	37	0.96	13.4^{x,z}	26.8	69
United Arab Emirates	79	70	15	-	0.9	19.2	59	0.96	-	22.7	25
Yemen	115	127	-	-	48.3^x	32.9	1 096^{x,z}	0.66	8.2^{x,y}	51	70
Latin America & Caribbean											
Antigua and Barbuda	-	-	19	53	-	-	-	-	-	-	-
Argentina	23	26	20	-	6.2^x	-	8	1.00	16.3	3	52
Bahamas	-	-	17	5	10.4^x	13.6^x	5^x	1.01	-	-	-
Barbados	8	1	16	23	19.9^x	0.2	0	1.00	14.2^{x,z}	0.3	51
Belize	77	48	23	59	6.0^x	3.8^x	2^{x,z}	0.97	-	23.1	49
Bolivia	76	74	25	-	9.2	5.8	76	0.99	14.3^x	13.3	74
Brazil	72	66	23	-	14.4	3.5	461	0.94	14.9	11.8	51
Chile	38	14	32	8	12.3	11.2	196^z	0.98	13.3^{x,z}	4.3	52
Colombia	86	45	26	-	31.9^x	13.3	621	0.99	10.7^x	7.9	51
Costa Rica	44	7	24	11	12.7	9.4	48	1.00	11^x	4.2	48
Cuba	30	23	14	0	8.3	4.3	42	0.96	12.8^x	3.1	52
Dominica	-	-	19	40	-	8.6^x	-	0.96	-	-	-
Dominican Republic	81	79	39	42	41.8^x	2.9	32	1.01	-	15.6	49
Ecuador	61	12	25	31	2.2^x	0.5	9	1.00	-	9	57
El Salvador	88	52	26	-	27.2^x	11.1	96	0.96	11^x	20.3	58
Grenada	-	-	22	30	-	15.8^x	-	0.95	-	-	-
Guatemala	98	91	30	0	36.0^x	15.0	288	0.92	-	30.1	62
Guyana	-	-	26	49	11.1	1.6	2^y	0.98	-	-	-
Haiti	-	-	-	-	77.9	-	-	-	-	48.1	54
Honduras	-	-	34	-	10.1^x	12.6^x	132^x	1.02	-	20	49
Jamaica	59	57	34	-	4.3	4.8	16	0.99	11.8^x	12.4	36
Mexico	48	53	27	-	1.2^x	0.6	85	0.99	12.3	9.5	62
Nicaragua	95	71	37	27	27.8	18.1	150	1.01	-	23.3	51
Panama	49	47	24	24	8.5	1.0	4	0.97	12.2^{x,y}	7.7	54
Paraguay	74	41	-	-	7.2	8.5	74^x	0.96	11.7^x	8.4	59

Table 7. Does lack of learning contribute to hunger in the country?

	Overall performance		Input		Participation					Outcomes	
	Education for All Development Index, rank	Gender-related EFA Index, rank	Pupil/ teacher ratio	Percentage of **untrained** teachers (%)	Net rate of **non-**enrolment to primary school (%)		Out-of-school children ('000)	Girls to boys ratio in primary schools	School life expectancy (years)	Adult **Illiteracy** rate (%)	Share of females among Illiterates (%)
	2001	2001	2001	2001	1990	2001	2001	2001	2001	2000-2004	2000-2004
Peru	66	75	29	-	12.2^x	0.1	4	1.00	14^x	15	69
Saint Kitts and Nevis	-	-	17	46	-	-	-	1.09	-	-	-
Saint Lucia	-	-	24	22	4.9^x	0.8	0^x	1.01	12.5^x	-	-
Saint Vincent and the Grenadines	-	-	17	-	-	8.1^x	1^x	0.96	-	-	-
Suriname	-	-	20	0	21.6^x	2.7	1^x	0.98	12.5^x	-	-
Trinidad and Tobago	28	51	19	22	9.1	13.2^x	9^x	0.99	12.1^x	1.5	69
Uruguay	57	69	21	-	8.1^x	10.5	35	0.98	14.6	2.3	43
Venezuela	50	72	-	-	11.9	7.6	253	0.98	11.2^x	6.9	53

Definitions of the Indicators:

Education for All Development Index (EDI): Composite index aiming at measuring overall performance towards Education for All. EDI = (GEI + NER + adult literacy rate + survival rate to grade 5) / 4.

Gender-related EFA Index (GEI): Composite index measuring relative achievement in gender parity in education. It is the average of the gender parity indexes (GGI) for gross enrolment ratios in primary and secondary education, and for adult literacy rates.

Pupil/teacher ratio: Average number of pupils per teacher in primary education based on headcounts.

Untrained teachers: Teachers who have not received the minimum organized teacher training normally required for teaching at primary education.

Net enrolment ratio (NER): Enrolment of the official age group for a given level of education, expressed as a percentage of the population at that age group.

Out-of-school children: Children in the official school-age range who are not enrolled.

School life expectancy (SLE): Number of years a child of school entrance age is expected to spend at school or university, including years spent on repetition.

Adult Illiteracy rate: Number of illiterate persons aged 15 and above, expressed as a percentage of the total population in that age group.

Share of females among illiterates: Share of females in the total number of illiterate adults.

Notes:

x: UIS estimation.

t: National estimation.

y: Data are for 1999/2000.

z: Data are for 2000/2001.

Main Sources:

All data: UNESCO, Education For All Global Monitoring Report 2003/04 and 2005.

Section III: Is the country doing its best to fight hunger?

Table 8. Are sufficient levels of basic nutritional, educational and health services provided?

	Public expenditure as percentage of GDP on			Proportion of population with access to			Proportion of routine EPI vaccines financed by the government (%)	Birth registration (proportion of births)	Prevalence of child labour (5-14 age group)
	Health	Education	Military[c]	Improved sanitation	Improved drinking water sources	Affordable essential drugs			
	2002	2000-02*	2003	2002	2002	1999	2003	1999-2003*	1999-2003*
Sub-Saharan Africa									
Angola	2.1	2.8[g]	4.7	30	50	0-49	10	29	22
Benin	2.1	3.3[g]	-	32	68	50-79	0	62	26[y]
Botswana	3.7	2.2	4.1	41	95	80-94	100	58	-
Burkina Faso	2.0	-	1.3	12	51	50-79	100	-	57[y]
Burundi	0.6	3.9	5.9	36	79	0-49	6	75	24
Cameroon	1.2	3.8	1.5	48	63	50-79	100	79	51
Cape Verde	3.8	7.9	0.7	42	80	80-94	80	-	-
Central African Republic	1.6	-	1.3	27	75	50-79	0	73	56
Chad	2.7	-	1.5	8	34	0-49	75	25	57
Comoros	1.7	3.9	-	23	94	80-94	0	83	27
Congo, Republic of	1.5	3.2[g]	1.4	9	46	50-79	0	-	-
Congo, Democratic Republic of	1.2	-	-	29	46	-	0	34	28[y]
Côte d'Ivoire	1.4	4.6[g]	1.5	40	84	80-94	58	72	35
Djibouti	3.3	-	-	50	80	80-94	85	-	-
Equatorial Guinea	1.3	0.6	-	53	44	0-49	0	32	27
Eritrea	3.2	4.1	19.4	9	57	50-79	0	-	-
Ethiopia	2.6	4.6[g]	4.3	6	22	50-79	18	-	43[y]
Gabon	1.8	3.9[g]	-	36	87	0-49	100	89	-
Gambia	3.3	2.8	0.5	53	82	80-94	63	32	22
Ghana	2.3	-	0.7	58	79	0-49	28	21	57[y]
Guinea	0.9	1.8[g]	-	13	51	80-94	20	67	-
Guinea-Bissau	3.0	-	-	34	59	0-49	0	42	54
Kenya	2.2	7.0	1.7	48	62	0-49	36	63	25
Lesotho	5.3	10.4[g]	2.6	37	76	80-94	10	51	17
Liberia	-	-	-	26	62	80-94	0	-	-
Madagascar	1.2	2.9[g]	-	33	45	50-79	12	75	30
Malawi	4.0	6.0	-	46	67	0-49	0	-	17
Mali	2.3	-	1.9	45	48	50-79	100	48	30
Mauritania	2.9	-	1.6	42	56	50-79	100	55	10[y]
Mauritius	2.2	4.7	0.2	99	100	95-100	100	-	-
Mozambique	4.1	-	1.3	27	42	50-79	21	-	-
Namibia	4.7	7.2	2.8	30	80	80-94	100	71	-
Niger	2.0	2.3[g]	-	12	46	50-79	100	46	65
Nigeria	1.2	-	1.2	38	60	0-49	100	68	39[y]
Rwanda	3.1	2.8[g]	2.8	41	73	0-49	50	65	31
Sao Tome and Principe	9.7	-	-	24	79	0-49	-	70	14
Senegal	2.3	3.6	1.5	52	72	50-79	100	62	33
Seychelles	3.9	5.2	1.7	-	87	80-94	100	-	-
Sierra Leone	1.7	3.7	1.7	39	57	0-49	20	46	57
Somalia	-	-	-	25	29	-	0	-	32
South Africa	3.5	5.3[g]	1.6	67	87	80-94	100	-	-
Sudan	1.0	-	2.4	34	69	0-49	0	64	13
Swaziland	3.6	7.1	-	52	52	95-100	100	53	8
Tanzania, United Republic of	2.7	-	2.1	46	73	50-79	30	6	32
Togo	1.1	2.6	1.6	34	51	50-79	0	82	60
Uganda	2.1	-	2.3	41	56	50-79	7	4	34
Zambia	3.1	2.0[g]	-	45	55	50-79	5	10	11
Zimbabwe	4.4	4.7[g]	2.1	57	83	50-79	0	40	26[y]

Table 8. Are sufficient levels of basic nutritional, educational and health services provided?

	Public expenditure as percentage of GDP on			Proportion of population with access to			Proportion of routine EPI vaccines financed by the government (%)	Birth registration (proportion of births)	Prevalence of child labour (5-14 age group)
	Health	Education	Military[c]	Improved sanitation	Improved drinking water sources	Affordable essential drugs			
	2002	2000-02*	2003	2002	2002	1999	2003	1999-2003*	1999-2003*
Asia & Oceania									
Afghanistan	-	-	-	8	13	-	0	10	8
Bangladesh	0.8	2.4	1.2	48	75	50-79	100	7	8[y]
Bhutan	4.1	5.2	-	70	62	80-94	0	-	-
Brunei Darussalam	2.7	9.1	-	-	-	95-100	100	-	-
Cambodia	2.1	1.8	2.5	16	34	0-49	7	22	-
China	2.0	-	2.3	44	77	80-94	100	-	-
Fiji	2.7	5.6[g]	1.6	98		95-100	100	-	-
Hong Kong, China (SAR)	-	4.4	-	-	-	-	-	-	-
India	1.3	4.1	2.1	30	86	0-49	100	35	14
Indonesia	1.2	1.2	1.5	52	78	80-94	90	62	4[y]
Kiribati	-	-	-	39	64	-	-	-	-
Korea, Dem. People's Rep. of	-	-	-	59	100	-	80	99	-
Korea, Republic of	2.6	4.2	2.5	-	92	95-100	100	-	-
Laos	1.5	2.8[g]	-	24	43	50-79	0	59	24
Malaysia	2.0	8.1	2.8		95	50-79	100	-	-
Maldives	5.1	-	-	58	84	50-79	98	73	-
Marshall Islands	-	-	-	82	85	-	-	-	-
Micronesia	-	-	-	28	94	-	6	-	-
Mongolia	4.6	9.0	-	59	62	50-79	22	98	30
Myanmar	0.4	-	-	73	80	50-79	0	39	-
Nauru	-	-	-	97	82	-	100	-	-
Nepal	1.4	3.4	1.6	27	84	0-49	65	34	-
Pakistan	1.1	1.8[g]	4.4	54	90	50-79	100	-	-
Palau	-	-	-	83	84	-	5	-	-
Papua New Guinea	3.8	2.3[g]	0.6	45	39	80-94	80	-	-
Philippines	1.1	3.1	0.9	73	85	50-79	3	83	11
Samoa	-	4.8	-	100	88	95-100	100	-	-
Singapore	1.3	-	5.2	-	-	95-100	100	-	-
Solomon Islands	4.5	3.4[g]	-	31	70	80-94	-	-	-
Sri Lanka	1.8	-	2.7	91	78	95-100	100	-	-
Thailand	3.1	5.2	1.3	99	85	95-100	100	-	-
Timor-Leste	6.2	-	-	33	52	-	0	22	-
Tonga	5.1	4.9[g]	-	97	100	-	100	-	-
Tuvalu	-	-	-	88	93	-	100	-	-
Vanuatu	2.8	11.0[g]	-		60	-	100	-	-
Viet Nam	1.5	-	-	41	73	80-94	55	72	23
Eastern and Southern Europe & CIS									
Albania	2.4	-	1.2	89	97	50-79	40	99	23
Armenia	1.3	3.2[g]	2.7	84	92	0-49	65	-	-
Azerbaijan	0.8	3.2	1.9	55	77	50-79	51	97	8
Belarus	4.7	6.0[g]	1.3	-	100	50-79	100	-	-
Bosnia and Herzegovina	4.6	-	2.9	93	98	80-94	70	98	11
Cyprus	2.9	6.3	1.5	100	100	95-100	25	-	-
Georgia	1.0	2.2	1.1	83	76	0-49	19	95	-
Kyrgyzstan	2.2	3.1[g]	2.9	60	76	50-79	40	-	-
Tajikistan	0.9	2.8	2.2	53	58	0-49	0	75	18
Turkey	4.3	3.7	4.9	83	93	95-100	100	-	-

Table 8. Are sufficient levels of basic nutritional, educational and health services provided?

	Public expenditure as percentage of GDP on			Proportion of population with access to			Proportion of routine EPI vaccines financed by the government (%)	Birth registration (proportion of births)	Prevalence of child labour (5-14 age group)
	Health	Education	Military	Improved sanitation	Improved drinking water sources	Affordable essential drugs			
	2002	2000-02*	2003	2002	2002	1999	2003	1999-2003*	1999-2003*
Turkmenistan	3.0	-	-	62	71	50-79	82	-	-
Uzbekistan	2.5	-	0.5	57	89	50-79	77	100	15
Middle East & North Africa									
Algeria	3.2	-	3.3	92	87	95-100	100	-	-
Bahrain	3.2	-	5.1	-		95-100	100	-	5
Egypt	1.8	-	2.6	68	98	80-94	100	-	6
Iran	2.9	4.9	3.8	84	93	80-94	100	-	-
Iraq	-	-	-	80	81	-	100	98	8
Jordan	4.3	-	8.9	93	91	95-100	100	-	-
Kuwait	2.9	-	9.0	-	-	95-100	100	-	-
Lebanon	3.5	2.7	4.3	98	100	80-94	100	-	6
Libyan Arab Jamahiriya	1.6	-	2.0	97	72	95-100	-	-	-
Morocco	1.5	6.5	4.2	61	80	50-79	100	-	-
Occupied Palestinian Territories	-	-	-	76	94	-	-	100	-
Oman	2.8	4.6[g]	12.2	89	79	80-94	100	-	-
Qatar	2.4	-	-	100	100	95-100	100	-	-
Saudi Arabia	3.3	-	8.7	-		95-100	100	-	-
Syria	2.3	-	7.1	77	79	80-94	100	-	8[y]
Tunisia	2.9	6.4	1.6	80	82	50-79	100	-	-
United Arab Emirates	2.3	1.6[g]	3.1	100	-	95-100	100	-	-
Yemen	1.0	9.5[g]	7.1	30	69	50-79	100	-	-
Latin America & Caribbean									
Antigua and Barbuda	3.3	3.8	-	95	91	50-79	100	-	-
Argentina	4.5	4.0	1.2		NA	50-79	100	-	-
Bahamas	3.4	-	-	100	97	80-94	-	-	-
Barbados	4.7	7.6	-	99	100	95-100	94	-	-
Belize	2.5	5.2	-	47	91	80-94	100	-	-
Bolivia	4.2	6.3	1.7	45	85	50-79	40	82	21
Brazil	3.6	4.2	1.6	75	89	0-49	100	76	7[y]
Chile	2.6	4.2	3.5	92	95	80-94	100	-	-
Colombia	6.7	5.2	4.4	86	92	80-94	100	91	5
Costa Rica	6.1	5.1	0.0	92	97	95-100	0	-	50[y]
Cuba	6.5	18.7	-	98	91	95-100	99	100	-
Dominica	4.6	-	-	83	97	80-94	70	-	-
Dominican Republic	2.2	2.3	-	57	93	50-79	65	75	9
Ecuador	1.7	1.0[g]	2.4	72	86	0-49	100	-	6[y]
El Salvador	3.6	2.9	0.7	63	82	80-94	100	-	-
Grenada	4.0	5.1	-	97	95	95-100	100	-	-
Guatemala	2.3	-	0.5	61	95	50-79	0	-	24[y]
Guyana	4.3	8.4	-	70	83	0-49	90	97	19
Haiti	3.0	-	-	34	71	0-49	30	70	-
Honduras	3.2	-	0.4	68	90	0-49	100	-	-
Jamaica	3.4	6.1	-	80	93	95-100	100	96	-
Mexico	2.7	5.3	0.5	77	91	80-94	100	-	16[y]
Nicaragua	3.9	3.1	0.9	66	81	0-49	74	-	10[y]
Panama	6.4	4.5	-	72	91	80-94	100	-	-
Paraguay	3.2	4.4	0.9	78	83	0-49	100	-	8[y]

Table 8. Are sufficient levels of basic nutritional, educational and health services provided?

	Public expenditure as percentage of GDP on			Proportion of population with access to			Proportion of routine EPI vaccines financed by the government (%)	Birth registration (proportion of births)	Prevalence of child labour (5-14 age group)
	Health	Education	Military[c]	Improved sanitation	Improved drinking water sources	Affordable essential drugs			
	2002	2000-02*	2003	2002	2002	1999	2003	1999-2003*	1999-2003*
Peru	2.2	3.0	1.3	62	81	50-79	100	-	-
Saint Kitts and Nevis	3.4	7.6	-	96	99	50-79	97	-	-
Saint Lucia	3.4	7.7[g]	-	89	98	50-79	100	-	-
Saint Vincent and the Grenadines	3.9	10.0	-	-	-	80-94	100	-	-
Suriname	3.6	-	-	93	92	95-100	100	95	-
Trinidad and Tobago	1.4	4.3[g]	-	100	91	50-79	100	95	2
Uruguay	2.9	2.6	1.6	94	98	50-79	100	-	-
Venezuela	2.3	-	1.3	68	83	80-94	100	92	7

Definitions of the Indicators:

Health expenditure, public: Current and capital spending from government (central and local) budgets, external borrowings and grants and social health insurance funds.

Education expenditure, public: Both capital expenditures and current expenditures. It covers such expenditures as staff salaries and benefits, services, books and teaching materials, welfare services, furniture and equipment, etc.

Military expenditure, public: All expenditures of the defence ministry and other ministries on recruiting and training military personnel as well as on construction and purchase of military supplies and equipment. Military assistance to other nations is included in the expenditures of the donor country.

Access to improved sanitation: 'Improved' sanitation technologies are: connection to a public sewer, connection to septic system, pour-flush latrine, simple pit latrine, ventilated improved pit latrine.

Access to improved water: Access to an 'improved' water supply, which provides 20 litres per capita per day at a distance no longer than 1000 metres.

Access to affordable essential drugs: The estimated percentage of the population for whom a minimum of 20 of the most essential drugs are continuously and affordably available at public or private health facilities or drug outlets within one hour's travel from home.

Government funding of EPI vaccines: Percentage of Expanded Programme on Immunization vaccines routinely administered in a country to protect children that are financed by the national government (including loans).

Birth registration: Percentage of children under 5 that were registered at the moment of the survey.

Child labour: Percentage of children aged 5 to 14 involved in child labour activities at the moment of the survey.

Main Sources:

Public expenditures: UNDP, Human Development Report 2005.

Access to sanitation and water: United Nations Statistics Division, Millennium Indicators Database (http://millenniumindicators.un.org).

Access to drugs: UNDP, Human Development Report 2003.

Vaccines, birth registration and child labour: UNICEF, State of the World's Children Report 2005.

Notes:

*: Data refer to the most recent year available during the period specified in the table heading.

y: Data differ from the standard definition or refer to only part of a country but are included in the calculation of regional and global averages.

c: As a result of a number of limitations in the data, comparisons of military expenditure data over time and across countries should be made with caution. For detailed notes on the data see SIPRI (Stockholm International Peace Research Institute) 2004. SIPRI Yearbook: Armaments, Disarmament and International Security. Oxford: Oxford University Press.

g: Data refer to UNESCO Institute for Statistics estimate when national estimate is not available.

Section IV: How much does the international community contribute to the fight against hunger?

Table 9. How much help does the country receive, and how much of it is food aid?

	Official Development Assistance (ODA) received					Global food aid deliveries in 2004				
	Net ODA receipts (US$ million)	Net ODA receipts (US$ million)	ODA/GNI (%)	ODA per capita (US$)	ODA related to agriculture (US$ million)	Global food aid deliveries ('000 tons)	Food aid deliveries per capita (Kg)	WFP's share (%)	Share of cereals (%)	Share of local purchases (%)
	2003	1999 - 2003 (average)	2002	2002	2003	2004	2004	2004	2004	2004
Sub-Saharan Africa										
Angola	499	1 903	4.5	32.1	7.7	120.6	9.2	78	75	0
Benin	294	1 233	8.1	33.0	20.4	16.9	2.6	17	87	11
Botswana	30	188	0.7	22.0	1.7	-	-	-	-	-
Burkina Faso	451	2 051	14.8	40.0	62.5	39.3	3.3	25	87	20
Burundi	224	701	24.2	24.3	3.4	81.5	11.5	84	75	10
Cameroon	884	2 794	6.6	38.6	33.6	33.2	2.1	32	98	9
Cape Verde	144	544	14.6	200.4	1.1	31.5	68.5	7	98	0
Central African Republic	50	370	5.8	15.7	5.1	5.9	1.5	100	73	0
Chad	247	981	11.6	27.5	10.6	45.9	5.5	91	88	13
Comoros	24	125	13.1	55.0	2.2	-	-	-	-	-
Congo, Republic of	70	378	2.6	15.7	0.6	8.3	2.3	51	62	0
Congo, Democratic Republic of	5 381	7 129	21.3	22.7	9.5	99.5	1.9	81	73	5
Côte d'Ivoire	252	2 291	9.6	64.7	8.9	56.3	3.4	51	71	29
Djibouti	78	360	12.9	112.7	2.7	13.4	19.4	46	86	0
Equatorial Guinea	21	95	0.0	42.1	1.5	-	-	-	-	-
Eritrea	307	1 143	30.8	53.6	5.4	304.3	70.8	52	89	1
Ethiopia	1 504	5 263	21.7	19.4	36.7	790.3	11.8	43	92	23
Gabon	-11	129	1.7	54.5	13.9	-	-	-	-	-
Gambia	60	256	15.3	43.6	6.1	13.8	9.9	15	79	15
Ghana	907	3 410	10.8	32.6	73.6	64.7	3.3	16	94	1
Guinea	238	1 159	7.9	32.2	19.8	27.9	3.6	46	63	14
Guinea-Bissau	145	397	30.5	41.0	1.5	4.8	3.3	100	88	8
Kenya	483	2 162	3.2	12.6	31.2	212.3	6.8	53	90	50
Lesotho	79	280	8.7	42.9	0.4	45.8	25.8	100	93	70
Liberia	107	360	11.0	15.9	0.9	82.8	25.1	89	88	2
Madagascar	539	1 967	8.6	22.7	59.6	52.6	3.2	36	73	7
Malawi	498	2 172	20.2	35.1	41.3	52.8	4.9	99	88	56
Mali	528	2 062	15.0	41.0	28.0	13.7	1.2	100	95	95
Mauritania	243	1 286	30.6	131.3	15.6	41.7	15.9	26	93	0
Mauritius	-15	93	0.5	19.8	1.2	-	-	-	-	-
Mozambique	1 033	5 701	60.3	111.4	24.5	158.4	8.6	56	93	8
Namibia	146	723	4.5	67.9	27.8	6.0	3.0	81	90	67
Niger	453	1 407	13.8	26.1	17.4	35.4	3.1	34	93	37
Nigeria	318	1 153	0.9	2.4	16.7	10.5	0.1	-	100	0
Rwanda	332	1 680	20.5	43.5	6.3	48.5	5.9	77	58	2
Sao Tome and Principe	38	164	56.0	173.4	1.1	3.0	20.2	6	96	1
Senegal	450	2 266	9.2	44.5	46.8	29.0	2.9	29	94	10
Seychelles	9	62	1.2	98.1	1.6	-	-	-	-	-
Sierra Leone	297	1 252	47.0	67.4	0.2	38.0	7.2	65	83	0
Somalia	175	737	0.0	20.8	2.8	44.2	4.7	61	89	0
South Africa	625	2 588	0.5	11.1	55.0	-	-	-	-	-
Sudan	621	1 626	2.5	10.7	4.8	388.8	11.9	89	85	35
Swaziland	27	121	1.8	20.6	4.1	13.0	11.9	69	78	27
Tanzania, United Republic of	1 669	6 185	13.2	35.0	53.1	125.5	3.6	92	90	12
Togo	45	281	3.8	10.7	5.4	-	-	-	-	-
Uganda	959	3 801	11.2	25.9	45.6	256.7	10.4	77	85	36

Table 9. How much help does the country receive, and how much of it is food aid?

	Official Development Assistance (ODA) received					Global food aid deliveries in 2004				
	Net ODA receipts (US$ million)	Net ODA receipts (US$ million)	ODA/GNI (%)	ODA per capita (US$)	ODA related to agriculture (US$ million)	Global food aid deliveries ('000 tons)	Food aid deliveries per capita (Kg)	WFP's share (%)	Share of cereals (%)	Share of local purchases (%)
	2003	1999 - 2003 (average)	2002	2002	2003	2004	2004	2004	2004	2004
Zambia	560	2 969	18.1	62.6	13.5	115.3	11.3	34	87	37
Zimbabwe	186	973	0.0	15.4	25.5	273.7	21.1	97	90	3

Asia & Oceania										
Afghanistan	1 533	3 510	0.0	45.9	9.2	233.9	8.4	78	74	7
Bangladesh	1 393	5 722	1.8	6.7	63.9	315.4	2.3	37	95	9
Bhutan	77	331	13.7	86.4	6.9	5.1	6.0	100	76	33
Brunei Darussalam	-	-	-	-	-	-	-	-	-	-
Cambodia	508	2 091	12.7	37.0	26.8	32.6	2.5	98	87	1
China	1 325	8 401	0.1	1.2	133.6	35.1	0.0	100	100	8
Fiji	51	175	1.9	41.5	5.2	-	-	-	-	-
Hong Kong, China (SAR)	-	0	-	-	-	-	-	-	-	-
India	942	7 106	0.3	1.4	75.8	139.1	0.1	15	70	39
Indonesia	1 743	8 305	0.8	6.2	134.0	168.1	0.8	44	93	0
Kiribati	18	90	22.9	208.8	4.3	-	-	-	-	-
Korea, Dem. People's Rep. of	167	830	0.0	11.9	3.3	676.3	30.1	56	92	0
Korea, Republic of	0	-55	0.0	-	-	-	-	-	-	-
Laos	299	1 399	16.2	50.3	18.5	25.5	4.6	43	99	1
Malaysia	109	412	0.1	3.5	13.5	-	-	-	-	-
Maldives	18	120	4.6	94.7	0.1	7.5	25.7	-	100	0
Marshall Islands	56	313	48.4	1 248.4	3.7	-	-	-	-	-
Micronesia	115	574	45.6	930.7	6.2	-	-	-	-	-
Mongolia	247	1 107	18.6	85.1	7.6	48.5	19.8	-	100	0
Myanmar	126	561	0.0	2.5	-	18.1	0.4	63	94	99
Nauru	16	46	0.0	1 172.0	0.7	-	-	-	-	-
Nepal	467	1 967	6.7	15.1	57.4	60.5	2.5	75	87	65
Pakistan	1 068	6 590	3.6	14.8	9.9	60.5	0.4	95	68	36
Palau	26	159	21.2	1 562.5	3.0	-	-	-	-	-
Papua New Guinea	221	1 119	7.6	37.8	23.7	-	-	-	-	-
Philippines	737	3 131	0.7	6.9	71.9	48.2	0.6	-	100	0
Samoa	33	164	14.3	207.1	3.2	-	-	-	-	-
Singapore	-	-	-	-	0.4	-	-	-	-	-
Solomon Islands	60	253	10.9	59.8	2.8	-	-	-	-	-
Sri Lanka	672	1 868	2.1	18.1	11.5	39.7	2.1	99	89	1
Thailand	-966	1 322	0.2	4.8	37.5	-	-	-	-	-
Timor-Leste	151	951	58.3	281.8	10.2	5.3	6.8	88	92	12
Tonga	27	110	16.4	222.7	1.3	-	-	-	-	-
Tuvalu	6	38	0.0	1 171.0	0.9	-	-	-	-	-
Vanuatu	32	175	11.9	131.0	1.9	-	-	-	-	-
Viet Nam	1 769	7 606	3.6	15.9	124.5	57.8	0.7	-	70	0

Eastern and Southern Europe & CIS										
Albania	342	1 728	6.2	98.2	13.7	33.8	10.7	25	74	0
Armenia	247	1 165	12.0	95.6	29.9	11.8	3.8	89	94	18
Azerbaijan	297	1 187	6.0	42.8	1.9	47.4	5.8	20	80	11
Belarus	-	-	-	-	0.3	-	-	-	-	-
Bosnia and Herzegovina	539	3 519	9.6	137.1	1.7	-	-	-	-	-
Cyprus	-	-	-	-	-	-	-	-	-	-
Georgia	220	1 247	9.4	60.3	16.3	98.2	19.0	13	88	3
Kyrgyzstan	198	1 071	12.0	37.2	15.4	2.3	0.5	-	30	0
Tajikistan	144	730	14.8	26.9	1.7	83.2	13.3	62	93	1

B. Data Compendium

Table 9. How much help does the country receive, and how much of it is food aid?

	Official Development Assistance (ODA) received					Global food aid deliveries in 2004				
	Net ODA receipts (US$ million)	Net ODA receipts (US$ million)	ODA/GNI (%)	ODA per capita (US$)	ODA related to agriculture (US$ million)	Global food aid deliveries ('000 tons)	Food aid deliveries per capita (Kg)	WFP's share (%)	Share of cereals (%)	Share of local purchases (%)
	2003	1999 - 2003 (average)	2002	2002	2003	2004	2004	2004	2004	2004
Turkey	166	1 084	0.2	5.9	11.3	-	-	-	-	-
Turkmenistan	27	195	0.9	8.5	0.1	-	-	-	-	-
Uzbekistan	194	878	2.0	7.5	6.5	82.1	3.2	-	88	0
Middle East & North Africa										
Algeria	232	1 124	0.6	10.5	4.5	50.7	1.6	89	85	0
Bahrain	38	179	1.0	100.8	0.2	-	-	-	-	-
Egypt	894	6 300	1.4	18.7	15.8	13.9	0.2	98	87	54
Iran	133	657	0.1	1.8	14.3	3.3	0.1	100	61	10
Iraq	2 265	2 680	0.0	4.8	79.1	10.4	0.4	100	14	0
Jordan	1 234	3 171	5.6	100.6	2.3	126.9	24.5	6	99	2
Kuwait	-	-	-	-	-	-	-	-	-	-
Lebanon	228	1 318	2.5	102.0	36.6	-	-	-	-	-
Libyan Arab Jamahiriya	0	7	0.0	-	0.5	-	-	-	-	-
Morocco	523	2 626	1.4	16.4	30.2	0.1	0.0	100	66	100
Occupied Palestinian Territories	972	4 611	42.9	500.5	-	183.9	56.9	-	92	17
Oman	45	173	0.2	16.1	5.7	-	-	-	-	-
Qatar	-	-	-	-	-	-	-	-	-	-
Saudi Arabia	22	136	0.0	1.2	0.2	-	-	-	-	-
Syria	160	784	0.4	4.8	5.6	20.6	1.2	50	87	20
Tunisia	306	1 423	1.3	27.1	9.6	-	-	-	-	-
United Arab Emirates	-	-	-	-	-	-	-	-	-	-
Yemen	243	2 011	6.3	31.4	0.7	191.4	10.3	9	94	2
Latin America & Caribbean										
Antigua and Barbuda	5	48	2.0	174.5	-	-	-	-	-	-
Argentina	109	520	0.1	2.3	24.5	-	-	-	-	-
Bahamas	-	-	-	-	-	-	-	-	-	-
Barbados	20	20	0.1	12.7	-	-	-	-	-	-
Belize	12	117	2.7	88.8	0.5	-	-	-	-	-
Bolivia	930	3 390	9.0	77.3	69.6	100.0	11.3	10	94	1
Brazil	296	1 484	0.1	1.9	76.8	-	-	-	-	-
Chile	76	245	0.0	-0.5	14.7	-	-	-	-	-
Colombia	802	2 113	0.6	10.1	5.1	13.1	0.3	92	42	92
Costa Rica	28	39	0.0	1.3	10.2	-	-	-	-	-
Cuba	70	287	0.0	5.4	6.8	5.0	0.4	84	13	82
Dominica	11	86	12.9	427.4	1.3	-	-	-	-	-
Dominican Republic	69	579	0.7	16.9	17.8	13.0	1.5	1	99	2
Ecuador	176	861	1.0	16.8	18.6	21.1	1.6	0	100	0
El Salvador	192	1 026	1.7	36.4	36.7	44.4	6.9	9	76	0
Grenada	12	60	2.6	97.2	2.1	0.0	0.1	-	0	0
Guatemala	247	1 279	1.1	20.7	13.2	69.1	5.8	16	71	0
Guyana	87	436	9.7	84.2	10.1	23.0	29.9	-	100	0
Haiti	200	998	4.7	18.8	25.9	138.4	16.7	20	89	1
Honduras	389	2 771	6.8	64.0	8.3	58.5	8.6	29	76	4
Jamaica	3	70	0.3	9.2	4.9	11.5	4.4	-	52	0
Mexico	103	297	0.0	1.3	25.5	-	-	-	-	-
Nicaragua	833	3 516	13.6	96.9	34.4	67.8	12.7	19	92	4
Panama	30	112	0.2	7.6	11.2	-	-	-	-	-
Paraguay	51	329	1.0	10.3	23.3	-	-	-	-	-

160

Table 9. How much help does the country receive, and how much of it is food aid?

	Official Development Assistance (ODA) received					Global food aid deliveries in 2004				
	Net ODA receipts (US$ million)	Net ODA receipts (US$ million)	ODA/GNI (%)	ODA per capita (US$)	ODA related to agriculture (US$ million)	Global food aid deliveries ('000 tons)	Food aid deliveries per capita (Kg)	WFP's share (%)	Share of cereals (%)	Share of local purchases (%)
	2003	1999 - 2003 (average)	2002	2002	2003	2004	2004	2004	2004	2004
Peru	500	2 301	0.9	18.5	46.8	89.7	3.4	3	63	1
Saint Kitts and Nevis	0	48	9.2	569.4	-	-	-	-	-	-
Saint Lucia	15	101	5.3	209.5	0.5	-	-	-	-	-
Saint Vincent and the Grenadines	6	42	1.4	43.5	2.8	-	-	-	-	-
Suriname	11	116	1.3	27.0	0.3	-	-	-	-	-
Trinidad and Tobago	-2	13	-0.1	-5.6	7.7	-	-	-	-	-
Uruguay	17	85	0.1	4.0	4.8	-	-	-	-	-
Venezuela	82	305	0.1	2.3	1.9	-	-	-	-	-

Definitions of the Indicators:

ODA receipts: Total net official development aid flows from DAC countries, multilateral organizations, and non-DAC countries.

GNI: Gross National Income.

Global food aid deliveries in 2004: Global food aid deliveries based on shipments during the given year expressed in thousand tons, cereals in grain equivalent.

WFP's share: Share in global food aid delivered by WFP in 2004 on a tonnage basis, expressed in percentage.

Share of cereals: Share of cereals in the total amount of food distributed in weight and grain equivalent expressed in percentage.

Share of local purchases: Share of food deliveries purchased in the country where the food is distributed.

Main Sources:

ODA receipts: OECD, Statistical Annex of the 2004 Development Co-operation Report.

ODA related to agriculture: OECD, DAC Statistics database.

Global food aid deliveries: International Food Aid System (INTERFAIS): www.wfp.org/interfais.

WFP's share in global food aid deliveries: WFP, Statistics 2004.

PART V: Annexes

Abbreviations & Acronyms

Glossary

Bibliography

International Alliance Against Hunger

Abbreviations and acronyms

ACC/SCN	Administrative Committee on Coordination/Subcommittee on Nutrition		**HDI**	Human Development Index
BASICS	Basic Support for Institutionalizing Child Survival		**HIPC**	Heavily-Indebted Poor Countries
BMI	body mass index		**ICDS**	Integrated Child Development Service
CIS	Commonwealth of Independent States		**ICRC**	International Committee of the Red Cross
CONPAN	Consejo Nacional para la Alimentación y Nutrición (Food and Nutrition National Council, Chile)		**IDP**	internally displaced person
			IFPRI	International Food Policy Research Institute
CONSEA	Conselho Nacional de Segurança Alimentar e Nutricional (Food Security Council, Brazil)		**IFRC**	International Federation of Red Cross and Red Crescent Societies
ECD	early childhood development		**IMCI**	Integrated Management of Childhood Illness
EDI	Education for All Development Index		**INTA**	Instituto de Nutrición y Tecnología de los Alimentos (National Nutrition Institute, Chile)
EFA	Education for All			
EMOP	emergency operation		**INTERFAIS**	WFP International Food Aid Information System
EPI	Expanded Programmes on Immunization			
FAO	Food and Agriculture Organization of the United Nations		**IPT**	intermittent preventive treatment
			IQ	intelligence quotient
FAS	USDA Foreign Agricultural Service		**LA-RAE**	Latin American School Feeding Network
FRESH	Focusing Resources on Effective School Health		**LBW**	low birthweight
GAM	Global Acute Malnutrition		**LIFD**	Low-income, food-deficit
GDP	gross domestic product		**MCHN**	mother-and-child health and nutrition
GEI	Gender-related EFA-Index		**MDG**	Millennium Development Goal
GFE	Global Food for Education		**MoP**	Measure of Progress
GNP	gross national product		**NCHS**	National Center for Health Statistics

NEDP	National Economic Development Plan
NER	net enrolment ratio
NESDP	National Economic and Social Development Plans
NFE	non-formal education
NFNP	National Food and Nutrition Plan
NGO	non-governmental organization
ODA	Official Development Assistance
OECD	Organisation for Economic Co-operation and Development
PAP	Poverty Alleviation Plan
PHI	Poverty and Hunger Index
PRSP	Poverty Reduction Strategy Paper
PVO	private voluntary organization
SFP	School Feeding Programme
SIPRI	Stockholm International Peace Research Institute
SLE	school life expectancy
SWAPs	Sector-Wide Approaches
UNAIDS	Joint United Nations Programme on HIV/AIDS
UNDAF	United Nations Development Assistance Framework
UNDP	United Nations Development Programme

UNESCO	United Nations Educational, Scientific and Cultural Organization
UNHCR	Office of the United Nations High Commissioner for Refugees
UNICEF	United Nations Children's Fund
UNSCN	United Nations Standing Committee on Nutrition
USAID	United States Agency for International Development
USDA	United States Department of Agriculture
VAM	Vulnerability Analysis and Mapping
WFP	World Food Programme
WFS	World Food Summit
WHS	World Hunger Series
WHO	World Health Organization

Glossary³⁹

Adulthood
As used in this report, the stage of life that begins when a person reaches 18 years of age.

Body mass index (BMI)
An indicator used to assess the nutritional status of adults and older children. It is derived by dividing the weight of an individual in kg by the square of the height measured in metres (weight/height^2).

Common Country Assessment
An analysis of the development situation in one country. It is undertaken by members of the United Nations system as the first step in the UNDAF (United Nations Development Assistance Framework) preparation process in collaboration with the government and in consultation with other development partners.

Early childhood
As used in this report, the period from zero to five years of age.

Emergency operation (as used in WFP)
A mechanism by which WFP, in response to a request from a government or the UN Secretary-General, provides emergency food aid and related assistance to meet the food needs of people affected by a disaster or other emergency.

Fertility rate
The average number of children a woman in a given population will have during her lifetime.

Food access (at household level)
A household's ability to regularly acquire adequate amounts of food through a combination of their own home production and stocks, purchases, barter, gifts, borrowing or food aid.

Food availability
The amount of food that is physically present in a country or area through all forms of domestic production, commercial imports and food aid.

Food insecurity
A condition that exists when people are hungry or vulnerable to hunger at some point in the future.

Food security
A condition that exists when all people at all times are free from hunger — that is, they have sufficient nutrients (protein, energy, and vitamins and minerals) required for fully productive, active and healthy lives.

Food utilization
This refers to the selection and in-take of food and the absorption of nutrients into the body.

Gross domestic product (GDP)
Sum of gross value added by all resident producers in the economy, including distributive trades and transport, plus any product taxes and minus any subsidies not included in the value of the products.

Growth faltering
Failure of a young child to grow to its potential after it is born, which is a physical indication that a child is not receiving the necessary nutrients.

Hunger
A condition in which people lack the required nutrients (protein, energy, and vitamins and minerals) for fully productive, active and healthy lives. Hunger can be a short-term phenomenon, or a longer-term chronic problem. It can have a range of severities from mild to clinical.

Infant mortality rate
Number of deaths per 1,000 live births up to, but not including, one year of age.

Intelligence quotient (IQ)
Score derived from a set of standardized tests that were developed with the purpose of measuring a person's cognitive abilities ('intelligence') in relation to their age group. It is expressed as a number normalized so that the average IQ in an age group is

Glossary

100 — in other words an individual scoring 115 is above-average when compared to similarly aged people.

International poverty line
The equivalent of US$1 per day in consumption expenditures converted using purchasing power parity. People living on less than this amount are considered very poor.

Intra-uterine growth retardation (IUGR)
Inadequate growth of the foetus during pregnancy, resulting in it being too small for its gestational age.

Livelihoods
All capabilities, assets (including both material and social resources) and activities required for a means of living.

Low birthweight
A birthweight under 2,500 grams.

Macronutrients
These nutrients include carbohydrates, protein and fat. They form the bulk of the diet and provide all energy needs. They are sometimes also referred to as protein-energy.

Malnutrition
A clinical condition in which people experience either nutritional deficiencies (undernutrition) or an excess of certain nutrients (overnutrition).
- Acute malnutrition
  Protein-energy malnutrition caused by a recent and severe lack of food intake or disease that has led to substantial weight loss or nutritional oedema. There are different degrees/stages of acute malnutrition, which are often categorized as: severe malnutrition, moderate malnutrition and global acute malnutrition.
- Global acute malnutrition (GAM)
  The percentage of children whose weight-for-height measurements fall below the cut-off of -2 standard deviations (or <- 80 percent median)

and/or who suffer from oedematous malnutrition. Note: GAM is sometimes referred to as 'total' malnutrition.
- Moderate malnutrition
  The percentage of children whose weight-for-height measurements fall below the cut-off of -3 to -2 standard deviations (or 70 to 80 percent median).
- Protein-energy malnutrition (PEM)
  A condition caused by insufficient consumption of macronutrients (carbohydrates, protein and fat).
- Severe malnutrition
  The percentage of children whose corresponding weight-for-height measurements fall below the cut-off of -3 standard deviations (or <-70percent median).

Maternal mortality rate
Number of deaths of women from pregnancy-related causes per 100,000 live births.

Micronutrients
These nutrients include all vitamins and minerals that in small amounts are essential for life and needed for a wide range of body functions and processes.

Neonatal mortality rate
Number of deaths per 1,000 live births in the first 28 days after birth.

Net enrolment ratio (NER)
Enrolment of the official age group for a given level of education, expressed as a percentage of the population at that age group.

Out-of-school children
Children in the official school-age range who are not enrolled in school.

Post-neonatal mortality rate
Number of deaths per 1,000 live births after the neonatal period in the first 28 days after birth and up to, but not including, one year of age, recorded within a given time period.

Poverty gap

Indicator to measure the mean shortfall from the poverty line (counting the non-poor as having zero shortfall), expressed as a percentage of the poverty line.

Protein energy malnutrition

The lack of sufficient energy or protein to meet the body's metabolic demands, as a result of either an inadequate dietary intake of protein, intake of poor quality dietary protein, increased demands due to disease or increased nutrient losses.

Purchasing power parity (PPP)

An exchange rate that accounts for price differences among countries, allowing international comparisons of real output and incomes. A given sum of money, when converted into US dollars at the PPP rate [PPP$], will buy the same basket of goods and services in all countries.

School enrolment

The official number of children recorded as enrolled in a school at the beginning of the school year.

School life expectancy (SLE)

Number of years a child of school-entrance age is expected to spend at school or university, including years spent on repetition, based on country average.

School-age population

Population of the age group which officially corresponds to the relevant level of education, whether enrolled in school or not.

Short-term hunger

A transitory non-clinical form of hunger that can affect short term physical and mental capacity. In this report, it often pertains to school children who have missed breakfast or have walked long distances to school on a relatively empty stomach.

Stunting

An indicator of chronic malnutrition, calculated by comparing the height-for-age of a child with a reference population of well-nourished and healthy children. The prevalence of stunting reflects the long-term nutritional situation of a population.

SWAPs (Sector-Wide Approaches)

An approach under which all spending for a sector (e.g. government, donor, private and international organizations) supports a single, comprehensive sector strategy under the recipient government's leadership.

Under 5 Mortality Rate

Number of deaths per 1,000 live births between birth and exactly five years of age.

Undernourishment

The condition of people whose dietary energy consumption is continuously below a minimum requirement for fully productive, active and healthy lives. It is determined using a proxy indicator that estimates whether the food available in a country is sufficient to meet the energy (but not the protein, vitamin and mineral) requirements of the population. Unlike undernutrition, the indicator does not measure an actual outcome.

Undernutrition

The clinical form of hunger that results from serious deficiencies in one or a number of nutrients (protein, energy, and vitamins and minerals). The deficiencies impair a person from maintaining adequate bodily processes, such as growth, pregnancy, lactation, physical work, cognitive function, and resisting and recovering from disease.

Underweight

A composite measure of someone's weight-for-age compared with a reference population. It reflects both chronic and acute hunger.

Vulnerability

As used in this report, the presence of factors that place people at risk of becoming hungry.

Wasting

An indicator of acute malnutrition that reflects a recent and severe process that has led to substantial weight loss. This is usually the result of starvation or disease and strongly related to mortality. It is calculated by comparing the weigh-for-height of a child with a reference population of well-nourished and healthy children.

Z-score

A measure that shows where an individual value lies relative to a reference population. It is the deviation of an individual's value from the median value of a reference population, divided by the standard deviation of the reference population.

Bibliography

Abadzi, H. 2003. "Improving Adult Literacy Outcomes: Lessons from Cognitive Research for Developing Countries". Washington DC, World Bank.

AED (Academy for Educational Development) 2006. "Welcome to PROFILES". Posted at: http://www.aedprofiles.org.

Ahmed, A.U. 2004. "Impact of Feeding Children in School: Evidence from Bangladesh". Washington DC, IFPRI.

Ahmed, A.U. 2003. "Do Crowded Classrooms Crowd Out Learning?: Evidence from the Food for Education Program in Bangladesh". Posted at: http://www.ifpri.org/divs/fcnd/briefs.htm.

Ahmed, M. 1975. *The Economics of Nonformal Education: Resources, Costs and Benefits*. New York, Praeger Publishers.

Alderman, H. & Christiaensen, L. 2001. "Child Malnutrition in Ethiopia: Can Maternal Knowledge Augment the Role of Income?" Africa Region Working Paper Series, No. 22. Washington DC, World Bank.

Algarín, C., Peirano, P., Garrido, M., Pizarro, F. & Lozoff, B. 2003. "Iron Deficiency Anemia in Infancy: Long-Lasting Effects on Auditory and Visual System Functioning". *Pediatric Research* 53: 217 — 223. Posted at: http://www.pedresearch.org/cgi/content/full/53/2/217

Allen, L.H. & Gillespie, S.R. 2001. *What Works? A Review of the Efficacy and Effectiveness of Nutrition Interventions*. Geneva and Manila, ACC/SCN and ADB (Asian Development Bank).

Allen, R.C., Backstrand, J.R., Stanek, E.j., Pelto, G.H., Chavez, A., Molina, E., Castillo, J.B. & Mata, A. 1992. "The Interactive Effects of Dietary Quality on the Growth and Attained Size of Young Mexican Children". *American Journal of Clinical Nutrition* 56: 353-364.

Anderson, J.W., Johnstone, B.M. & Remley, D.T. 1999. "Breast-feeding and Cognitive Development: A Meta-analysis". *American Journal of Clinical Nutrition* 70 (3): 525 — 535.

Appleton, S. & Song, L. 1999. "Income and Human Development at the Household Level: Evidence from Six Countries". University of Oxford, Centre for the Study of African Economies, Mimeo.

Barro, R. 1998. *Determinants of Economic growth: A Cross-country Empirical Study*. Cambridge, MA, MIT Press.

Beaton, G.H., Martorell, R. & L'Abbé, K.A. 1993. "Effect of vitamin A Supplementation in the Control of Young Child Morbidity and Mortality in Developing Countries". Nutrition Policy Discussion Paper No. 13. Geneva, ACC/SCN.

Begley, S. 1996. "Your child's brain". *Newsweek*, 19 February 1996. Posted at: http://www.gymboree.ch/pdf/articles/your_childs_brain_newsweek.pdf.

Behrman, J.R., Alderman, H. & Hoddinott, J. 2004. "Hunger and Malnutrition: Copenhagen Consensus Challenge Paper". Posted at: http://www.copenhagenconsensus.com/Files/Filer/CC/Papers/Hunger_and_Malnutrition_070504.pdf.

Belik, W. & Del Grossi, M. 2003. "Brazil's Zero Hunger Program in the Context of Social Policy". São Paulo, Brasil, University of Campinas.

Black, M.M., Sazawal,S., Black, R.E., Khosla, S., Kumar, J. & Menon, V. 2004. "Cognitive and Motor Development Among Small-for-gestational-age Infants: Impact of Zinc Supplementation, Birth Weight, and Caregiving Practices". *Pediatrics* 113(5): 1297 — 1305.

Black, R.E. 1998. "Therapeutic and Preventive Effects of Zinc on Serious Childhood Infectious Diseases in Developing Countries". *American Journal of Clinical Nutrition* 68 (Supplement): S476 — 479.

Bruns, B., Mingat, A. & Rakotomalala, R. 2003. "Achieving Universal Primary Education by 2015: A Chance for Every Child". Washington DC, World Bank.

Caulfield, L.E., Huffman, S.L. & Piwoz, E.G. 1999a. "Interventions to Improve Intake of Complementary Foods by Infants 6 to 12 Months of Age in Developing Countries: Impact on Growth and on the Prevalence of Malnutrition and Potential Contribution to Child Survival". *Food and Nutrition Bulletin* 20 (2): 183 — 200.

Caulfield, L.E., Zavaleta, N., Figueroa, A. & Leon, Z. 1999b. "Maternal Zinc Supplementation Does Not Affect Size at Birth or Pregnancy Duration in Peru". *Journal of Nutrition* 129: 1563 — 1568.

Ceesay, S.M., Prentice, A.M., Cole, T.J., Foord, F., Weaver, L.T., Poskitt, E.M. & Whitehead, R.G. 1997. "Effects on Birth Weight and Perinatal Mortality of Maternal Dietary Supplements in Rural Gambia: 5 Year Randomised Controlled Trial". *British Medical Journal* 315: 786 — 790.

Chandler, A.M., Walker, S.P., Connolly, K. & Grantham-McGregor, S.M. 1995. "School Breakfast Improves Verbal Fluency in Undernourished Jamaican Children". *Journal of Nutrition* 125(4): 894 — 900.

Chavez, A., Martinez C., & Soberanes B. 1995. "The Effect of Malnutrition on Human Development: A 24-year Study of Well-nourished and Malnourished Children Living in a Poor Mexican Village". In Scrimshaw, N.S., ed., *Community-based Longitudinal Nutrition and Health Studies: Classical Examples from Guatemala, Haiti and Mexico.* Boston, International Nutrition Foundation for Developing Countries.

Choularton, R. 2005. "Contingency Planning and the Asian Tsunami". Posted at: http://www.odihpn.org.

Collier, P., Elliot, L., Hegre, H., Hoeffler, A., Reynal-Querol, M. & Sambanis, M. 2003. *Breaking the Conflict Trap: Civil War and Development Policy.* Oxford and New York, Oxford University Press for the World Bank.

Corbett, J. 1988. "Famine and Household Coping Strategies". *World Development* 16 (9): 1009 — 1112.

Coutsoudis, A., Pillay, K., Spooner, E., Kuhn, L. & Coovadia, H. M. 1999. "Influence of Infant-feeding Patterns on Early Mother-to-Child Transmission of HIV-1 in Durban, South Africa: A Prospective Cohort Study. South African Vitamin A Study Group". *Lancet* 354 (9177): 288 — 293.

CRED EM-DAT 2005. "The CRED International Disasters Database 2005". Posted at: http://www.em-dat.net/.

Cueto, S. 2001. "Breakfast and Performance". *Public Health Nutrition* 4(6A): 1429 — 1431.

de Onis, M., Blossner, M. & Villar, J. 1998. "Levels and Patterns of Intrauterine Growth Retardation in Developing Countries". *European Journal of Clinical Nutrition* 52 (Supplement): S5 — S15.

de Onis, M., Frongillo, E.A. & Blössner, M. 2000. "Is Malnutrition Declining? An Analysis of Changes in Levels of Child Malnutrition Since 1980". *Bulletin of the World Health Organization* 78(10): 1222 — 1233.

Deininger, K. 2003. "Does Cost of Schooling Affect Enrollment by the Poor? Universal Primary Education in Uganda." *Economics of Education Review* 22 (3): 291 — 305.

Del Rosso, J. M. 1999. "School Feeding Programs: Improving Effectiveness and Increasing the Benefit to Education: A Guide for Program Managers". Oxford, Partnership for Child Development.

Del Rosso, J.M. & Marek, T. 1996. "Class Action: Improving School Performance in the Developing World through Better Health and Nutrition". Washington DC, World Bank.

Delange, F. 2000. "The Role of Iodine in Brain Development". *Proceedings of the Nutrition Society* 59: 75-79.

Desmond, D., Grieshop, J. & Subramaniam, A. 2004. *Revisiting Garden-based Learning in Basic Education*. Rome and Paris, Food and Agriculture Organization and International Institute for Educational Planning.

Drake, L., Maier, C., Jukes, M., Patrikios, A., Bundy, D., Gardner, A. & Dolan, C. 2002. "School-Age Children: Their Nutrition and Health". SCN News 25: 4 — 30.

Drèze, J. & Sen, A. 1989. *Hunger and Public Action*. Oxford, Clarendon Press.

Economist 2004. "Through a Glass Darkly". Posted at: http://www.economist.com/world/asia/displayStory.cfm?story_id=2502961.

Eisemon, T. 1989. "Becoming a 'Modern' Farmer: The Impact of Primary Schooling on Agricultural Thinking and Practices in Kenya and Burundi". In Warren, D., Slikkerveer, L. & Titilola, S., eds., *Indigenous Knowledge Systems: Implications for Agriculture and International Development*. Iowa, Iowa State University.

FAO (Food and Agriculture Organization) 1996. "Rome Declaration on the World Food Security and the World Food Summit Plan of Action". Adopted at the World Food Summit, November 13-17, Rome.

____ 1998. *The Right to Food in Theory and Practice*. Rome, FAO.

____ 2001. "Improving Nutrition through Home Gardening: A Training Package for Preparing Field Workers in Africa". Rome, FAO.

____ 2003. *The State of Food Insecurity in the World 2003*. Rome, FAO.

____ 2004. *The State of Food Insecurity in the World 2004*. Rome, FAO.

FAS Online 2003. "McGovern-Dole International Food for Education and Child Nutrition Program". Posted at: http://www.fas.usda.gov/excredits/FoodAid/FFE/mcdfactsheet.htm.

____ 2005. *Global Food for Education Program; Special Emphasis on Girls*. Posted at: http://www.fas.usda.gov/excredits/FoodAid/FFE/gfe/2004/wo5.htm.

Fernald, L., Ani, C.C. & Grantham-McGregor, S. 1997. "Does School Breakfast Benefit Children's Educational Performance?". *African Health* 19(6): 19 — 20.

Fiedler, J. 2003. "A Cost Analysis of the Honduras Community-Based Integrated Child Care Program". Health, Nutrition and Population Discussion Paper. Washington DC, World Bank.

Fogel, R. 2004. "Health, Nutrition and Economic Growth". *Economic Development and Cultural Change* 52 (3): 643-658.

Foster, A. & Rosenzweig, M. 1996. "Technical Change and Human Capital Returns and Investments: Evidence from the Green Revolution". *American Economic Review* 86 (4): 931-953.

FRESH (Focusing Resources on Effective School Health) 2005. "Focusing Resources on Effective School Health: A FRESH Start to Improving the Quality and Equity of Education". Posted at: http://www.freshschools.org/whatisFRESH.htm.

Garner, P., Kramer, M.S., & Chalmers, I. 1992. "Might Efforts to Increase Birthweight in Undernourished Women Do More Harm than Good?" *Lancet* 340(8826): 1021 — 3.

Gentilini, U. & Webb, P. 2005. "How are We Doing on Poverty and Hunger Reduction? A New Measure of Country-Level Progress". Working Papers in Food Policy and Applied Nutrition, Friedman School of Nutrition Science and Policy. Posted at: http://nutrition.tufts.edu/academy/fpan.

Gillespie, S. & Kadiyala, S. 2005. "HIV/AIDS and Food and Nutrition Security". Food Policy Review No. 7. Washington DC, IFPRI. Posted at: http://www.ifpri.org/pubs/fpreview/fpreview07.htm,

Gillespie, S., Mason, J. & Martorell, R. 1996. "How Nutrition Improves". ACC/SCN State of the Art Series. Nutrition Policy Discussion Paper No. 15. Geneva, ACC/SCN.

Glewwe, P. & Jacoby, H. 1994. "An Economic Analysis of Delayed Primary School Enrolment and Childhood Nutrition in Ghana". LMS Working Paper 98. Washington DC, World Bank.
_____ 1995. "An Economic Analysis of Delayed Primary School Enrolment in a Low Income Country: The Role of Childhood Nutrition". *Review of Economics and Statistics* 77(1): 156 — 169.

Glewwe, P. & Kremer, M. 2005. "Schools, Teachers, and Education Outcomes in Developing Countries". CID Working Papers No. 122. Posted at: http://www.cid.harvard.edu/cidwp/122.htm

Grantham-McGregor, S.M., Walker, S.P. & Chang, S. 2000. "Nutritional Deficiencies and Later Behavioural Development". *Proceedings of the Nutrition Society* 59(1): 47 — 54.

Grantham-McGregor, S.M., Powell, C.A., Walker, S.P. & Himes, J.H. 1991. "Nutritional Supplementation, Psychosocial Stimulation, and Mental Development of Stunted Children: The Jamaican Study". *Lancet* 338 (8758): 1 — 5.

Grantham-McGregor, S.M., Chang, S., & Walker, S.P. 1998. "Evaluation of School Feeding Programs: Some Jamaican Examples". *American Journal of Clinical Nutrition* 67 (4): 785S — 789S.

Grantham-McGregor, S.M., Powell, C., Walker, S., Chang, S. & Fletcher, P. 1994. "The Long-term Follow-up of Severely Malnourished Children Who Participated in an Intervention Program". *Child Development* 65 (2): 428-439.

Haddad, L., Webb, P. & Slack, A. 1997. "Trouble Down on the Farm: What Role for Agriculture in Meeting World Food Needs by 2020?" *American Journal of Agriculture Economics* 5: 1476 — 1479.

Heaver, R. 2005. *Strengthening Country Commitment to Human Development: Lessons from Nutrition*. Washington DC, The World Bank.

Heaver, R. & Kachondam, Y. 2002. "Thailand's National Nutrition Program: Lessons in Management and Capacity Development". Washington DC, The World Bank.

Heckman, J.J. & Carneiro, P. 2003. "Human Capital Policy". *In* J.J. Heckman & A. Krueger, eds. *Inequality in America: What Role for Human Capital Policy?* Cambridge, MA, MIT Press.

Herz, B. & Sperling, G. 2004. *What Works in Girls' Education: Evidence and Policies from the Developing World*. New York, Council on Foreign Relations.

Ho, T.J. 1985. "Economic Issues in Assessing Nutrition Projects: Costs, Affordability and Cost Effectiveness". PHN Technical Note 85-14. Washington DC, World Bank.

Holman, D.J. & Grimes, M.A. 2001. "Colostrum Feeding Behavior and Initiation of Breastfeeding in Rural Bangladesh". *Journal of Biosocial Science* 33: 139 — 154.

Horton, S. & Ross, J. 2003. "The Economics of Iron Deficiency". *Food Policy* 28: 51 — 75.

Horton, S., Sanghvi, T., Phillips, M., Fiedler, J., Perez-Escamilla, R., Lutter, C., Rivera, A. & Segall-Correa, A.M. 1996. "Breastfeeding Promotion and Priority Setting in Health". *Health Policy Planning* 11(2): 156 — 168.

Horton, S. 1999a. "Opportunities for Investments in Nutrition in Low-Income Asia". *Asian Development Review* 17(1,2): 246 — 273.
____ 1999b. "The Economics of Nutritional Interventions". *In* Semba, R.D. & Bloem, M.W., eds., *Nutrition and Health in Developing Countries*. Totowa, NJ, Humana Press.
____ 1993. "Cost Analysis of Feeding and Food Subsidy Programmes". *Food Policy* 18(3): 192 — 199.
____ 1992. "Unit Costs, Cost-Effectiveness, and Financing of Nutrition Interventions". Washington DC, World Bank.

Iannotti, L. & Gillespie, S. 2002. "Successful Community Nutrition Programming: Lessons from Kenya, Tanzania, and Uganda". Washington DC, Kampala, New York, Academy for Educational Development, Makerere University Medical School, UNICEF.

IFRC (International Federation of Red Cross and Red Crescent Societies) 2004. *World Disaster Report 2004*. London, Eurospan.

Ismail, S., Immink, M., Mazar, I. & Nantel, G. 2003. *Community-based Food and Nutrition Programmes: What Makes Them Successful — A Review and Analysis of Experience*. Rome, FAO. Posted at: http://www.fao.org/documents/show_cdr.asp?url_fil e=/DOCREP/006/Y5030E/Y5030E00.HTM.

Jones, G., Steketee, R.W., Black, R.E., Bhutta, Z.A., Morris, S.S. & the Bellagio Child Survival Study Group 2003. "How Many Child Deaths Can We Prevent This Year?" *Lancet* 362 (9377): 65 — 71.

Jukes, M., McGuire, J., Method, F. & Sternberg, R. 2002. "Nutrition and Education". In *Nutrition: A Foundation for Development*. Geneva, ACC/SCN.

Kanarek, R.B. & Marks-Kaufman, R. 1991. *Nutrition and Behavior: New Perspectives*. New York, Van Nostrand Reinhold Publisher.

Keys, A., Brozek, J., Henschel, A., Mickelsen, O. & Longstreet, H.T. 1950. *The Biology of Human Starvation*. Minneapolis, University of Minnesota Press.

Klasen, S. 1999. "Does Gender Inequality Reduce Growth and Development? Evidence from Cross-Country Regressions". Policy Research on Gender and Development, Working Paper No. 7. Washington DC, World Bank.

Kleinman, R.E., Hall, S., Green, H., Korzec-Ramirez, D., Patton, K., Pagano, M.E. & Murphy, J.M. 2002. "Diet, Breakfast, and Academic Performance in Children". *Annals of Nutrition Metabolism* 46 (Supplement 1): 24 — 30.

***Lancet* Editor** 2003. "The World's Forgotten Children: Editorial". *Lancet* 361 (9351): 1.

Landry, S.H. 2001. "Supportive Cognitive Development in Early Childhood". Posted at: http://www.ed.gov/news.

Lauglo, J. 2001. "Engaging With Adults: The Case for Increased Support to Adult Basic Education in Sub-Saharan Africa". Africa Region Human Development Working Paper Series. Washington DC, World Bank.

Bibliography

Laxmaiah, A., Rameshwar Sarma, K.V., Hanumantha Rao, D., Gal Reddy, Ch., Ravindranath, M., Vishnuvardhan Rao, M. & Vijayaraghavan, K. 1999. "Impact of Mid-day Meal Programme on Educational and Nutritional Status of School Children in Karnataka". *Indian Pediatrics* 36 (12): 1221 — 1228.

Levinger, B. 1996. *Critical Transitions: Human Capacity Development Across the Lifespan.* Newton, MA & New York: Education Development Center & United Nations Development Programme.

Lin, S. 1997. "Education and Economic Development: Evidence from China". *Comparative Economic Studies* XXXIX (3-4): 66 — 85.

Lockheed, M.E. & Verspoor, A.M. 1991. *Improving Primary Education in Developing Countries*. Oxford, Oxford University Press.

Lozoff, B., Jimenez, E., Hagen, J., Mollen, E. & Wolf, A.W. 2000. "Poorer Behavioral and Developmental Outcome More Than 10 Years After Treatment for Iron Deficiency in Infancy". *Pediatrics* 105(4): e51.

Lucas, R.E. 1988. "On the Mechanics of Economic Development". *Journal of Monetary Economics* 22: 3 — 42.
_____ 1990. "Why Doesn't Capital Flow from Rich to Poor Countries?" *AEA Papers and Proceedings* 80 (2): 92 — 96.

Mahendra Dev, S., Ravi, C., Viswanathan, B., Gulati, A. & Ramachander, S. 2004. "Economic Liberalisation, Targeted Programmes and Household Food Security: A Case Study of India". Washington DC, IFPRI.

Mason, J., Hunt, J., Parker, D. & Jonsson, U. 2001. "Improving Child Nutrition in Asia". ADB Nutrition and Development Series No. 3. Manila, Asian Development Bank.

Mendez, M. & Adair, L.S. 1999. "Severity and Timing of Stunting in the First Two Years of Life Affect Performance on Cognitive Tests in Late Childhood". *Journal of Nutrition* 129(8): 1555 — 62.

Mingat, A. 1998. "The Strategy Used by High-performing Asian Economies in Education: Some Lessons for Developing Countries". *World Development* 26 (4): 695 — 715.

Mohammed, K. 2000. "Iron Supplementation in Pregnancy". *Cochrane Data Base of Systematic Reviews* 2:CD000117.

Mönckeberg, F. 2005. "Poverty and Malnutrition in Chile: Case Study". Rome, Mimeo.

Morley, S. & Coady, D. 2003. "From Social Assistance to Social Development: A Review of Targeted Education Subsidies in Developing Countries". Washington DC, Center for Global Development and IFPRI.

Myers, R.G. 1984. "Going to Scale". Paper prepared for UNICEF for the Second Inter-Agency Meeting on Community-based Child Development (29-31 October 1984). New York, UNICEF.

Natsios, A. 2001. *The Great North Korean Famine: Famine, Politics, and Foreign Policy*. Washington, D.C., United States Institute for Peace Press.

Ndure, K.S., Maty, N.S., Micheline, N. & Serigne, M.D. 1999. "Best Practices and Lessons Learned for Sustainable Community Nutrition Programming". Posted at: www.pronutrition.org/files/Best%20Practices.pdf.

Nordtveit, B.H. 2005. "The Role of Civil Society Organizations in Developing Countries: A Case Study of Public-Private Partnerships in Senega"l. Dissertation, University of Maryland. Posted at: http://hdl.handle.net/1903/2193.

Noriega, J.A., Ibanez, S.E., Ramos, M.O. & Carbajal, M.M. 2000. "Evaluation of the Effects of a School Breakfast Program on Attention and Memory". *Archivos Latinoamericanos de Nutricion* 50 (1): 35 — 41.

Osrin, D., Vaidya, A., Shrestha, V., Baniya, R.B., Manandhar, D. S., Adhikari, R.K., Filteau, S., Tomkins, A. & Costello, A. 2005. "Effects of Antenatal Multiple Micronutrient Supplementation on Birthweight and Gestational Duration in Nepal: Double-blind, Randomised Controlled Trial". *Lancet* 365 (9463): 955-962.

Oxenham, J., Diallo, A.H., Katahoire, A.R., Petkova-Mwangi, A. & Sall, O. 2002. "Skills and Literacy Training for Better Livelihoods : A Review of Approaches and Experience". Africa Region Human Development Working Paper Series. Washington DC, World Bank.

Okech, A., Carr-Hill, R.A., Katahoire, A.R., Kakooza, T., Ndidde, A.N. & Oxenham, J. 2001. "Adult Literacy Programme in Uganda - An Evaluation". Washington DC, World Bank.

Pak, S. 2004. "The Biological Standard of Living in the Two Koreas". *Economics and Human Biology* 2 (2004): 511-521.

Parlato, M. & Seidel, R., eds. 1998. "Large-Scale Application of Nutrition Behavior Change Approaches: Lessons from West Africa". Arlington, VA, Basic Support for Institutionalizing Child Survival (BASICS) Project.

Pelto, G., Dicken, K. & Engle, P. 1999. "A Critical Link: Interventions for Physical Growth and Psychological Development". Geneva, WHO.

Pollitt, E. 1990. "Malnutrition and Infection in the Classroom: Summary and Conclusions". *Food and Nutrition Bulletin* 12(3): 178-190.

Pollitt, E., Cueto, S. & Jacoby, E.R. 1998. "Fasting and Cognition in Well and Undernourished Schoolchildren: A Review of Three Experimental Studies". *American Journal of Clinical Nutrition* 67(4): 779S — 784S.

Pollitt, E., Jacoby, E. & Cueto, S. 1996. "School Breakfast and Cognition Among Nutritionally At-risk Children in the Peruvian Andes". *Nutrition Review* 54 (4 Pt 2): S22 — 26.

Pollitt, E., Gorman, K., Engle, E., Martorell, R. & Rivera, J. 1993. "Early supplementary feeding and cognition: effects over two decades". Society for Research in Child Development Monograph, Serial No. 235, Vol. 58. Chicago, University of Chicago Press.

Pollitt, E., Hathirat, P., Kotchabhakdi, N.J., Missell. L. & Valyasevi, A. 1989. "Iron deficiency and educational achievement in Thailand". *American Journal of Clinical Nutrition* (Suppl) 50: 687 — 696.

Putnam, R. 1993. *Making Democracy Work: Civic Traditions in Modern Italy.* Princeton, NJ, Princeton University Press.

Quisumbing, A. 1996. "Male-Female Differences in Agricultural Productivity: Methodological Issues and Empirical Evidence". *World Development* 24(10): 1579 — 95.

Rahmato, D. 1991. *Famine and Survival Strategies.* Uppsala, The Scandinavian Institute of African Studies.

Richards, M., Hardy, R., Kuh, D. & Wadsworth, M.E.J. 2001. "Birth Weight and Cognitive Function in the British 1946 Birth Cohort: Longitudinal Population Based Study". *British Medical Journal* 322: 199 — 203.

Richards, M., Hardy, R., & Wadsworth, M.E.
2002. "Long-term Effects of Breast-feeding in a
National Birth Cohort: Educational Attainment and
Midlife Cognitive Function". *Public Health Nutrition*.
5(5): 631 — 5.

Roll Back Malaria 2005. "Preventing Malaria
During Pregnancy". Geneva, Roll Back Malaria
Global Partnership. Posted at:
http://www.rbm.who.int.

Romer, P.M. 1986. "Increasing Returns and
Long-run Growth". *Journal of Political Economy* 94:
1002 — 1037.
_____ 1993. "Idea Gaps and Object Gaps in
Economic Development". *Journal of Monetary
Eonomics* 32: 543 — 573.

Ross, J.S. 1997. "PROFILES Guidelines: Calculating
the Effects of Malnutrition on Economic Productivity
and Survival". Washington DC, Academy for
Educational Development.

Ruel, M. 2005. "Translating Research into Action:
Using Operations Research to Strengthen Food Aid".
Washington DC, IFPRI.

Rush, D. 2000. "Nutrition and Maternal Mortality in
the Developing World". *American Journal of Clinic
Nutrition* 72(Supplement): 212S — 240S.

**Sachs, J., McArthur, J., Schmidt-Traub, G.,
Bahadur, C., Faye, M. & Kruk, M.** 2004. "MDG
Needs Assessment: Country Case Studies of
Bangladesh, Cambodia, Ghana, Tanzania, and
Uganda". January draft of UN Millennium Project
Working Paper. New York, UN Millennium Project,
Mimeo.

Sachs, J. 2001. *Macroeconomics and Health:
Investing in Health for Economic Development.*
Posted at:
www.cid.harvard.edu/cidcmh/CMHReport.pdf.

Saito, K., Mekonen, H. & Spurling, D. 1994.
"Raising the Productivity of Women Farmers in Sub-
Saharan Africa". World Bank Discussion Paper No.
230. Washington DC, World Bank.

Schleifer, A. 1998. "State Versus Private
Ownership". NBER Working Paper Series. Posted at:
http://www.nber.org/papers/w6665.

Schlein, L. 2005. "UNICEF Survey Finds Malnutrition
Among Tsunami-affected Indonesian Children".
Asean News Network. Posted at:
http://www.aseannewsnetwork.com.

Schultz, T. 1971. *Investment in Human Capital:
The Role of Education and of Research.* New York,
Free Press.

Schultz, T.P. 2004. "School Subsidies for the Poor:
Evaluating the Mexican PROGRESA Poverty
Program". *Journal of Development Economics* 74 (1):
199 — 250

Scrimshaw, N.S. 1997. "The Lasting Damage of
Early Malnutrition". In *Ending the Inheritance of
Hunger.* Rome, WFP.

**Seal, A., Kafwembe, E., Kassim, I., Hong, M.,
Wesley, A., & van den Briel, T.** 2006. "Local-level
Maize Meal Fortification is Associated with Improved
Nutritional Status in a Food Aid Dependent Refugee
Population". Mimeo.

Sen, A. 1999. *Development As Freedom.* New York,
Alfred A. Knopf.

Sheshadri, S. & Golpaldas, T. 1989. "Impact of
Iron Supplementation on Cognitive Functions in
Preschool and School-Aged Children: The Indian
Experience". *American Journal of Clinical Nutrition*
50: 675 — 86.

Shrimpton, R. 2001. "The East Asian Nutrition Enigma: An Analysis of the Patterns and Causes of Child Malnutrition in Countries of the East Asia and Pacific Region, Together with Extensive External Comparisons, and Recommendations for Programmes to Accelerate Declines in Stunting". Bangkok, UNICEF Regional Office for East Asia and Pacific Region, Mimeo.

____ 2002. "Nutrition and Communities". In *Nutrition: A Foundation for Development*. Geneva, ACC/SCN.

Shrimpton, R., Thorne-Lyman, A., Tripp, K., Sullivan, K. & Tomkins, A. 2003. "Birth Weight, Food and Nutrition among Bhutanese refugees in Nepal". London, Centre for International Child Health, Institute of Child Health, Mimeo.

Shrimpton, R., Victora, C.G., de Onis, M., Lima, R.C., Blossner, M. & Clugston, G. 2001. "Worldwide Timing of Growth Faltering: Implications for Nutritional Interventions". *Pediatrics* 107(5): e75: 1 — 7.

Silvereano-Velis, J.P. 2003. "Evaluation à mi-parcours du programme de pays du PAM au Burkina Faso (2000-2004). Examen de l'activité BFK 6310 'Soutien à l'éducation de base: alphabétisation'". Ouagadougou, UNESCO and WFP.

SIPRI 2005. "Patterns of Major Armed Conflicts". Posted at: www.sipri.org/contents/conflict/MAC_patterns.html.

Simeon, D.R. and Grantham-McGregor, S. 1989. "Effects of Missing Breakfast on the Cognitive Functions of School Children of Differing Nutritional Status". *American Journal of Clinical Nutrition* 49: 646 — 53.

Simeon, D.T. 1998. "School Feeding in Jamaica: A Review of its Evaluation". *American Journal of Clinical Nutrition* 67(4): 790S — 794S.

Simondon, K.B., Simondon, F., Simon, I., Diallo, A., Bénéfice, E., Traissac, P. & Maire, B. 1998. "Preschool Stunting, Age at Menarche and Adolescent Height: A Longitudinal Study in Rural Senegal". *European Journal of Clinical Nutrition* 52: 412 — 418. Cited in Drake et al. 2002.

Smith, L.C. & Haddad, L. 2000. "Explaining Child Malnutrition in Developing Countries: A Cross-Country Analysis". Research Report No. 111. Washington DC, IFPRI.

Smith, L.C., Ramakrishnan, U., Ndiaye, A., Haddad, L. & Martorell, R. 2003. "The Importance of Women's Status for Child Nutrition in Developing Countries". *Food and Nutrition Bulletin* 24 (3): 287 — 288.

Strauss, J. & Thomas, D. 1998. "Health, Nutrition and Economic Development". *Journal of Economic Literature*. 36(2): 766-817.

Tontisirin, T. & Gillespie, S. 1999. "Linking Community-Based Programmes and Service Delivery for Improving Maternal and Child Nutrition". *Asian Development Review* 17(1,2): 33 — 65.

UCLA International Institute 2004. "School Children in the Developing World: Health, Nutrition and School Performance". Los Angeles, University of California. Posted at: http://www.international.ucla.edu/article.asp?parentid=8943.

UIS (UNESCO Institute of Statistics) 2003. "Estimated Number of Out-of-school Children, by Gender and by Region". Posted at: http://portal.unesco.org/education/en/file_download.php/31f369abb771db2f164f3246d5832d76table2.10.pdf.

UN Millennium Project 2005a. *Halving Hunger: It Can Be Done.* UN Millennium Project's Task Force on Hunger. New York, Earthscan Publications.
____ 2005b. *Towards Universal Primary Education: Investments, Incentives, and Institutions.* UN Millennium Project's Task Force on Education and Gender Equality. New York, Earthscan Publications.

UNDP (United Nations Development Programme) 2004. *Human Development Report: Cultural Liberty in Today's Diverse World.* Oxford, Oxford University Press.

UNESCO (United Nations Educational, Scientific and Cultural Organization) 1997. *Adult Education in a Polarizing World.* Paris, UNESCO.
____ 2003. *EFA Global Monitoring Report 2003-2004. Gender and Education for All: The Leap to Equality.* Paris, UNESCO.
____ 2004. *EFA Global Monitoring Report 2005. Education for All: The Quality Imperative.* Paris, UNESCO.

UNESCO (United Nations Educational, Scientific and Cultural Organization), UNICEF (United Nations Children's Fund), WHO (World Health Organization) & World Bank 2000. "Focusing Resources on Effective School Health: a FRESH Start to Enhancing the Quality and Equity of Education". Paris, UNESCO.

UNHCR (United Nations High Commissioner for Refugees) 2003. *Statistical Yearbook.* Geneva, UNHCR.

UNICEF (United Nations Children's Fund) & Micronutrient Initiative 2004. *Vitamin & Mineral Deficiency: A Global Progress Report.* New York, UNICEF.

UNICEF (United Nations Children's Fund) 2001. "Children on the Edge: Protecting children from sexual exploitation and trafficking in East Asia and the Pacific". Bangkok, UNICEF East Asia and Pacific.
____ 2002a. "Case Studies on Girls' Education".
New York, UNICEF.
____ 2002b. "Quality Education for All: From a Girl's Point of View". New York, UNICEF..
____ 2002c. "U.N. Special Session on Children". Posted at:
http://www.unicef.org/specialsession/activities/healthy-mothers-report.htm.
____ 2004. *The State of the World's Children 2005.* New York, UNICEF.

UNSCN (United Nations Standing Committee on Nutrition) 2004. *5th Report on the World Nutrition Situation: Nutrition for Improved Development Outcomes.* Geneva, UNSCN.

Valerio, A. 2003. "Estimating the Economic Benefits of Adult Literacy Programs: The Case of Ghana". PhD Dissertation, Columbia University.

VAM (Vulnerability Analysis and Mapping) 2002. "Mali: Rural Community and Household Food Security Profiles". Rome, WFP.

Vanderpas, J. &Thilly, C.H. 1994. "Endemic Neonatal, Infantile, and Juvenile Hypothyrodism in Ubangi, Northern Zaire". In Stanbury, J.B., ed., *The Damaged Brain of Iodine Deficiency.* Elmsford, Cognitive Communications Corporation.

Walker, P. 1989. *Famine Early Warning Systems: Victims and Destitution.* London, Earthscan Publications.

Webb, P. & Block, S. 2004. "Nutrition Information and Formal Schooling as Inputs to Child Nutrition". *Economic Development and Cultural Change* 52 (4): 801 — 820.

Webb, P. & Harinarayan, A. 1999. "A Measure of Uncertainty: The Nature of Vulnerability and its Relationship to Malnutrition". *Disasters* 23(4): 292 — 305.

Webb, P. & Rogers, B. 2003. "Addressing the 'In' in Food Insecurity". USAID Occasional Paper No. 1. Posted at http://www.dec.org/pdf_docs/PNACS926.pdf.

WFP (World Food Programme) 2001. "School Feeding Works for Girls' Education". Rome, WFP.
____ 2002. "VAM (Vulnerability Analysis & Mapping) Standard Analytical Framework Guideline: Role and Objectives of VAM Activities to Support WFP Food-Oriented Interventions". Rome, WFP.
____ 2004a. "WFP and World Vision Target Schools to Help Keep Children HIV/AIDS Free". News Release. Posted at:
http://www.wfp.org/newsroom/subsections/preview.asp?content_item_id=2043&item_id=1133&section=13
____ 2004b. "WFP Survey: More than One-fifth of Darfur Children are Malnourished". News Release. Posted at: www.wfp.org/newsroom.
____ 2004c. "What It Would Cost per Child to Meet the Needs of Some 300 Million Hungry Children?". Rome, WFP. Mimeo.
____ 2004d. *WFP in Statistics*. Rome, WFP.
____ 2004e. *Food and Nutrition Handbook*. Rome, WFP.
____ 2005a. "Regional EMOP 10405.0: Assistance to Tsunami Victims in Sri Lanka, Indonesia, Maldives and Other Countries in the Indian Ocean Region". Rome, WFP.
____ 2005b. "Emergency Operation Sudan: EMOP 10339.1: Food Assistance to Population Affected by War in Greater Darfur, West Sudan". Rome, WFP.
____ 2005c. "A Front-line Defence Against HIV/AIDS". Posted at:
http://www.wfp.org/aboutwfp/introduction/hiv.html.
____ 2005d. "Case study Report — Uganda". Rome, WFP, Mimeo.
____ 2005e. *Global School Feeding Report 2005*. Rome, WFP.

WFP (World Food Programme) & UNICEF (United Nations Children's Fund) 2005. "Emergency Food Security and Nutrition Assessment in Darfur, Sudan 2005: Provisional Report". Rome and New York, WFP and UNICEF.

WFP (World Food Programme), UNESCO (United Nations Educational, Scientific and Cultural Organization) & WHO (World Health Organization) 1999. *School Feeding Handbook*. Rome, WFP.

WHO (World Health Organization) 1998. "Health Nutrition: An Essential Element of a Health-Promoting School". WHO Information Series on School Health, Document Four. Geneva, WHO.
____ 1999. "Preventing HIV/AIDS/STI and Related Discrimination: An Important Responsibility of a Health-promoting School". WHO Information Series on School Health, Document Six. Geneva, WHO.
____ 2001. "IMCI: A joint WHO/UNICEF Initiative". Posted at: http://www.who.int/child-adolescent-health/New_Publications/IMCI/imci.htm.
____ 2004. *The World Health Report: Changing History.* Geneva, WHO.
____ 2005a. "Report of the Third Global Meeting of the Partners for Parasite Control: Deworming for Health and Development". Geneva, WHO.
____ 2005b. *The World Health Report: Make Every Mother and Child Count.* Geneva, WHO.

Wijngaarden, J. & Shaeffer, S. 2002. "The Impact of HIV/AIDS on Children and Young People: Reviewing Research Conducted and Distilling Implications for the Education Sector in Asia". Paper prepared for the workshop on Anticipating the Impact of AIDS on the Education Sector in Asia, 12-14 December 2002, Bangkok, Thailand. Mimeo.

Woolcock, M. 1998. "Social Capital and Economic Development: Towards a Theoretical Synthesis and Policy Framework". *Theory and Society* 27: 1 — 57.

World Bank 1993. *The East Asian Miracle: Economic Growth and Public Policy*. Washington DC, Oxford University Press.
____ 2000. *World Development Report 1999/2000*. Washington DC, Oxford University Press.
____ 2002. "Hundreds of Thousands in Madagascar Receive Critical Nutritional Treatment: The Role of the Education Sector in Reaching the Poorest."

_____ 2003. "Bangladesh: Female Secondary School Assistance Project". Washington DC, World Bank.

_____ 2004. *World Development Indicators 2004*. CD-ROM.

_____ 2005a. *Reshaping the Future: Education and Postconflict Reconstruction*. Washington DC, World Bank.

_____ 2005b. "Early Child Development. Why Invest in ECD: Brain Development". World Bank Internet Site. Posted at: http://web.worldbank.org/WBSITE/EXTERNAL/TOPICS /EXTEDUCATION/EXTECD/0,,contentMDK:20207747 ~menuPK:527098~pagePK:148956~piPK:216618~t heSitePK:344939,00.html.

_____ 2005c. *Economic Growth through Improved Nutrition*. Washington DC, World Bank, Mimeo.

Xu, L-S., Pan, B-J., Lin, J-X., Chen, L-P., Yu, S-H. & Jones, J. 2000. "Creating Health-promoting Schools in Rural China: A Project Started from Deworming". *Health Promotion International* 15 (3): 197 — 206.

International Alliance Against Hunger

Joint statement of the Rome-based Organizations, 13 October 2003

Working together we can stop hunger

Responding to the call made by the World Food Summit: Five Years Later held in Rome in 2002, we, the Rome-based organizations dealing with food and agriculture — FAO (Food and Agriculture Organization of the United Nations), IFAD (International Fund for Agricultural Development), IPGRI (International Plant Genetic Resources Institute) and WFP (World Food Programme) — have joined the International Alliance Against Hunger. We want to maximize our efforts to work together at both national and international levels, with other international organizations, food producers and consumers, scientists, academics, religious groups, NGOs and civil society organizations, donors and policymakers, to halve hunger by 2015, the target set by the 1996 World Food Summit and reiterated in the Millennium Development Goals. The Alliance will also help to keep the plight of the poor and the hungry in the spotlight and strongly encourages nations and the international community to honour their commitments to fight hunger and poverty.

The Alliance will work towards building a hunger and poverty reduction constituency within countries and at the international level to support sustainable livelihoods and advocate relentlessly for urgent action towards eradicating hunger and poverty. In so doing, the Alliance plans to leverage the influence of broad segments of societies and of the international community to encourage donor and recipient countries alike to exert their political will and devote their resources to this end.

The Rome-based organizations are determined to mobilize their energies to work towards this shared goal. We invite all stakeholders to join us in the battle against hunger.

Notes

1 This terminology is used for convenience. In fact, protein, carbohydrates and fat are all sources of energy. So, properly speaking, protein and energy should not be separate categories. However, protein is such an important source of energy (because it contains essential amino acids) that it is broken out here, with energy referring to carbohydrates and fats.

2 A 'major armed conflict' is defined as: "the use of armed force between the military forces of two or more governments, or of one government and at least one organized armed group, resulting in battle-related deaths of at least 1000 people in any single calendar year and in which the incompatibility concerns control of government and/or territory" (SIPRI 2005).

3 It was also known to slow mental development during infancy.

4 The optimal birthweight for cognitive function appears to be 3.5-4.0 kilograms. Lower (and higher) birthweights for gestational age seem to be associated with decreases in ability, though caution must be used in interpreting the results of a single study.

5 Even moderate vitamin A deficiency increases a child's risk of severe infection and death, while severe vitamin A deficiency causes night blindness and other conditions, that can lead to permanent blindness (Beaton and others 1993). Ill health and blindness obviously impair a child's ability to learn (in addition to the other damage they cause). A lack of vitamin B12 can reduce growth and cognitive function (Allen and Gillepsie 2001). The effect of zinc deficiency on development beyond its contribution to frequent childhood illness (R.E. Black 1998) is not yet clear (M.M. Black and others 2004).

6 A writer for *The Economist* magazine (11 March 2004) made this point on a visit to a classroom in North Korea.

7 This phrase is borrowed from World Bank 2005c.

8 The incident described in this paragraph was remembered by several aid workers familiar with the area, but the supporting documentation has not been identified. It appears, however, to be broadly illustrative of similar situations. For example, a VAM study (2002) recommended education programmes for several food insecure communities.

9 It should be noted that there was much less difference in productivity in areas where new technologies were not introduced.

10 While the evidence points to the value of food supplementation for increasing birthweight, several qualifications need to be made (Allen and Gillepsie 2001). In these studies, the supplementation had its greatest effect when targeted to women with the lowest weights and lowest energy intakes. The results were less pronounced in better nourished women. Moreover, the supplements that provide additional energy (rather than more protein) appear to have the largest effects. In terms of timing, improvements occurred when the supplements were given in either the second or third trimesters of the pregnancy. Finally, in cases where access to food is sufficient, it is probably more important to make households aware of a woman's need for additional food intake, rather than to provide external assistance.

11 The supplement was given during the second and third trimesters of pregnancy. The single supplements were iron and folic acid.

Notes

[12] About half of all pregnant women in developing countries are anaemic, and iron supplementation during pregnancy helps to prevent severe anaemia. Although this seems likely to have an effect on the foetus, there is little or mixed evidence of beneficial effects of iron supplements on foetal growth (Mohammed 2000). Zinc supplementation does not appear to help reduce the incidence of low birthweight or increase the duration of time towards a full-term birth (Caulfield and others 1999b). Iodine supplementation does appear to contribute to greater birthweight (Allen and Gillepsie 2001). One concern about any of these supplements is that by increasing the size of the baby, they may lead to obstructed labour (Garner and others1992; Rush 2000). But the evidence suggests that the harmful effects are more related to the mother's age than the size of the baby.

[13] The health provider can help the woman determine if she needs supplementary food (through weighing) or micronutrient (sometimes through blood tests) interventions.

[14] In malaria endemic areas, it is recommended that women in endemic areas take anti-malarials as a precaution during pregnancy (IPT, intermittent preventive treatment) and sleep under an insecticide-treated mosquito net (Roll Back Malaria 2005).

[15] Although choices for infant feeding are more complex in areas with a high HIV prevalence, for many women who choose to breastfeed, exclusive breastfeeding may be the safest choice for their infant (Coutsoudis and others 1999).

[16] It should be noted that when the child is no longer an infant, but not yet ready for school, the diet must change to meet the nutritional requirements of new growth and greater activity. Nutritional supplements may also be necessary to ensure that growth does not falter during this critical interval. Caregivers need to be informed of how and what to feed their children and, if required, to give nutritional supplements.

[17] However, there were other factors that potentially contributed to the increase in birthweight. For instance, girls' education increased in the camps and may have led to delays in pregnancy or improved antenatal health.

[18] A related concern is that parents may simply view the school meal as a substitute for normal meals and reduce the amount of food given to the child at home. However, recent studies suggest that this does not generally occur (Glewwe and Kremer 2005).

[19] In some locations, parents take a role on committees that supervise food stocks, provide condiments for meals or assist in the preparation of the food. Without community involvement, the cost of the programme can escalate, and there is less accountability and greater risk of abuse of the programme by those who run it.

[20] Some authors (cf. Glewwe and Kremer 2005) have urged caution in the interpretation of these figures. They point out that many of the fee reduction programmes are accompanied by other initiatives that may account for part of the increase. They also indicate that a surge in enrolment will not lead to lasting attendance, if the capacity and quality of the schools is not sufficient.

[21] Two studies in Jamaica showed that school children who received breakfast at school,

particularly those undernourished, improved some cognitive functions (Grantham-McGregor and others 1998). In Mexico a school breakfast programme for four to six year old poor children improved response, speed, fine motor skills and behaviour executions (Noriega and others 2000).

22 This greater immediacy may explain the differences in retaining knowledge from the courses. A longitudinal study of a literacy project in Senegal found that the success rates of reading skills was 35 percent, writing skills 26 percent, math and problem-solving skills 20 percent, and income-generating skills 68 percent (Nordtveit 2005).

23 This may be due to several difficulties with adult literacy classes, including infrequent attendance, poor quality instruction, and the lack of an environment that values and requires literacy to help stimulate the learning process. Too often, literacy classes have been conducted in isolation — implemented as ends, not as means to improving livelihoods and addressing hunger.

24 Height is often used as a proxy for the nutritional well-being in a society at large. However, other factors, including the health environment, socio-economic conditions and genetics, also play a role.

25 There was a positive and statistically significant correlation between investments in primary education at the start of their countries' development processes and future economic growth (Mingat 1998). A study from thirty provinces in China found similar results (Lin 1997). Of course, the correlation could run in reverse, with higher levels of economic growth leading to more education. However, by focusing on education levels in initial years, these studies were able to control for this effect to a great extent.

26 As mentioned in the previous footnote, there is evidence that the level of schooling contributes significantly to economic growth and not just vice-versa.

27 One complicating factor is that improved health conditions led to a reduction in infant mortality rates in many countries. In Asia, the fertility rate decline reached 40-50 percent, which more than offset the increase in population due to reduced infant mortality. However, in parts of Latin America, and especially in Africa, fertility did not decline quickly enough, leading to overall increases in population growth.

28 Technically, this is called a lower youth-dependency ratio. Of course, there can be a trade-off between the absolute size of the labour force and its quality. In general, however, a lower youth-dependency ratio has been associated with higher levels of economic growth.

29 Fogel implies that these improvements helped to explain the reduction of paupers and beggars on the streets of nineteenth century England.

30 Losses are also associated with decreased cognitive capacity. Although the estimates have to be treated with caution, this type of malnutrition has been associated with a 15 point loss in intelligence quotients and a consequent decrease of 10 percent in wages and productivity (Horton 1999). Vitamin and mineral deficiencies — including iron and iodine deficiencies — contribute to the significant productivity losses. Childhood anaemia is associated with a 4 percent decrease in real hourly earnings (Horton 1999). Estimates indicate that the reduced cognitive ability from anaemia in selected South Asian countries has led to a 3.5 percent reduction in GDP (Horton and Ross 2003). The effect of cognitive impairment is five to six times higher than the losses in physical productivity. Iodine deficiency (sometimes

referred to as goitre) causes similarly staggering losses. It is estimated that children born to mothers with goitre suffer on average a 10 percent productivity loss, as a result of reduced cognitive potential (Ross 1997, cited in Horton 1999).

[31] 'Health capital' is a term used to describe the direct impact of health conditions on economic growth. Fogel argues that his 'physiological capital' is a distinct input into economic growth that has not been properly analysed.

[32] It also helped that communities felt that they owned the programme, which used locally produced food and other inputs.

[33] A recent study prepared for the Copenhagen Consensus supports this view (Behrman, Alderman and Hoddinott 2004). It analysed the benefit-cost ratio of various nutritional interventions (table below). Benefits include the future gains in productivity, converted into current amounts. The costs relate to the requirements for implementing the programmes over the specified period of time. If the value for the benefit-cost ratio exceeds 1, the benefits outweigh the costs. For example, the intervention for iron supplementation has a benefit-cost ratio ranging from 6.1 to 14.0. This means that the economic benefits of making these interventions outweigh the costs by somewhere in the range of 6 to 14 times.

[34] At the time that she makes this statement, she is not yet aware that he is trying to gather knowledge for that purpose.

[35] The table on the next page identifies some of the key indicators for issues related to hunger and learning for each age group. International comparisons are also provided, where available, to offer a sense of the severity of the problem.

TABLE: Benefit-cost ratios for interventions to reduce hunger

Interventions and targeted populations	Benefit-cost ratio
Reducing low birthweight where there is a high risk (particularly in South Asia)	
Treatment for women with asymptomatic bacterial infections	0.6 - 4.9
Treatment for women assumed to have sexually transmitted diseases	1.3 - 10.7
Drugs for women with poor obstetric history	4.1 - 35.2
Improving infant and child nutrition in populations with a high prevalence of malnutrition	
Breastfeeding promotion in hospitals in which the norm has been the promotion of infant formula	4.8 - 7.4
Integrated childcare programmes	9.4 - 16.2
Intensive preschool programme with considerable nutrition for poor families	1.4 - 2.9
Reducing micronutrient deficiencies in populations with high prevalence	
Iodine (women of childbearing age)	15.0 - 250.0
Iron (whole population)	176.0 - 200.0
Iron (pregnant women)	6.1 - 14.0

Source: Behrman and others 2004

TABLE: Assessing problems related to hunger and learning

Age Group/Issue	Indicator	Benchmarks
Early childhood		
Low birthweight	Percent low birthweight	Top: 0-7, Upper mid: 7-11, Lower mid: 11-15; Low: 15-32
Growth faltering	Percent stunting (low height-for-age)	Top: 1.3-12; Upper mid: 12-25; Lower mid: 25-39; Low: 39-57
	Percent underweight children	Top: 0.8-7; Upper mid: 7-17.5; Lower mid: 17.5-31; Low: 31-50
	Percent of children exclusively breastfed for first six months	Top: 73-86; Upper mid: 56-73; Lower mid: 36-56; Low: 8-36
Micronutrient deficiencies	Percent goitre (total population)	Top: 4-11; Upper mid: 11-17; Lower mid: 17-24; Low: 24-48
	Percent iron deficient anaemia	Top: 8-36; Upper mid: 36-56; Lower mid: 56-73; Low: 73-86
Stimulation	Psychomotor development scales	NA
School age		
School attendance	Net primary school enrolment	Top: 96-100; Upper mid: 86.5-96; Lower mid: 70-86.5; Low: 34-70
	School life expectancy	Top: 12.5-16; Upper mid: 11-12.5; Lower mid: 8-11; Low: 3-8
Attention spans	NA	NA
Micronutrient deficiencies	Percent goitre in total population	Top: 4-11; Upper mid: 11-17; Lower mid: 17-24; Low: 24-48
	Percent iron deficient anaemia	NA
Specific skills and knowledge	Knowledge, attitudes and practice survey	NA
Adult		
Adult literacy	Adult literacy rate	Top: 93-99.7; Upper mid: 83-93 Lower mid: 60-83; Low: 13-60
Livelihoods	Percent living below US$1 per day	Top: 0-2; Upper mid: 2-15; Lower mid: 15-36; Low: 36-85
Specific skills and knowledge	Knowledge, attitudes and practice survey	NA
Attendance and concentration	NA	NA

[36] Estimates of costs for various interventions are provided below:

Early childhood	Annual Cost per Person
Food supplementation	US$ 36-172 to provide 1000 kcal/day (a)
Iodine fortification	US$ 0.02-0.05 (b)
Iodine supplementation (through capsules) per child/mother	US$ 0.50-2.80 (c)
Iodine supplementation (through oil injections)	US$ 0.8-2.75 (d)
Iron fortification	US$ 0.09-1.00 (e)
Iron supplementation through tablets per person	US$ 0.55-US$ 5.30 (f)
Breastfeeding promotion in hospitals	US$ 0.30-0.40 if infant formula removed; US$ 2-3 if not (g)
Community-based growth monitoring	US$ 1.60-10 without food US$ 11-18 with food (h)
Early child development /child care	US$ 250-412 with food (Bolivia) US$ 2-3 without food (Uganda) (i)

School Age	Annual Cost per Person
School meals (660 kcal a day and 200 school days)	US$ 20 (j)
Local food fortification (including the premix, milling and bagging) in SF programmes	less than US$ 30 a tonne or less than US$ 1/child (k)
Costs of combined deworming and micronutrient supplementation in SF programs	US$ 1-4 (l)

Adulthood	Annual Cost per Person
Nutrition education	US$ 2.5 (m)
Microcredit and nutrition education	NA
Take-home rations	NA

Sources: (a) Horton 1993, 1999; (b) Caulfield and others 2005, as cited in World Bank 2005c; (c) As cited in World Bank 2005c; (d) Caulfield and others 2005, as cited in World Bank 2005c; (e) Caulfied and others 2005, as cited in World Bank 2005c; (f) Horton 1992, Mason and others 2001, Caulfield and others 2005, as cited in World Bank 2005c; (g) Horton and others 1996; (h) Fielder 2003, Ianotti and Gillespie 2002; Gillespie and others 1996; Mason and others 2001; (i) World Bank 2002, 2005c; (j) WFP 2004c; (k) WFP 2004c; (l) WFP 2004c; (m) Ho 1985. *Note:* This compilation of costs and sources is derived in large part from World Bank 2005c.

37 An extreme case is when the '1990' values are equal to the '2015' values. This happens if a country, for example, has a rate of 0 for poverty in 1990. Then, the '1990' value will be 1, and the corresponding 2015 value will be 1 as well. If the rate of poverty is 0 also the '2000' (and the dimensional value is therefore 1) then the assigned value for that dimension will be 1, meaning that the dimension is not a problem — a country has to continue maintaining such a level. In the case that poverty increased from 0 in 1990 to a certain percentage in 2000 (e.g. 3 percent), than the Ni for poverty will be negative, and the magnitude will be expressed as the distance from the value 1 in 2015 (e.g. -0.03).

38 United Nations Statistics Division, Millennium Development Goal Indicators Database.

39 The definitions in this glossary have been adapted or taken from a range of UN and other sources, including UNESCO, WFP, FAO, UN Millennium Project, and the Bretton Woods Project, among others.

Map B — Hunger across the world measured by undernourishment and underweight

Prevalence of underweight

Countries with underweight prevalence above 30%

Prevalence of undernourishment

Extremely low: less than 2.5%

Very low: 2.5% to 5%

Moderately low: 5% to 20%

Moderately high: 20% to 35%

Very high: more than 35%

NA

The boundaries and the designations used on this map do not imply any official endorsement or acceptance by the United Nations.
Map produced by WFP VAM.

Data source: FAO, WHO